# Distributed-Processor Communication Architecture

# Distributed-Processor Communication Architecture

**Kenneth J. Thurber**
Sperry Univac and
The University of Minnesota

**Gerald M. Masson**
The Johns Hopkins University

**LexingtonBooks**
D.C. Heath and Company
Lexington, Massachusetts
Toronto

**Library of Congress Cataloging in Publication Data**

Thurber, Kenneth J
    Distributed-processor communication architecture.

    Includes index.
    1. Computer networks. 2. Computer architecture. 3. Electronic data processing—Distribution processing. I. Masson, Gerald joint author. II. Title.
TK5105.5.T49                    621.3819'592                    79-1563
ISBN 0-669-02914-9

Published simultaneously in Canada.

Printed in the United States of America.

International Standard Book Number: 0-669-02914-9

Library of Congress Catalog Card Number: 79-1563

*To*
*Martie, Megan,*
*and*
*Betsy*

# Contents

# List of Figures

# List of Tables

# Preface and Acknowledgments

This book is an introductory-level text on the subject of digital path and interconnection switch architecture for intercomputer communication for distributed-processor architectures. The book deals with switches, paths, and their system implications. It is meant to be architecture-oriented and therefore does not attempt to dogmatically form a complete taxonomy of the communication techniques used in networks or distributed processing systems. Rather, it describes the communication techniques used in distributed processors and networks, forming or using previously formulated taxonomies whenever possible to provide a structured approach to the subject.

Functional topology issues of distributed and network systems are discussed. The implementation of their data-transfer mechanisms via paths and switches is evaluated from the viewpoint of their architecture tradeoffs. Detailed interface and transmission techniques are discussed. A chapter about some of the architectural aspects of network systems is included.

Before pursuing the topics discussed in this book, students should have some prerequisites, namely, at least one quarter of each of the following type of course: (1) a high-order language such as FORTRAN, (2) a course dealing with the assembly-language-level description of processors and computers including input/output (I/O), and (3) a first-level course in switching theory. Although prerequisites 1 and 3 are not mandatory, these three prerequisites describe a level of maturity which the student should attain before attempting the material contained here. Further, the students should understand fundamental concepts of set theory and graph theory.

This book has been used in seminars taught at the University of Minnesota in the Computer Science Department in the form of class notes. Selected chapters were taught in a one-quarter seminar course during the Spring quarters of 1976, 1977, and 1978 at the University of Minnesota. The book is structured in a "top-down fashion." That is, it begins with a chapter of distributed-processor system configurations (chapter 2); moves to three architecture chapters (chapters 3, 4, and 5) which discuss message and packet switching, circuit switching, and bus structures; contains a chapter (chapter 6) on hardware implementation considerations, followed by a chapter (chapter 7) containing example systems; and concludes with a summary chapter (chapter 8).

Based on the teaching experience with the book, the authors recommend that the book be used in one of two ways. First, if the students are basically computer science majors, we suggest that in addition to the three previously mentioned prerequisites, they should also have had an introductory course in operating-system design. The student should study in a top-down fashion, taking the chapters in this order: 1, 2, 3, 4, 5, 7, and 8. We suggest that computer science majors skip chapter 6.

Second, if the students are basically electrical engineering majors, then they would benefit by having had an additional prerequisite, an introductory electronics course. The students should study in a bottom-up fashion, taking the chapters in this order: 1, 6, 5, 4, 3, 2, 7, and 8.

We feel that these suggestions will structure the material so that maximum benefit is gained by the students based on their particular backgrounds.

This is a book about computer architecture. This is not a book about networks or queuing theory. There are forms of distributed processors other than networks; however, packet-switched networks are one important form of a distributed processor and thus some architecture strategies for their design have been included. The intent of the book is to enumerate architecture possibilities and tradeoffs, not to pick the world's best architecture. References to detailed implementation concepts are given. Additionally, the exercises have been built as an extension of concepts introduced in the book. You will not find the answer to the exercises simply by looking back in the text. You will have to work for the solution(s). To further emphasize (and to conclude) the point, from the architecture viewpoint buses, circuit switches, and packet switches are all important technologies; and systems based upon them are extensively enumerated in this book.

The authors wish to thank Dave Albee, Jack Lipovski, Doug Jensen, Larry Jack, Don Moran, and Don Anderson for discussions which contributed substantially to the concept and structure of this book. Particular thanks go to G. Michael Schneider for his extensive help in the network architecture area.

# 1 Introduction

## Distributed Systems

There are many and varied definitions of distributed systems. In this discussion we use a simple definition with which a large number of researchers [1, 2, 3, 4, 5] tend to agree. A *distributed system* is a system in which a processing load is distributed across a number of *processing elements* (PEs), defined as a processor-memory pair, which are physically interconnected but allow varying amounts of software intercommunication. Generally, there is a time delay in transmitting information between elements. Typical computer systems which could be considered distributed are general-purpose computers (which are realized from multiple microprocessors), computers with dedicated adjuncts which perform specific functions (such as fast Fourier transforms), and array processors such as ILLIAC IV, multiprocessors, and computer networks.

Research in the area of distributed processors is proceeding mainly in three areas: network systems [6], special-purpose systems [7], and high-performance general-purpose systems [8]. Further, research in this area has been proceeding in two main contexts—computer communications and computer architecture [6, 9, 10, 11]. This book is written from the architecture viewpoint.

The major benefits of distributed processors include resource sharing, high system availability, load leveling, improved throughput capability, improved response time, greater modularity, and improved fault tolerance. Not all these advantages may be realized in the same system, but the potential advantages of distributed processing are enormous [1, 3, 6, 8].

There are three main architectural issues in the design of distributed processing systems: (1) interprocess communications design, (2) intercomputer communications design, and (3) application and system process partitioning and assignment [12]. Interprocess communications design is a fairly well-understood function since it has a strong background in the operating-system works of Dijsktra and others [13, 14, 15, 16]. Intercomputer communications design is also a fairly well-understood subject. In fact, some design techniques are amenable to the construction of classification schemes [9, 10, 17, 18, 19]. Process partitioning for general distributed processors has only recently begun to be developed, and researchers are beginning to construct the vocabulary and terminology of such issues [1, 12].

This book explores in detail the design issues involved with intercomputer communications techniques as applied to distributed processing systems and networks. This book covers the interconnections design from system architecture design all the way to detailed data-link design issues. The importance of this problem cannot be overstressed because regardless of whether researchers are trying to interconnect microprocessors or minicomputers to form distributed systems, the intercomputer communications problems of bus design, channel design, I/O design, and so on continue to be with us. To make this book highly usable, it deals with the general architectural techniques necessary to make computers communicate. Thus the designer of a minicomputer network should find the book as useful as someone who is trying to interconnect main-frame computers. Further, both designers will find that by carefully following the techniques described in the text they realize two major advantages:

1. For any design problem the book presents a number of architectures so that if a designer considers the techniques described, he can feel confident of having considered a large number of the major design tradeoffs.
2. The designer should get a good perspective of how to organize his system structurally because the book structurally develops an overview of intercomputer communication architecture techniques for networks and distributed processors.

Figure 1-1 gives a rudimentary description of a hierarchial view of a distributed system. Since a distributed system has multiple processes that run in it, the system may be viewed as a set of cooperating processes communicating over a subnetwork via a hierarchy of hardware and software protocols. Figure 1-1 indicates a simple view of the concept of distributed processing in which there are processing elements (hosts—host processing elements) that communicate via a communication subnetwork. Both actual and virtual communication occurs in the system. A particular system may have more levels than shown in figure 1-1.

In this book we are concerned with the architectures of communication subnetworks that are specifically useful in building networks and distributed processors. Precisely, the book contains one chapter devoted to system design issues and models encountered in the design of distributed processors and networks (chapter 2). It also contains three chapters that detail the architectures of the most common types of communication subnetworks encountered in distributed systems, that is, message and packet switches (chapter 3), circuit switches (chapter 4), and buses (chapter 5). Chapter 6 deals with the hardware details inherent in the design of the actual hardware transmission paths. Example systems are discussed in chapter 7, and future trends in the area of distributed processing systems are treated in chapter 8. The remainder of this chapter discusses the evolution of digital communication system architecture and three examples of simple distributed systems.

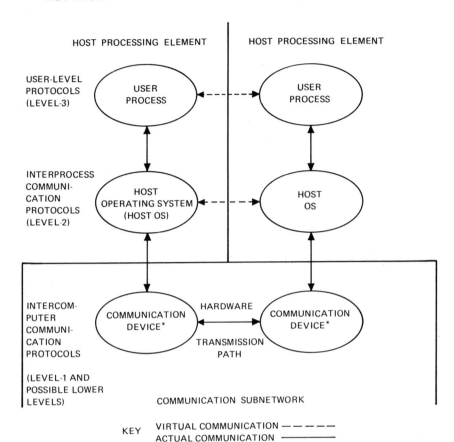

**Figure 1-1.** General Hierarchical Communication System Model. Reprinted with permission from K.J. Thurber, "Computer Communication Techniques," COMPSAC, IEEE Computer Society, 1978: 589-594.

## Evolution of Digital Communication System Architecture

Throughout history people have had to communicate. Various techniques have been used ranging from drums and smoke signals to satellite data links. Modern communication techniques can be traced from the telegraph to torn tape units to teletypewriters.

As computer technology increased over the past fifteen to twenty years, computer systems needed to send and receive messages. As computer uses expanded with the advent of time-sharing systems and minicomputer networks, communication techniques took on larger importance. Because of the complexity and cost of some digital bus concepts, various other communication-link techniques were developed that were more cost-effective [3, 6, 8, 20, 21]. As this growth of technology continues, communications technology must grow with computer technology. Communication subnetwork design is one of the foundations of the interface between computer and communication systems [1].

Originally computers were produced and thought of strictly in terms of central site installations [17, 20]. All peripherals and the computer existed at a single physical location, the local site. Later developments (more sophisticated peripheral complexes) made it possible for some peripherals to be located at physically remote sites. As system technology developed further, networks of minicomputers allowed different system components to communicate with one another [6].

One of the first historical steps in computer communications was to connect a large number of peripherals at a single site. If the operating system is appropriately structured, terminals can be designed so that they appear interactive. If desired, the terminals may be physically distributed. Thus a simple time-sharing system can be constructed with a local-site capability for batch processing and a number of remote terminal sites. The remote terminal sites may be connected either by buses or by phone lines with dial-up capability to the main computer site. This processing node may then be used by many users interactively. Each user has the ability to share the system's resources. Further, the remote sites may be located hundreds of miles from the actual computer installation. Time-sharing systems encouraged numerous people of unrelated disciplines to solve a variety of problems with computers.

Multiprocessor/multicomputer systems are another example of the growth of digital communications technology. Multiprocessor systems typically contain a number of processors which communicate over a bus structure to a shared memory (figure 1-2). This provides greater resource availability and fail safe-fail soft operation. It also provides two techniques of digital communications: one is on the bus to memory, and the other is the depositing of information in memory locations which can later be read by another program. This shared-memory communication concept has some problems with synchronization of reading and writing, which has led to the use of test and set and semaphore operations in computer systems. This synchronization problem is not discussed in this book. A good description of the problem and its solutions can be found in Lorin [13]. A similar system is shown in figure 1-3. This is commonly known as a *multicomputer*, or *federated, system*. Its primary means of communication is via an interprocessor link. Each processor has its own memory.

An expansion of the previous system types is a computer network or resource-sharing network [3, 6], shown in figure 1-4. A computer network

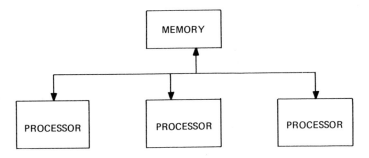

**Figure 1-2.** Global Bus Multiprocessor: An Example of a Distributed System.

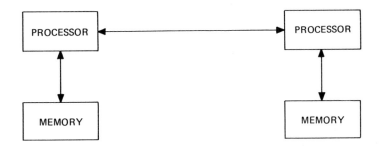

**Figure 1-3.** Federated System: An Example of a Distributed System.

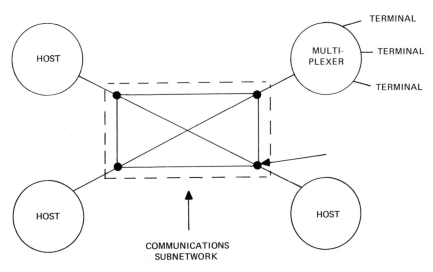

**Figure 1-4.** Network Architecture: An Example of a Distributed System.

can be described as an interconnected group of computers. Usually at least two distinct functions are performed by these computers, potentially in single physical processor. One function is the general-purpose processing function performed by the host processor. The other function consists of a communication and control function. The units that perform the control and communication function are stored program processors commonly known as the *message switch* or *packet switch* [6].

The primary reasons for the emergence of networks are several:

1. The user gains the ability to update the system in piecemeal fashion rather than having to replace a large central computer with an even larger central computer every few years.
2. The user can access a variety of services that may not be available at the local site (for example, ILLIAC IV on the ARPANET [9]).
3. The total processing power of the network may be larger than any single available computer.
4. The topology of the network can be tailored to applications.
5. The software for complex applications can be easily and clearly segmented and therefore should be easier to develop.
6. The network with its large pool of resources should be more fault-tolerant than a single machine.
7. A network should be easier to develop than a very large single machine.

Not all distributed systems explicitly contain all the protocol levels implied in figure 1-1. Recently, as a result of the potential impact of microprocessors on real-time military systems, some researchers have been looking at the problem of specialized distributed systems [1]. These systems tend to differ from networks and more general-purpose distributed processors in that the communication processing functions may be implicitly or even explicitly built into the hardware (in which case, all communication paths could be hard-wired and all communication protocols and traffic could be prearranged and fixed). Such distributed-system architectures are usually oriented toward a specific application. They may differ from networks in that the application may be distributed logically and not physically [2].

One of the main advantages of networks is their ability to share entities such as physical devices, files, programs, data, and peripheral facilities without having the entities actually at the local site. This provides a large service capability without a large hardware investment at the local site.

Good surveys of the entire field of distributed-system architectures written from a systems perspective may be found by reading references 1, 4, 11, 12, 13, and 22.

**Communication Subnetworks**

A *digital communication subnetwork* is any digital subsystem that can be used to interconnect digital devices. It may be as simple as a dedicated link connecting the register set of a computer to the computer's arithmetic and logic unit, or as complex as a complete computer along with memory which is used in a store-and-forward communication switching environment. Architecture design decisions for communication subnetworks should involve at least the following main areas:

1. *System topology*—the definition of the overall system and its architectural structure and a decision whether to implement the communication subnetwork using paths (no routing) or switches (using routing strategies).
2. *Message and packet switch design*—the implementation of the system architecture's communication structure using communication processors or systems of processors performing either message- or packet-switching functions.
3. *Circuit switch design*—the implementation of the system architecture's communication structure using crossbar-switch or time-division multiplexer devices to perform circuit switching functions.
4. *Subnetwork bus or path design*—the implementation of the system architecture's communication structure using dedicated links, shared buses, or shared memories.

Typical architectural topologies are rings, stars, and point-to-point connected systems. Computer architecture topology is implemented through the use of paths and switches. Paths are the media by which messages are transferred and may be dedicated links, shared buses, or common memories. However, because of their hardware complexity buses are the most interesting from the design standpoint. The major decisions in path design involve how a device receives control of a path and how messages are communicated over the path. Switches intervene between message source and destination to establish routing, and they may be circuit switches or message and packet switches (processors or even systems of interconnected computers such as the Bolt, Beranek, and Newman (BBN) Pluribus IMP [23]). Switches eventually must transfer information over a hardware transmission path, as shown in figure 1-1. Thus figure 1-1 could be broken down further by changing the intercomputer communication level into two levels—one associated with the switching algorithm and one associated with the control of the data path.

Circuit switches are generally used when portal-to-portal speed is important and routing decisions are simple. Message switches are generally slower than circuit switches but allow more complex routing decisions.

**Summary and Conclusion**

This chapter briefly reviewed some important concepts in the development of digital communications technology. It discussed networks and distributed systems and their uses and advantages. The remaining chapters deal with the types of networks as seen via examination of their communication structure and the construction of such communication subnetworks.

It is important to note that the model of a distributed processor chosen for this book provides for device (host) independence. Thus, using the techniques described here, the designer could either develop several forms of minicomputer networks or use the concepts to develop the communication scheme for a system built with multiple microprocessors. It is up to the designer to select which of the described communication techniques is most cost-effective for the system requirements.

The interconnection of computers to peripheral devices, to other computers, and to communication systems has been a significant and neglected design problem for a number of years. Yet, like I/O, hardware designers have been connecting digital devices for many years with little attempt to provide an integrated perspective of this vital area. There exist a smaller number of key papers and books in this area. To date, there has been one attempt [11] to develop a survey of the entire area of communication networks. Other researchers [9, 10, 23 to 30] have attempted to unify the present theories in some of the specialty areas in communication networks such as message switching, distributed-processor taxonomies, bus structures, distributed-processor models, and circuit switching.

With the growing complexity of digital systems, the advent of large communication networks, increasingly complex I/O devices, and microprocessor technology growth, the ad hoc development of communication subnetwork theory cannot be encouraged. To date, research and development, of interest in this book, has occurred on three unique levels in the area of interconnection design:

1. *System level* [11, 20, 23 to 27, 31 to 39] —concentration on design of network and system configurations of processors
2. *Paths* [9, 11, 25] —design of buses, shared-memory communication, and data links
3. *Switches* [3, 6, 8, 19 to 21, 23, 28 to 39] —design of circuit switches (time-division multiplexer and crossbar switches) [19] and message switches [3, 23]

The orientation of this book is toward the architect. It attempts to unify the design perspective of communication subnetworks and their resultant system impacts. Each of the major design parameters is discussed separately in its own chapter. Within each chapter all the tradeoffs necessary to totally describe the parameter or design issue are enumerated. Whenever possible, design theory is developed. In chapters where theories cannot be developed, the design issues are enumerated in a systematic fashion that attempts to cover all known, practical, and important possibilities. However, the book is not about queuing theory and does not try to discuss the mathematical models of the described design techniques.

## References

[ 1] E.D. Jensen, "The Influence of Microprocessors on Computer Architecture: Distributed Processing," Proceedings of the ACM National Conference 1975: 125-128.

[ 2] K.J. Thurber, "Computer Communication Techniques," *COMPSAC, IEEE* Computer Society, 1978: 589-594.

[ 3] S.R. Kimbleton and G.M. Schneider, "Computer Communications Networks: Approaches, Objectives, and Performance Considerations," *Computing Surveys* September 1975: 129-173.

[ 4] K.J. Thurber and H.A. Freeman, "Local Computer Network Architectures," *COMPCON*, Spring 1979: 258-261.

[ 5] *Proceedings of the IEEE*, Special issue on packet communication networks, 66 (November 1978).

[ 6] L.G. Roberts, "The Evolution of Packet Switching," *Proceedings of the IEEE* 66 (November 1978): 1307-1313.

[ 7] K.J. Thurber, *Large Scale Computer Architecture: Parallel and Associative Processors* (Rochelle Park, N.J.: Hayden, 1976).

[ 8] W.A. Wulf and C.G. Ball, "C.mmp: A Multi-Mini-Processor," 1972 *Fall Joint Computer Conference*, 765-777.

[ 9] K.J. Thurber et al., "A Systematic Approach to the Design of Digital Busing Structures," *Proceedings of the FJCC*, 1972: 719-740.

[10] K.J. Thurber, "Circuit Switching Technology: A State-of-the-Art Survey," *COMPCON*, Fall 1978: 116-124.

[11] E.D. Jensen, K.J. Thurber, and G.M. Schneider, "A Review of Systematic Methods in Distributed Processor Interconnection," *International Communications Conference*, 1976: 7.17-7.22.

[12] E.D. Jensen and W.E. Bobert, "Partitioning and Assignment of Distributed Processing Software," *COMPCON East*, 1976.

[13] H. Lorin, *Parallelism in Hardware and Software: Real and Apparent Concurrency* (Englewood Cliffs, N.J.: Prentice-Hall, 1972).

[14] E.W. Dijsktra, "The Structure of the 'The' Multiprogramming System," *Communications of the ACM*, May 1968.

[15] P.B. Hansen, "The Nucleus of a Multiprogramming System," *CACM*, April 1970.

[16] L.P. Rivas, H.C. Ludlam, and R.T. Braden, "An Implementation of the MSG Interprocess Communication Protocol," AD A041630, National Technical Information Center.

[17] C.G. Bell and A. Newell, *Computer Structures: Readings and Examples* (New York: McGraw-Hill, 1971).

[18] E.C. Luczak, "Global Bus Computer Communication Techniques," *Proceedings of the 1978 Computer Networking Symposium*, 58-67.

[19] G.M. Masson, "On Rearrangeable and Non-blocking Switching Networks, *ICC*, 1976.

[20] Digital Equipment Corporation, *Distributed Systems Handbook* (Maynard, Mass.: Digital Press, 1978).

[21] G. Falk, "A Comparison of Network Architectures: The ARPANET and SNA," *NCC*, 1978, pp. 755-763.

[22] G. LeLann, "Distributed Systems—Towards a Formal Approach," *Proceedings of the International Federations of Information Processing Societies*, 1977, pp. 155-160.

[23] F.E. Heart et al., "A New Minicomputer/Multiprocessor for the ARPA Network," *NCC* 42 (1973), pp. 529-537.

[24] G.A. Anderson and E.D. Jensen, "Computer Interconnection: Taxonomy, Characteristics, and Examples," *ACM Computing Surveys*, December 1975.

[25] R.C. Chen, "Bus Communication Systems" (Ph.D. diss., Carnegie-Mellon, 1974).

[26] D.P. Siewiorek, "Modularity and Multi-Microprocessor Structures," *Proceedings of the Seventh Annual Workshop on Microprogramming*, October 1974.

[27] D.P. Siewiorek, "Modularity and Multi-Microprocessor Structures," *Infotech State-of-the-Art Report on Distributed Processing*, 1976.

[28] M.J. Marcus, "Designs for Time Slot Interchanges," *Proceedings of the National Electronics Conference* 1970, 812-817.

[29] N. Pippenger, "On Crossbar Switching Networks," *IEEE Trans. on Comm.*, June 1975.

[30] V.E. Benes, *Mathematical Theory of Connecting Networks and Telephone Traffic* (New York: Academic Press, 1965).

[31] R. Rice, "A Project Overview," *COMPCON*, 1972.

[32] R.J. Swan, S.H. Fuller, and D.P. Siewiorek, "*Cm\*—A* Modular, Multi-microprocessor," *NCC*, 1977.

[33] S. Fuller, D. Siewiorek, and R. Swan, "Computer Modules—An Architecture for a Modular Multi-Microprocessor," *Proceedings of the 1975 ACM National Conference*.

[34] Phillip H. Enslow, ed., *Multiprocessors and Parallel Processors* (New York: John Wiley & Sons, 1974).

[35] P.H. Enslow, "Multiprocessor Organization—A Survey," *ACM Computer Surveys*, March 1977, pp. 103-129.

[36] R.M. Metcalfe and D.R. Boggs, "Ethernet: Distributed Packet Switing for Local Computer Networks," *CACM* 19 (July 1976), pp. 395-404.

[37] David J. Farber and Kenneth C. Larson, "The System Architecture of the Distributed Computer System—The Communications System," *Proc. Symposium on Computer-Communications Networks and Teletraffic, April 1972* (Brooklyn, N.Y.: Polytechnic Press, 1972).

[38] *Proceedings of the IEEE*, Special issue on circuit switching, September 1977.

[39] *Computer*, Special issue on circuit switching, June 1979.

# 2 System Topology Concepts Based on Communication Considerations

## Introduction

To date, the authors know of many different conceptualizations of distributed processing systems. Most fit within the simple concept presented in chapter 1: a *distributed processor* is a system in which a processing load is distributed across a number of processing elements that are physically interconnected but allow varying amounts of software intercommunication. Clearly, a multiprocessor fits this definition, as does a network. Is there a way to categorize such systems and intuit the essential architecture that would allow the reader to develop a general feel for the most basic properties of distributed-processor architectures? The answer is emphatically yes! However, the answer is clouded by the context of the reader.

The idea of a distributed processor touches many disciplines such as networking, efficient usage of microprocessor technology, computer communication principles and so on [1]. There are five important taxonomies and studies which describe distributed-processor architecture: Enslow [2] contends that a distributed processor must have distributed hardware processors, distributed data base, and distributed system control; Thurber and Freeman [3] purport that distributed processors are closely related and intersect the architectural concepts of local computer networks; Chen [4] takes a topological view of distributed processors; Siewiorek [5] describes distributed processors in terms of their topology and communication concepts; and Anderson and Jensen [6] view the architectures of distributed processors from the concept of message communications. From these perspectives it is clear that distributed-processor architecture encompasses many possible concepts, and the communication between processing elements is principally implemented using bus structures (and I/O connections), circuit switches, and packet switches. The remainder of this chapter pursues system-level architectural concepts and tradeoffs. Later chapters deal with the communications architectures.

## Model Basis

The Anderson and Jensen [6] model is based on three simple concepts:

*Message*—a unit of information transferred between processes executing on processors

*Path*—the media over which information is transferred, for example, bus, data link, and so on

*Switch*—an intervening intelligent device which routes a message between a sender and a receiver

Considering the consequences of the definitions, it can be seen that the communication of a message between process A and process B may be characterized as being either a direct communication over a path or an indirect communication through a switch in which some intervention occurs such as message routing or address transformation. Further, the switch could be either centralized or decentralized. These two design decisions represent system strategies. No distinction between message, packet, or circuit switching is necessary at this level as long as the reader understands that this communications process can be broken down further than illustrated in figure 1-1 and that switches at the next-lower level will actually switch some type of line. Anderson and Jensen next suggest that two tactical decisions must be made—whether the transfer structure is to be dedicated or shared, and the system topology. The resultant taxonomy is shown in figures 2-1 and 2-2 with important extant system concepts indicated for the system architectures.

## Additional Issues

The additional points suggested for consideration during examination of Anderson and Jensen's taxonomy may encompass expansions to the original goal and thus are not meant as criticisms but as issues that the reader should keep in mind for a truly comprehensive understanding of the importance and limitations of Anderson and Jensen's taxonomy.

Additional considerations for Anderson and Jensen's taxonomy necessary for in-depth understanding of the remainder of this chapter include the following:

1. Communications orientation of the model
2. Generic nature of model
3. Lack of consideration of I/O, memory, software control hierarchies, processing element-system interface, and interprocess communication problems
4. Lack of discussion of hybrid systems

With regard to issue 1, the model assumed that communication was via message. Yet, it glosses over the fact that a message transmitted over a bus may be different from a message transmitted in a switched communication environment. The reader should note that a message may be viewed simply as a string of bits divided into three parts—a header or identifier, a body or text, and a trailer or terminator. Messages may differ in path- and switch-oriented systems

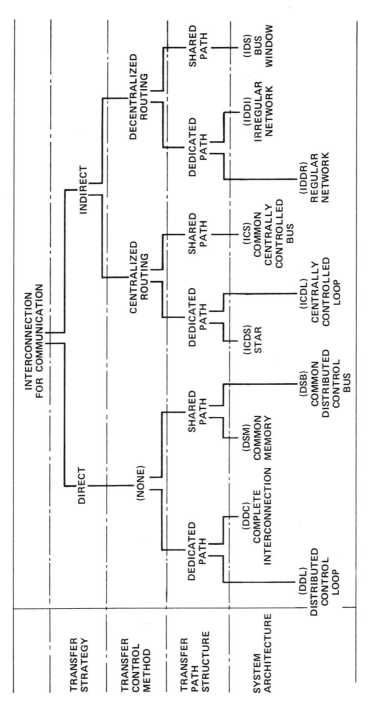

**Figure 2-1.** Communication System Models: Anderson and Jensen's Taxonomy.

```
TRANSFER STRATEGY: DIRECT
    PATH: DEDICATED
        TOPOLOGY: DISTRIBUTED CONTROL LOOP
        TOPOLOGY: COMPLETE INTERCONNECTION
    PATH: SHARED
        TOPOLOGY: COMMON MEMORY
        TOPOLOGY: COMMON DISTRIBUTED
                  CONTROL BUS
TRANSFER STRATEGY: INDIRECT
    ROUTING: CENTRALIZED
        PATH: DEDICATED
            TOPOLOGY: STAR
            TOPOLOGY: CENTRALLY CONTROLLED
                      LOOP
        PATH: SHARED
            TOPOLOGY: COMMON CENTRALLY
                      CONTROLLED BUS
    ROUTING: DECENTRALIZED
        PATH: DEDICATED
            TOPOLOGY: REGULAR NETWORK
            TOPOLOGY: IRREGULAR NETWORK
        PATH: SHARED
            TOPOLOGY: BUS WINDOW
```

**Figure 2-2.** Outline Representation of Anderson and Jensen's Taxonomy. Reprinted with permission from K.J. Thurber, Computer Communication Techniques," COMPSAC, IEEE Computer Society, 1978: 589-594.

as a result of the allowable sizes of each message portion, the technique used to separate the portions, and whether the header and/or trailer is implicit or explicit. For example, in a system made up of dedicated links and synchronized processing elements, messages may not require a header or a trailer. Further, a distinction is not made between circuit and message or packet switches in the Anderson and Jensen model. This assumption is reasonable as long as the reader notes that switches control paths or links at some lower level. The model is a generic one describing the most rudimentary levels of communication and their practical implementations. Thus in many cases it glosses over details which the reader will find in later chapters of this book (issue 2). The model does not discuss the concept of superposition, that is, that two generic concepts could be combined to form a hybrid system having the mutual advantageous properties of each of the generic systems (issue 4). Indeed, one could conceive of systems in which each of the main system functions (I/O, memory-PE connection, backend memory hierarchy storage connections, and so on) uses a different communication technique. Anderson and Jensen do, however, point out some examples of hybrid systems.

We will also ignore many of the issues pointed out in issue 3, for example, interprocess communication. Later chapters address issues involving I/O, control hierarchies, and PE-system interface as part of the path design problem.

## Comparison of System Concepts

We choose for consideration of the system-level design issues the same measures of effectiveness chosen by Anderson and Jensen: (1) modularity (cost modularity and placement modularity), (2) connection flexibility, (3) fault tolerance, (4) logical complexity, and (5) and bottlenecks (or congestion). These concepts are defined as follows.

*Cost modularity* (CM) is the incremental cost of adding a processing element (PE). In some systems this could be free (zero cost); in other systems it could require that $n - 1$ paths be added to accept the $n$th PE.

*Placement modularity* (PM) is the degree to which the function or location of an element is restricted. In some systems a path, switch, or PE can be easily added to improve performance. In other systems, for example a STAR, the central switch is not amenable to place modularity. In this case addition of a switch would change the architecture to another category in the taxonomy.

*Connection flexibility* (CF) is primarily important in message-switched systems. It is a measure of the alternative costs associated with adding a PE. When a processor is added, whether extra long-distance connection paths or extra local paths have to be added is one measure of the connection flexibility. This issue is similar to the modularity tradeoffs associated with path-oriented systems.

*Fault Tolerance* (FT) is the measure of the effect of a fault in a system. In system configurations, this manifests itself in terms of how is the system reconfigured (fail-soft) in terms of either architecture or performance. Typically, systems with decentralized control would be most amenable to fault-tolerant design.

*Local complexity* (LC) deals with a measurement of the amount and complexity of decisions necessary to route information (send a message) within a system.

*Bottleneck* (B) problems deal with resource performance limitations created by saturation or congestion of a system facility such as a data link due to system-resource demand.

Each of the ten system concepts of Anderson and Jensen is discussed.

## Design Tradeoffs

A number of architecture design tradeoffs are not explicitly discussed by Anderson and Jensen. They are implicit in some of the systems Anderson and Jensen discussed. Some of these issues are:

1.  System level
    Must a system have homogeneous PEs or can the PEs be nonhomogeneous?

    Must a system have homogeneous switches (buses, data links, and so on) or can the switches be nonhomogeneous?

Are communication links bidirectional or unidirectional?

Can full duplex transmission occur?

Can multiple communication facilities be added to a system?

2. Processing element
   What type of buffering capabilities does a PE have?

   If a PE has $n$ input/output ports, can a PE receive $n$ messages, transmit $n$ messages, and process simultaneously?

3. Messages
   How are transmission errors detected and processed?

   What happens to a message sent to a nonexistent PE (process)?

   Are message acknowledgments transmitted PE to PE or only from PE source to PE destination?

   Can more than one message be in transit simultaneously in a system?

**System Types**

*Loop Architecture*

Loop systems (figure 2-3) use a direct transfer strategy, no transfer control, and dedicated paths [7, 8, 9]. They have typically evolved from a data communication context. In a typical loop system, each PE connects to its two nearest neighbors. Data traffic could conceptually flow in clockwise and/or counterclockwise directions in such a system. Most implemented loop systems, however, tend to be unidirectional. The system operation is very simple—A processing element (the source) transmits a message to its neighbor PE (the destination). This procedure continues until the message arrives at its final destination. Before arriving at the final destination, the message may have passed through many intermediate destinations. If a message comes into a destination but must be retransmitted to another PE, the transmitting PE acts as a relay or buffer. Thus, PEs must act as both sources and destinations. Some system architecture options include:

1. A routing strategy which either allows only one message to circulate at a given time or allows more than one message to circulate at a given time based on PE buffering-capability tradeoffs
2. Allowing both fixed or variable message lengths
3. Allowing bidirectional communication
4. Allowing bit serial or parallel communication
5. Allowing virtual-message addressing (sending a message to a logical process rather than a physical processor, thus allowing communication to be independent of the number of processors or the assignment of processes to processors)

```
TRANSFER STRATEGY: DIRECT
    PATH: DEDICATED
        TOPOLOGY: DISTRIBUTED CONTROL LOOP
        TOPOLOGY: COMPLETE INTERCONNECTION
    PATH: SHARED
        TOPOLOGY: COMMON MEMORY
        TOPOLOGY: COMMON DISTRIBUTED
                  CONTROL BUS
TRANSFER STRATEGY: INDIRECT
    ROUTING: CENTRALIZED
        PATH: DEDICATED
            TOPOLOGY: STAR
            TOPOLOGY: CENTRALLY CONTROLLED
                      LOOP
        PATH: SHARED
            TOPOLOGY: COMMON CENTRALLY
                      CONTROLLED BUS
    ROUTING: DECENTRALIZED
        PATH: DEDICATED
            TOPOLOGY: REGULAR NETWORK
            TOPOLOGY: IRREGULAR NETWORK
        PATH: SHARED
            TOPOLOGY: BUS WINDOW
```

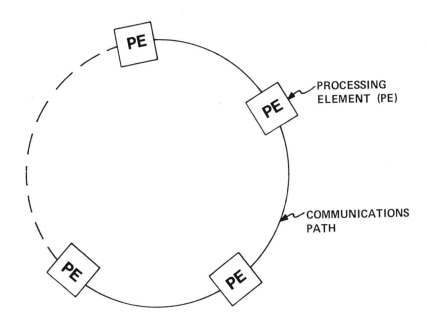

**Figure 2-3.** Loop Systems.

6.  Providing multiple loops in a system
7.  Dedicating a loop to a specific form of traffic
8.  Providing subloops in a system
9.  Providing a set of hierarchical loops in which the loops run at different speeds

The main properties of a loop system are as follows:

1.  CM is very good; an additional PE is easy to add although total loop delay increases; cost is a single path.
2.  PM is very good; any type of PE can be added without restriction.
3.  CF is fixed.
4.  FT is poor, susceptible to single point failures, and solvable by providing redundant sets of paths and bypass switches.
5.  LC is low; a PE must be able only to recognize, accept/buffer, and transmit messages.
6.  Bottleneck is potentially bad; bandwith of loop dictates whether the system will have a bottleneck.

*Complete Interconnection Architecture*

Completely interconnected systems (figure 2-4) use direct transfer strategy, no transfer control, and dedicated paths [10, 11]. Typically, such systems have evolved from groups interconnecting their currently existing computers into a system. By definition, in a typical system all PEs are connected by a dedicated link to every other PE. Messages are transferred between PEs on the dedicated connections. Acting as source, PEs select the proper transmission path; PEs acting in destination mode must be able to arbitrate the reception of the many possible incoming messages; and PEs acting as sources may desire to be able to transmit multiple messages.

Some system options and restrictions include (1) restrictions on PE transmit and reception capabilities to tune system performance; (2) location-only message addressing (otherwise transmission would be indirect); (3) the possibility, dependent on link type, of bidirectional simultaneous communication between any two PEs; (4) ability to have direct PE-to-PE error processing; and (5) ability to have variable-capacity data links between any two PEs. The main properties of a complete interconnection architecture are:

1.  CM is very poor; addition of a PE requires the addition of *n* links if the system previously contained *n* PEs, dependent on PE port limitations.
2.  PM is very good; any type of PE can be added without restriction, dependent on PE port limitations.
3.  CF is fixed.

```
TRANSFER STRATEGY: DIRECT
     PATH: DEDICATED
          TOPOLOGY: DISTRIBUTED CONTROL LOOP
          TOPOLOGY: COMPLETE INTERCONNECTION
     PATH: SHARED
          TOPOLOGY: COMMON MEMORY
          TOPOLOGY: COMMON DISTRIBUTED
                    CONTROL BUS
TRANSFER STRATEGY: INDIRECT
     ROUTING: CENTRALIZED
          PATH: DEDICATED
               TOPOLOGY: STAR
               TOPOLOGY: CENTRALLY CONTROLLED
                         LOOP
          PATH: SHARED
               TOPOLOGY: COMMON CENTRALLY
                         CONTROLLED BUS
     ROUTING: DECENTRALIZED
          PATH: DEDICATED
               TOPOLOGY: REGULAR NETWORK
               TOPOLOGY: IRREGULAR NETWORK
          PATH: SHARED
               TOPOLOGY: BUS WINDOW
```

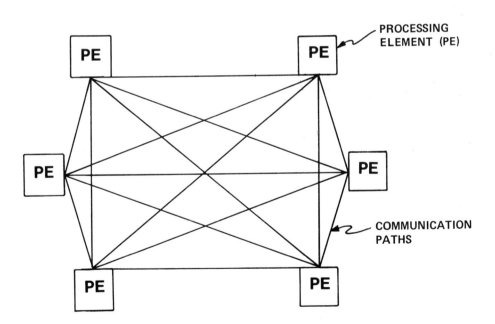

**Figure 2-4.** Complete System Interconnection.

4. FT is good; many paths are available to provide alternative routing (failed link) or masking out of a failed PE if routing is or can be supported by a PE.
5. LC is low; PEs transmit messages directly to one another.
6. Bottleneck is good; bandwidth of paths and number of PEs can be sized to the specific job.

*Multiprocessor Architecture*

Central memory multiprocessors (figure 2-5) use direct transfer strategy, no transfer control, and a shared transfer path (memory). Multiprocessors are a very common architecture that evolved from system concepts in which PEs used shared memory for communication or from systems requiring significant redundancy of processing capability [12, 13, 14]. In terms of systems actually used in the field, multiprocessors are probably the most common system type. The key concept is the use of memory as a communication path versus simply using memory for shared storage.

Typical system restrictions or options include (1) use of a special (separate) memory for communication, (2) use of bus or multiport techniques to connect PEs to the memory, (3) dividing the memory into banks with function dedicated to a specific bank, and (4) use of direct-memory-access ports to provide I/O capability.

The main properties of a shared-memory multiprocessor include the following:

1. CM is highly dependent on the technique for connecting the path to the memory: multiporting (good), direct (poor), or bus structure (good). (*Note*: A bus structure may be viewed as one form of a multiport.)
2. PM is very good; processors may be added arbitrarily (constrained by the memory design), and memory may be increased to fit the increased load, depending on the number of ports and their size.
3. CF is fixed.
4. FT is variable. Depending on the physical constraints of the system and isolation capabilities, FT can be good in terms of impact of failed processor or poor in terms of a failed central memory (potential software failure problems also arise due to centralization of the program and data storage).
5. LC is variable—low for simple software concepts, but can be extremely complex in large systems.
6. Bottleneck is bad. Typical implemented systems suffer severe performance degradation due to lack of sufficient memory bandwidth when typically four or more PEs are in the system; this can be corrected via use of local cache memory.

TRANSFER STRATEGY: DIRECT
    PATH: DEDICATED
        TOPOLOGY: DISTRIBUTED CONTROL LOOP
        TOPOLOGY: COMPLETE INTERCONNECTION
    PATH: SHARED
        TOPOLOGY: COMMON MEMORY ⟵
        TOPOLOGY: COMMON DISTRIBUTED
                  CONTROL BUS
TRANSFER STRATEGY: INDIRECT
    ROUTING: CENTRALIZED
        PATH: DEDICATED
            TOPOLOGY: STAR
            TOPOLOGY: CENTRALLY CONTROLLED
                      LOOP
        PATH: SHARED
            TOPOLOGY: COMMON CENTRALLY
                      CONTROLLED BUS
    ROUTING: DECENTRALIZED
        PATH: DEDICATED
            TOPOLOGY: REGULAR NETWORK
            TOPOLOGY: IRREGULAR NETWORK
        PATH: SHARED
            TOPOLOGY: BUS WINDOW

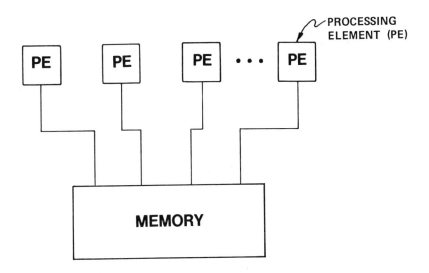

Figure 2-5. Central Memory Multiprocessor.

*Global Bus Architecture*

The global bus architecture (figure 2-6) uses direct transfer strategy, no transfer control, and a shared path [15, 16]. This type of system is common in many military, space, and process control environments. Sometimes it is called a federated system. Typical military systems use a bit serial bus which may be replicated for fault tolerance or throughput considerations. Access to the bus is arbitrated by a bus controller, and PEs share bus bandwidth.

Communication occurs directly between the PE in control of the bus (source) and the PE to receive the message (destination). Typically, the

```
TRANSFER STRATEGY: DIRECT
    PATH: DEDICATED
        TOPOLOGY: DISTRIBUTED CONTROL LOOP
        TOPOLOGY: COMPLETE INTERCONNECTION
    PATH: SHARED
        TOPOLOGY: COMMON MEMORY
        TOPOLOGY: COMMON DISTRIBUTED
                  CONTROL BUS
TRANSFER STRATEGY: INDIRECT
    ROUTING: CENTRALIZED
        PATH: DEDICATED
            TOPOLOGY: STAR
            TOPOLOGY: CENTRALLY CONTROLLED
                      LOOP
        PATH: SHARED
            TOPOLOGY: COMMON CENTRALLY
                      CONTROLLED BUS
    ROUTING: DECENTRALIZED
        PATH: DEDICATED
            TOPOLOGY: REGULAR NETWORK
            TOPOLOGY: IRREGULAR NETWORK
        PATH: SHARED
            TOPOLOGY: BUS WINDOW
```

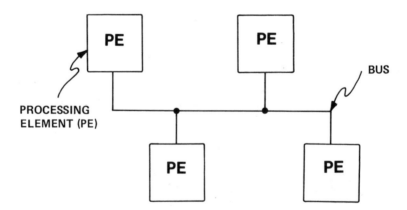

**Figure 2-6.** Global Bus Architecture.

destination must recognize that a message is intended for it. Virtual-message transmission is possible.

Typical system options include (1) time-slotting the bus to fix message size (time-division multiplexing), (2) letting message size be variable, (3) use of virtual (process-oriented) messages or placement (PE-oriented) messages, (4) replication of the bus for redundancy or throughput, (5) bit serial or parallel communication, (6) bus allocation schemes to guarantee service rates to specific PEs or processes, and (7) use of the bus structure to provide the facilities for bus arbitration.

The main properties of the global bus concept are:

1. CM is variable—good with respect to the PEs if the bus has been designed to allow for addition of PEs and potentially poor with respect to the bus since bus bandwidth tends to be fixed and adding PEs may require bus replication or complete bus redesign.
2. PM is variable—good with respect to the PEs and potentially poor with respect to the bus since the bus may have difficulty coping with high-speed processors or PEs which are geographically separated.
3. CF is fixed.
4. FT is variable—good with respect to the ability to replicate PEs and potentially good if the bus design allows for bus replication to remove the possible single-point failure.
5. LC is dependent on protocol and interface complexity but is typically low; usually the PEs communicate with simple protocols, and the system is operated in a near-dedicated mode, thus making the system-operation concept very simple. LC can be very low if logical communication (associative-process addressing) is not used.
6. Bottleneck is potentially poor. The global bus can represent a potential single-point failure; it could be solved by use of a passive bus, say, Ethernet.

*Star Architecture*

The star architecture (figure 2-7) uses an indirect transfer strategy, centralized message routing, and dedicated path. This type of architecture is the foundation of many time-sharing systems and simple data communication networks. The reader should note that not all people view this system as distributed. Also, some simple point of sale systems resembles this architecture; however, in such systems the switch also serves as a computation device, and the PEs may be "smart" terminals. In the star each PE connects (bidirectionally) to a central switch. A process on a PE communicates to another process by sending a message to the switch. The switch acts as an intervener. It appears to be the intermediate destination for all messages, and it also appears to the final destination as the "source" of all messages. When the switch receives a message, it determines the appropriate destination and routes the message to the destination.

```
TRANSFER STRATEGY: DIRECT
    PATH: DEDICATED
        TOPOLOGY: DISTRIBUTED CONTROL LOOP
        TOPOLOGY: COMPLETE INTERCONNECTION
    PATH: SHARED
        TOPOLOGY: COMMON MEMORY
        TOPOLOGY: COMMON DISTRIBUTED
                  CONTROL BUS
TRANSFER STRATEGY: INDIRECT
    ROUTING: CENTRALIZED
        PATH: DEDICATED
            TOPOLOGY: STAR
            TOPOLOGY: CENTRALLY CONTROLLED
                      LOOP
        PATH: SHARED
            TOPOLOGY: COMMON CENTRALLY
                      CONTROLLED BUS
    ROUTING: DECENTRALIZED
        PATH: DEDICATED
            TOPOLOGY: REGULAR NETWORK
            TOPOLOGY: IRREGULAR NETWORK
        PATH: SHARED
            TOPOLOGY: BUS WINDOW
```

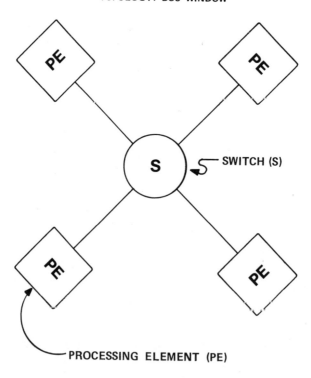

Figure 2-7. Star Architecture.

The properties of the star are similar to those of the multiprocessor and global bus system. These properties are summarized.

The two major options available on such systems are associative location addressing and switch replication for fault tolerance. The main properties of the star concept are:

1. CM is variable—good with respect to PEs but there exist potential problems involving the switch, depending on bandwidth and number of ports.
2. PM is variable—good with respect to PEs but there are potential problems involving the switch, depending on protocol requirements and throughput limitations.
3. CF is fixed. Each PE much have a switch port to the central switch, and each process must provide appropriate message-routing information.
4. FT is poor. Not only is there a single-point failure, but also the routing table must be preserved.
5. LC is moderate; communication protocols and routing algorithms must be provided.
6. Bottleneck is poor. The switch and its routing tables present a severe bottleneck which is aggravated by having to send both a message header of control information and the message body for each message, routing the message, and retransmitting it. This is always a problem with all indirect-transfer-oriented systems.

*Loop with Central Switch*

This architecture (figure 2-8), like the star architecture, uses an indirect transfer strategy, centralized routing, and dedicated paths [18]. Its topology is that of a loop. Thus it has many of the features of the loop (nearest-neighbor connections only) and of the star (a switch-oriented system). In this system (like in the star system) the switch acts to the final destination as the source, and to the source it acts as an intermediate destination of all messages. The switch performs all routing. Probably the most interesting tradeoff in this system concept is that of system bandwidth versus flexibility provided via the switch. In a system with unidirectional inter-PE links, the message must make almost one more complete trip around the loop than if the system were a direct transfer loop without a central switch.

If the switch is a program which runs on a PE, then maybe this architecture is a specialization of the loop system in which one of the PEs acts as a switch. It may also be possible for the switch to migrate from one PE to another in such a case.

Since the properties of this system can be easily derived by looking at those of a loop and a star, no further attention is given to the concept.

```
TRANSFER STRATEGY: DIRECT
    PATH: DEDICATED
            TOPOLOGY: DISTRIBUTED CONTROL LOOP
            TOPOLOGY: COMPLETE INTERCONNECTION
    PATH: SHARED
            TOPOLOGY: COMMON MEMORY
            TOPOLOGY: COMMON DISTRIBUTED
                        CONTROL BUS
TRANSFER STRATEGY: INDIRECT
    ROUTING: CENTRALIZED
        PATH: DEDICATED
            TOPOLOGY: STAR
            TOPOLOGY: CENTRALLY CONTROLLED
                        LOOP
        PATH: SHARED
            TOPOLOGY: COMMON CENTRALLY
                        CONTROLLED BUS
    ROUTING: DECENTRALIZED
        PATH: DEDICATED
            TOPOLOGY: REGULAR NETWORK
            TOPOLOGY: IRREGULAR NETWORK
        PATH: SHARED
            TOPOLOGY: BUS WINDOW
```

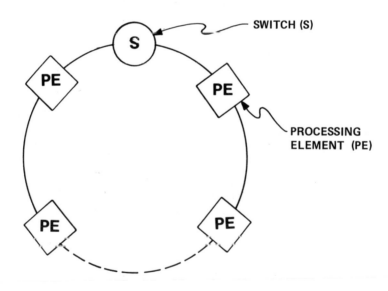

**Figure 2-8.** Loop with a Central Switch.

*Bus with Central Switch*

The bus with a central switch (figure 2-9) uses indirect transfer strategy, centralized routing, and shared path [19]. However, one could implement this system using a switch which just arbitrates. Like the loop with the central switch, the properties of this architecture can be derived by looking at the properties of the global bus concept and the star concept. In this system a PE wishing to transmit a message obtains control of the bus and sends the message to the switch which reroutes the message. Unfortunately this causes a bus bandwidth of about twice that of a global bus system. However, many of the connection links associated with a star are eliminated by the use of the global bus.

*Regular Network*

The regular network (figure 2-10) uses indirect transfer strategy, decentralized routing, and dedicated paths [20]. This system contains a number of PEs interconnected with dedicated paths in a regular fashion. Figure 2-10 shows a nearest-neighbors connection structure. However, any reasonable tessalation could be employed. The IMS hypercube system uses a cubic structure. Typically, regular network systems are based on a four nearest-neighbor interconnection scheme, and they have evolved from academic studies of highly parallel system structures.

System operation occurs as follows. A message is routed through the network via a set of transmissions from PE to PE. Each intermediate destination which intervenes between the initial source and final destination must determine which of its neighbors will be next to receive the message.

Alternatives and restrictions which are useful in regular networks include:

1. Different interconnection strategies: trees, cubes, and various planar tessalations (rectangular, hexagonal, and so on)
2. Restriction of transmission direction to unidirectional, that is, in a four nearest-neighbor configuration restriction of transmission to up and left only
3. Using the "edge PEs" to introduce special system end conditions as dictated by a specific application

The main properties of the regular network are:

1. CM is high because of the need to maintain the regular structure.
2. PM is high because of the need to maintain the regular structure.
3. There is no CF.
4. FT can be very good depending on the technique used for message routing and disconnection of the PEs in case of a PE failure. Reconfiguration is very poor unless all hardware is provided in duplicate; otherwise, the network must reconfigure to an irregular-network concept.

```
TRANSFER STRATEGY: DIRECT
    PATH: DEDICATED
        TOPOLOGY: DISTRIBUTED CONTROL LOOP
        TOPOLOGY: COMPLETE INTERCONNECTION
    PATH: SHARED
        TOPOLOGY: COMMON MEMORY
        TOPOLOGY: COMMON DISTRIBUTED
            CONTROL BUS
TRANSFER STRATEGY: INDIRECT
    ROUTING: CENTRALIZED
        PATH: DEDICATED
            TOPOLOGY: STAR
            TOPOLOGY: CENTRALLY CONTROLLED
                LOOP
        PATH: SHARED
            TOPOLOGY: COMMON CENTRALLY
                CONTROLLED BUS
    ROUTING: DECENTRALIZED
        PATH: DEDICATED
            TOPOLOGY: REGULAR NETWORK
            TOPOLOGY: IRREGULAR NETWORK
        PATH: SHARED
            TOPOLOGY: BUS WINDOW
```

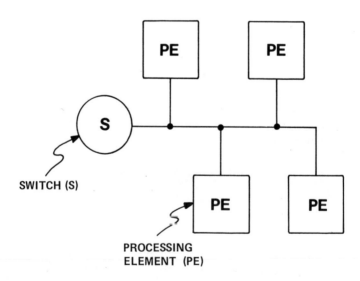

**Figure 2-9.** Bus with a Central Switch.

```
TRANSFER STRATEGY: DIRECT
    PATH: DEDICATED
        TOPOLOGY: DISTRIBUTED CONTROL LOOP
        TOPOLOGY: COMPLETE INTERCONNECTION
    PATH: SHARED
        TOPOLOGY: COMMON MEMORY
        TOPOLOGY: COMMON DISTRIBUTED
                  CONTROL BUS
TRANSFER STRATEGY: INDIRECT
    ROUTING: CENTRALIZED
        PATH: DEDICATED
            TOPOLOGY: STAR
            TOPOLOGY: CENTRALLY CONTROLLED
                      LOOP
        PATH: SHARED
            TOPOLOGY: COMMON CENTRALLY
                      CONTROLLED BUS
    ROUTING: DECENTRALIZED
        PATH: DEDICATED
            TOPOLOGY: REGULAR NETWORK
            TOPOLOGY: IRREGULAR NETWORK
        PATH: SHARED
            TOPOLOGY: BUS WINDOW
```

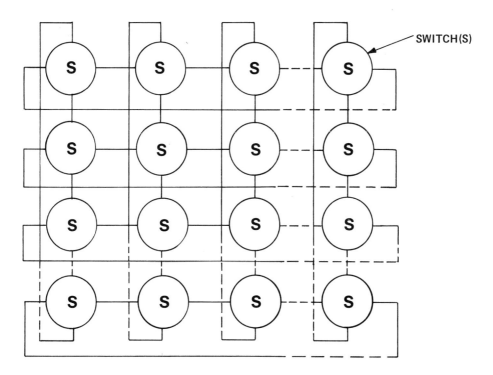

Figure 2-10. Regular Network.

5. LC is medium. The regularity of structure can cause simplification of potential routing algorithms.
6. Bottleneck is low; there are a large number of available routing paths.

*Irregular Network*

The irregular network (one example is shown in figure 2-11) uses indirect transfers, decentralized routing, and dedicated paths [21, 22]. The concept of an irregular network has evolved from the development of computer networks for data communications, for example, ARPANET. Routing is performed in the switches. Concepts useful in irregular networks are examined in detail in chapter 3.

The main properties of irregular network are:

1. CM is extremely good since PEs may be arbitrarily added.
2. PM is extremely good since PEs of any complexity or type may be arbitrarily added.
3. CF: connections can be arbitrarily added.
4. FT is good since arbitrary levels of redundancy and reconfiguration capabilities can be provided.
5. LC is high because of complex routing algorithms necessary for system operation.
6. Bottleneck is low since the system can be tailored to a specific application or throughput demands.

*Bus Window*

The bus window architecture (figure 2-12) uses indirect transfer, decentralized routing, and shared paths [23]. This architecture evolved out of attempts to design systems composed of hierarchies of interconnected minicomputers. A typical architecture consists of a set of switches connected to paths which are shared by multiple PEs. Messages are transmitted to the switches from a PE and then routed to the appropriate destination by the switch.

The main tradeoffs to be considered concern the issues of (1) unidirectional or bidirectional paths, (2) address mapping in the system, (3) time of address binding (static or dynamic), (4) number of elements allowed on a bus, (5) routing strategies, and (6) number of levels in the system hierarchy.

Typical properties of the bus window architecture are

1. CM is good since PEs can be added subject to limitations imposed by the bus structure.

```
TRANSFER STRATEGY: DIRECT
     PATH: DEDICATED
          TOPOLOGY: DISTRIBUTED CONTROL LOOP
          TOPOLOGY: COMPLETE INTERCONNECTION
     PATH: SHARED
          TOPOLOGY: COMMON MEMORY
          TOPOLOGY: COMMON DISTRIBUTED
                    CONTROL BUS
TRANSFER STRATEGY: INDIRECT
     ROUTING: CENTRALIZED
          PATH: DEDICATED
               TOPOLOGY: STAR
               TOPOLOGY: CENTRALLY CONTROLLED
                         LOOP
          PATH: SHARED
               TOPOLOGY: COMMON CENTRALLY
                         CONTROLLED BUS
     ROUTING: DECENTRALIZED
          PATH: DEDICATED
               TOPOLOGY: REGULAR NETWORK
               TOPOLOGY: IRREGULAR NETWORK
          PATH: SHARED
               TOPOLOGY: BUS WINDOW
```

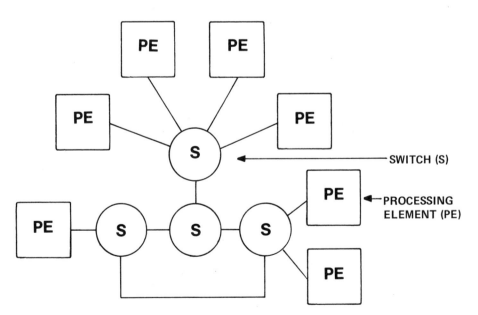

**Figure 2-11.** Irregular Network.

```
TRANSFER STRATEGY: DIRECT
    PATH: DEDICATED
        TOPOLOGY: DISTRIBUTED CONTROL LOOP
        TOPOLOGY: COMPLETE INTERCONNECTION
    PATH: SHARED
        TOPOLOGY: COMMON MEMORY
        TOPOLOGY: COMMON DISTRIBUTED
                  CONTROL BUS
TRANSFER STRATEGY: INDIRECT
    ROUTING: CENTRALIZED
        PATH: DEDICATED
            TOPOLOGY: STAR
            TOPOLOGY: CENTRALLY CONTROLLED
                      LOOP
        PATH: SHARED
            TOPOLOGY: COMMON CENTRALLY
                      CONTROLLED BUS
    ROUTING: DECENTRALIZED
        PATH: DEDICATED
            TOPOLOGY: REGULAR NETWORK
            TOPOLOGY: IRREGULAR NETWORK
        PATH: SHARED
            TOPOLOGY: BUS WINDOW ⟨▷
```

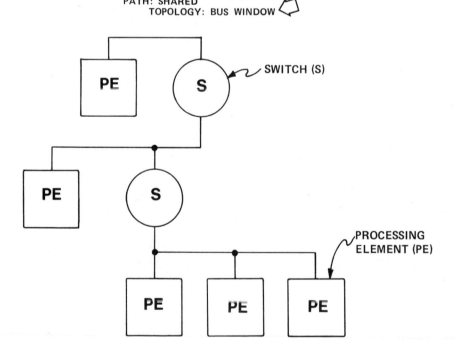

Figure 2-12. Bus Window.

2. PM is good since arbitrary PE designs can be added subject to limitations imposed by the bus structure.
3. CF: connections can be added conveniently by adding a switch; bus structures tend to be fixed.
4. FT is poor because of the possible failure of buses.
5. LC is high because of the complexities of systems that can be constructed; the complexity is proportional to the number of levels constructed in the system.
6. System is susceptible to bottlenecking because of the bus structures.

## Summary and Conclusion

This chapter used Anderson and Jensen's taxonomy to discuss significant system concepts in distributed-processor systems. The taxonomy is based on observations as to the nature of communications and the implications of communication strategies in terms of implementation, that is, paths and switches. The Anderson and Jensen taxonomy concept fits into a more general view of the levels of a hierarchically structured system employing a communication subsystem (subnetwork).

The view of systems as perceived through Anderson and Jensen's taxonomy provides a common ground for the examination of distributed systems from a communications perspective. If one classifies system concepts based on their dominant architectural features and the intent of the system concept, the taxonomy gives a very good analysis of the majority of "distributed-system concepts." Certain refinements, however, could be made. Some are alluded to in the text. The major change that would be useful is to establish a quantitative procedure of handling system-hybrid system tradeoffs.

Further, by relating the taxonomy to the hierarchical system structure (derived from the Kimbleton and Schneider survey [24]), we can attempt to provide further refinement in the way one thinks of the taxonomy. That is, using the Kimbleton and Schneider communication hierarchy corresponding to figure 1-1, one can more visibly separate the logical and physical aspects of communication and see how the Anderson and Jensen taxonomy fits into a structured system concept based solely on packet-switch network communication considerations.

The Anderson and Jensen taxonomy is the most innovative distributed-system model available. It provides a vehicle that allows comparison of ten fundamental system concepts. Further, it lends insight into how one can measure the cost of various system features (for example, modularity) and system performance (for example, throughput). It would also seem to provide a good basis for the development of comparative system simulators for more detailed simulation, analysis, and prediction of actual application performance, assuming quantitative metrics could be developed.

In our view, the taxonomy accurately reflects the fundamental communication concepts of computer communications from the architecture viewpoint. The remaining chapters discuss specific implementations of various types of switches and paths which would be used in previously described distributed-processor systems. Another, dimension from which to view communication concepts would be to develop and analyze the major architecture tradeoffs as seen from the implementations of contemporary communication processors. An excellent description and summary of such an approach is found in reference 25.

## Exercises

1. For each of the generic system concepts, determine alternative techniques and their system impact to provide the system with I/O facilities, memory external to a PE, and a memory hierarchy for the system concept.

2. Construct a tradeoff chart which compares and ranks all the generic system concepts in terms of PM, CM, CF, LC, FT, and B characteristics.

3. Develop a model for generic circuit-switch systems.

4. Design a loop system which can send fixed-length messages over serial data links with transmissions occurring bit serial and bidirectionally over full duplex links. Consider using I/O channels or direct memory access channels to construct the input/output terminals. Discuss all design tradeoffs. Discuss Anderson and Jensen's comment [6] that bidirectional loop systems are difficult to implement.

5. Design a variable-length parallel transfer message system for a completely interconnected system with nonhomogeneous PEs. Discuss all design assumptions and tradeoff decisions.

6. Assume you are given a central main-memory multiprocessor. Assume that for throughput reasons a "cache buffer memory" is to be added to the system. Discuss the impact of this addition on the system when the cache is centralized (that is, one cache is shared by all PEs) and when the cache consists of a series of cache memories (that is, there is one cache local to each PE in the system). What type of data interlock and synchronization problems occur in the latter concept and how can such problems be solved?

7. Repeat exercise 4 for the following architectures: generic global bus, loop with a central switch, and global bus with a central switch.

8. Repeat exercise 5 for generic star and regular-network architectures.

9. Develop a design tradeoff analysis technique oriented to evaluate message-routing strategies for an irregular-network architecture. Design three routing strategies for the irregular network: one to use global routines, one to use local routing, and one to use a combined global/local concept. Compare these strategies using the previously developed tradeoff analysis technique.

10. Repeat exercise 9 for the architecture of a generic bus window.

**References**

[ 1] K.J. Thurber and G.M. Masson, "Recent Advances in Microprocessor Technology and Their Impact on Interconnection Design in Computer Systems," *ICC*, 3 (1977), pp. 216-220.

[ 2] P.H. Enslow, "What Is a 'Distributed' Data Processing System?" *Computer*, January 1978, pp. 13-21.

[ 3] K.J. Thurber and H.A. Freeman, "Local Computer Network Architectures," *COMPCON*, Spring 1979, pp. 258-261.

[ 4] R.C. Chen, *Bus Communication Systems* (Ph.D. diss., Carnegie-Mellon, 1974).

[ 5] D.P. Siewiorek, "Modularity and Multi-microprocessor Structures," *Proceedings of the Seventh Annual Workshop on Microprogramming*, October 1974.

[ 6] G.A. Anderson and E.D. Jensen, "Computer Interconnection: Taxonomy, Characteristics, and Examples," *ACM Computer Surveys*, December 1975.

[ 7] David J. Farber and Kenneth C. Larson, "The System Architecture of the Distributed Computer System—The Communications System," *Proc. Symposium on Computer-Communications Networks and Teletraffic, April 1972* (Brooklyn, N.Y.: Polytechnic Press, 1972).

[ 8] D.L. Nelson and R.L. Gordon, "Computer Cells—A Network Architecture for Data Flow Computing," *COMPCON*, Fall 1978.

[ 9] Cecil C. Reames and Ming T. Liu, "Transmission of Variable-Length Messages," *Proc. Symposium on Computer Architecture*, (New York: IEEE, 1975).

[10] IBM, *IBM System/360 and System/370 Attached Support Processor Version 3 Asymmetrical Multiprocessor System, General Information Manual*, GH20-1173.

[11] William D. Becher and Eric M. Aupperle, "The Communications Computer Hardware of the MERIT Computer Network," *IEEE Transactions on Communications* 20 (June 1972), pp. 516-526.

[12] William A. Wulf and C. Gordon Bell, "C. mmp—A Multi-mini-processor," *Proceedings of the Fall Joint Computer Conference* (Montvale, N.J.: AFIPS Press, 1972).

[13] J.E. Jensen and J.L. Baer, "A Model of Interference in a Shared Resource Multiprocessor," *Third Annual Computer Architecture Conference*, IEEE Computer Society, 1976.

[14] P.H. Enslow, "Multiprocessor Organization—A Survey," *ACM Computer Surveys*, March 1977, pp. 103-129.

[15] E. Douglas Jensen, "A Distributed Function Computer for Real-Time Control," *Proceedings of the Second Symposium on Computer Architecture, January 1975* (New York: IEEE, 1975).

[16] U.S. Air Force, *Military Standard Aircraft Internal Time Division Multiplex Data Bus*, August 1973, MIL-STD-1553.

[17] Douglas B. McKay and Donald P. Karp, "IBM Computer Network/440," *Computer Networks—Proc. Courant Institute Symposium, November 1970* (Englewood Cliffs, N.J.: Prentice-Hall 1972).

[18] A.G. Fraser, "Spider—An Experimental Data Communications System," *Proceedings of the International Conference on Communications, June 1974* (New York: IEEE, 1974).

[19] Norman Abramson, "The Aloha System," *Computer-Communication Networks* (Englewood Cliffs, N.J.: Prentice-Hall, 1973).

[20] Richard J. Goodwin. *A Design for Distributed-Control Multiple-Processor Computer System*, National Technical Information Service, AD-772 883, December 1973.

[21] F.E. Heart et al., "The Interface Message Processor for the ARPA Computer Network," *Proceedings of the Spring Joint Computer Conference* 36 (1970), pp. 551-567.

[22] A.M. Despain and D.A. Patterson, "X-Tree: A Tree Structured Multiprocessor Computer Architecture," *Fifth Annual Computer Architecture Symposium*, IEEE Computer Society, 1978, pp. 144-151.

[23] F.W. Heart et al., "A New Minicomputer/Multiprocessor for the ARPA Network," *Proc. AFIPS 1973 National Computer Conf.* (Montvale, N.J.: AFIPS Press, 1973), pp. 529-537.

[24] S.R. Kimbleton and G.M. Schneider, "Computer Communications Networks: Approaches, Objectives, and Performance Consideration," *AMC Computing Surveys*, September 1975, pp. 129-173.

[25] D.P. Agrawal, T. Feng, and C. Wu, "A Survey of Communication Processor Systems," *COMPSAC*, 1978.

# 3

# Network Communications: Message and Packet Switching

## Introduction

In chapter 2 we discussed a number of system configurations useful for distributed processing which were derived based on a communications view of system architecture. A number of the previous configurations fall into the category of system usually known as network [1, 2, 3], that is, loop (ring), star, and irregular network (figure 3-1). One does note, however, that not all people view a star as distributed system [4]. In some star systems, the "points" of a star are simply terminals. These terminals then connect into the central main-frame computer. This type of configuration would not meet our previous definition of a distributed processor. If the "points" of the star were processing elements, as described in chapter 2, then the star system would be a distributed processor. In this chapter, we are interested in the communication technology which makes the various system configurations into a network; but more specifically, the technologies described provide for the capability to have the network meet our previous description of a distributed processor. Networks which do not have the property of being distributed are not of interest to us.

A *computer communications network* (figure 3-2) is a collection of host computers (which provide services to either another host or an end user) and a communications subnetwork that provides communication links between hosts, users, or both [5]. One of the major justifications for networking is resource sharing (sharing of programs, data, and/or hardware resources). Other important justifications are the ability to provide capabilities for distributed processing and remote communications facilities. Sharing is very important, particularly when unique resources are involved (that is, ILLIAC IV on the ARPANET).

Information in a network must be transmitted on some physical medium. A *circuit* is the physical path over which information is transmitted. A *channel* is the logical path over which connections are made between users, hosts, or hosts and users [5]. Circuits may be multiplexed to support several channels [6]. Also, a channel may be constructed using several circuits. Circuits represent physical interconnections of hardware. Channels represent logical or virtual interconnections which are constructed using circuits but which interconnect functional entities (nodes, users, or nodes and users).

Figure 3-2 shows a particular type of switch used to connect circuits known as a *packet switch*. We discuss packet switching extensively in this chapter.

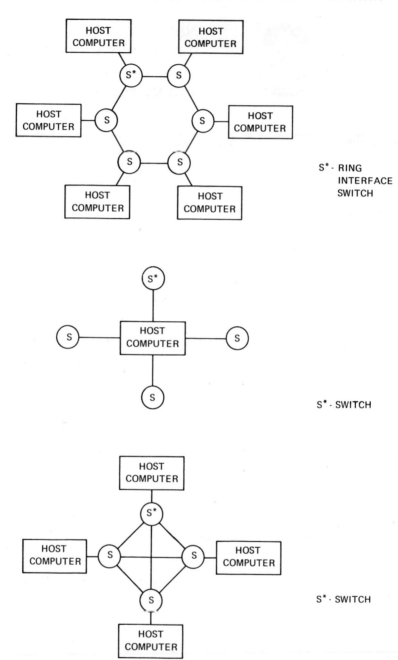

**Figure 3-1.** Typical Network Configurations: Ring, Star, and Irregular Network.

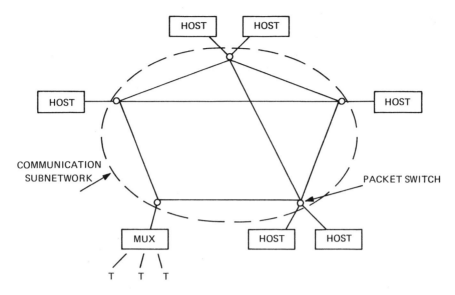

**Figure 3-2.** Model of a Resource-Sharing Computer Network. Reprinted
with permission from K.J. Thurber, "Computer Communications Techniques," COMPSAC, IEEE Computer Society,
1978, pp. 589-594.

Circuit connections in distributed networks can be of two major types: broadcast and point to point. Broadcast communication subnetworks permit simultaneous transmission or reception to or from a variety of sources. Sometimes
two transmitters may transmit simultaneously and their information may
interfere, causing an information collision. Colliding information must be
retransmitted. Broadcast techniques have been implemented in several systems
(for example, radio, coax, and satellite). Broadcast techniques are discussed
later in this chapter [7, 8]. Point-to-point and multipoint communication
techniques allow transmission and reception only between clearly defined host
nodes. Multipoint techniques tend to be associated with "centralized networks,"
and we ignore them because they are not distributed. Examples of such systems
are copper wire, telephone network, and coaxial cable. Three main switching
techniques are used in communication subnetworks [5]: (1) circuit switching
(CS), (2) message switching (MS), and (3) packet switching (PS). Further variations on these techniques are possible. TYMNET used a virtual circuit-switching scheme [9].

Circuit-switch design is discussed in detail in chapter 4. Both time-division
multiplexing and crossbar-switch techniques are considered. The basic idea of
circuit-switch techniques is to establish dedicated circuits to support host-to-host

or user-to-host communication. An example of a circuit-switch subnetwork is the use of phone (dial-up) connections in time-sharing systems. A modem (chapter 6) is used to convert digital data to analog signals for transmission over phone lines. Chapter 4 describes the detailed design issues of the circuit switch, its connection algorithms, and hardware minimization techniques. Before the switch can be designed, a number of detailed system-level design issues need to be considered: circuit setup time, circuit bandwidth considerations, circuit multiplexing, line utilization, message arrival rate, message size, line-busy periods, line-idle periods, and message delay. These system-level requirements can (and must) be derived for each individual communication subnetwork to establish the switch size and performance requirements before the switch itself can be designed. The telephone system is a classic example of circuit-switch technology.

A *message* may be defined as a logical unit of information, for example, telegram or data record from a data file. In MS techniques, a message is placed into the communications subnetwork. The subnetwork establishes a channel, the message is transmitted, and the channel is released. The main advantage of MS over CS is increased circuit utilization. The main disadvantage of MS in comparison to CS is the facilities required to set up the MS environment. The MS subnetwork may be viewed as a collection of physical circuits interconnected via switches (stored program computers) which are used to store and forward individual messages.

A message is routed between the source and destination via any available circuits. The MS system routes the message. Since a circuit may be involved in carrying traffic for any source-destination pairs, MS may provide increased circuit utilization. An example of an MS-oriented system is given in reference 10. Analysis of MS subnetworks is difficult because messages can vary in size. Kleinrock [11, 12, 13] has utilized queuing theory to model such systems. The most important design issues in MS systems involve balancing resource utilization against delay and giving "short" messages reasonable service. Obviously, the message must contain information concerning its source and destination. Further, the message may pass through many intermediate nodes before reaching its destination.

Packet-switching concepts attempt to solve the problems of variable-length messages in MS concepts by dividing a "message" into "packets." A *packet* is a subdivision of a message prefaced with an identifier containing suitable address information and information that will allow the message to be reconstructed. Importantly, packets are independent message subdivisions which can make their own way through the network; that is, packets can travel independently over different channels. Packet switching is important because it promises a way to provide effective support to many different types of message traffic simultaneously. This chapter concentrates on PS techniques.

Conceptually one would like to consider a packet as a fixed-length subdivision of a message (in a sense analogous to a page in a virtual memory system) and a message as a logical entity which is of arbitrary length (in a sense analogous to a segment in a virtual memory system). However, because of the emerging state of the art in computer communication systems and certain technical issues, this distinction is not as precise as a designer would like. For example, in the ARPANET if a host had a message for transmission, the host could deliver a "message" to the interface message processor (IMP) for transmission and this "message" was restricted to a maximum of 8,095 bits. Obviously, if a host had a message which was longer than the "message" allowed to be transmitted to the IMP, the host would have to transmit it in pieces of 8,095 bits or less. The host message is converted into a set of packets for transmission by the communication subnetwork; that is, a message in the IMP is broken into eight packets of up to 1,008 data bits (plus a 168-bit control field). Note that packets are not necessarily of fixed length. However, to ease memory buffer-allocation problems, typically the packet is treated as a fixed-length entity with regard to buffer allocation with a length of 1,176 bits (like a page in a virtual memory system) although the actual packet which is transmitted can be of variable length. This procedure simplifies memory allocation in the packet switch and keeps the actual amount of information transferred to a minimum, thus minimizing required transmission bandwidth. Obviously, a technique to determine packet length must then be included in the packet control fields to ensure that only the actual information is read from the packet-switch buffer memory when a message is being reassembled.

Packet-switching concepts have been used in ring (loop) networks and in irregular networks [14, 15]. No routing decisions are necessary in ring networks. Rings may be envisioned as a set of circulating packet frames. A packet is simply dropped into a frame at the source and emptied at the destination. Each node examines every packet. If the packet is for the host associated with the node, then the packet is captured; otherwise, the packet is forwarded to the next node. The ring topology is the key to the simplicity of this concept.

ARPANET [15] is an example of an irregular distributed packet-switched network. Within a resource-sharing computer network, it is most typical for the individual hosts to contain none of the software or hardware facilities required for managing the network's communication responsibility. All communication control resides within a unit typically termed the *packet switch*. This unit has been variously titled an IMP in the ARPANET, the communications computer in MERIT, the TAC in TELENET, or the ring interface in DCS. Regardless of its title, the packet switch is typically a dedicated minicomputer (or its functional equivalent) performing its operations independent of the associated host(s), as indicated in figure 3-2.

The classic paradigm of a network packet switch was described within the context of the design and implementation of the ARPA network [15, 16]. A similar functional organization can be seen on the description of the packet switch currently utilized by the MERIT network [17]. A multiprocessor packet switch has been implemented for ARPANET [18,19]. This multiprocessor arrangement should allow an easy expansion or contraction of the effective workload range simply by varying the number of processors within any given packet switch.

## Functional Network Forms

There are three major functional forms of a computer network:

1.  RAN (remote-access network)
2.  VAN (value-added network)
3.  MON (mission-oriented network) [5]

RANs are designed to support interaction between an end user and a host computer. The RAN usually provides two categories of service—remote batch and terminal access. Typically RANs have been implemented by using circuit-switch (CS) techniques. RANs are well understood and are available in many commercial forms [20].

VANs are designed to provide communication between host computers in many cases over common carrier lines. RAN capabilities can be provided within a VAN context by using a minicomputer interface between terminals and host computers (for example, terminal IMP, TIP, in the ARPANET) [21]. VAN services can be much broader than RAN services and can include file transfers, remote data-base manipulation, and distributed processing (using geographically distributed processors). Usually in VANs interaction between hosts proceeds based on individually defined and arranged agreements, although some standardization is evolving (for example, the X25 packet network interface standard). Thus, the hosts and communication subnetwork may be regarded as organizationally independent.

MONs are networks in which there exists a close organizational coupling of the host computers and the communication subnetwork [5]. VANs and MONs may be implemented in either distributed or centralized forms. We consider only distributed forms.

Kimbleton and Schneider [5], however, raise an issue not discussed by earlier researchers which stands to greatly affect the future design requirements of packet-switched networks. This is the issue of the administrative relationship between the hosts and the communication subnetwork. As mentioned earlier, the original design of packet switches has proceeded on an independence relationship (that is, connecting extant hosts), thus forcing the packet-switch design to conform to the existing host structure. There is, however, current interest in the design of mission-oriented networks (MONs), in which both the host subnetwork and communication subnetwork are under the control of a single administrative organization.

We can, if desired, impose restrictions on terminal access and allowable host organization (for example, geography, main-frame manufacturers, and data-base allocation) to facilitate the design and implementation of the subnetwork, including the packet switch. Kimbleton and Schneider [5] discuss the technological issues relating to the efficient utilization of a MON and its effect on the design of the communications subnetwork.

## Traffic Types

Networks tend to support four levels of traffic: (1) high-throughput traffic (HTT), (2) low-delay traffic (LDT), (3) real-time traffic (RTT), and (4) guaranteed-bandwidth traffic (GBT) [5, 22]. These traffic types differ in their requirements for host-to-host delay, transmission rate, and reliability. The requirements of the traffic type are:

1. HTT (for example, transmission of large data files): Transmission delay is relatively unimportant, throughput must be maximized, high reliability is required.
2. LDT (for example, interactive computing transactions): Transmission delay must be minimized; throughput is relatively unimportant; high reliability is required.
3. RTT (for example, remote telemetry for process control): There is low delay; constant throughput should be a goal; reliability does not have to be high since redundant data can be sent.
4. GBT (for example, digital speech transmission or picturephone®): There is low delay; constant throughput must be guaranteed; reliability does not have to be high since redundant data is sent (late-arriving data can thus be discarded).

The importance of packet switching is that it can simultaneously provide support to all traffic levels.

## Packet Switches

Within the environment of a distributed computer network, the decisions relating to packet routing, flow control, error detection, and error correction are enormously complex. However, the time constraints imposed on the information throughput are usually quite low—on the order of milliseconds or even seconds. Therefore, the environment of a computer communication network becomes ideal for stored-program processors handling all communication responsibilities independent of the associated host. In the literature these switches have been variously referred to as message switches, packet switches, front-end processors (FEPs), or interface message processors (IMPs).

The basic paradigm of the packet switch was first described in a series of classic papers by Roberts and Wessler [17] and Heart et al. [10]. These papers were reporting on the initial work done by the Bolt, Beranek, and Newman (BBN) group in the design of a generalized communication processor for the ARPANET. Until that time, the design of communication processors had proceeded primarily on an ad hoc basis, usually by subsuming the communication responsibilities into the host software and letting each node take individual responsibility to implement the necessary protocols.

The design requirements of the ARPA network, however, mandated that the individual host be insulated from all network-related communication problems and, conversely, that the communication subnetwork by divorced from any political or administrative relationship with its host. Furthermore, this independence relationship required that the subnetwork adapt to the geographical and organizational structure of the network as it stood—topological changes could not be made to facilitate the implementation of the packet switches. The original design of the ARPA packet switch (termed an IMP) is described quite fully in reference 9, 23, and 24. It was based on identical Honeywell 316 (later 516) minicomputers located at each node and performing the operations of message buffering and transmission, message assembly/disassembly, routing, error handling, and flow control. The shortcomings in the original design, however, quickly became apparent. The cost of the packet switch ($100,000) made it prohibitive to use either in the environment of a one-to-one relationship between hosts and switches or in a network with nodes without local processing capabilities (that is, terminals). Ornstein et al. [21] describe the work that was done at BBN in the design of terminal-oriented packet switches. Essentially these TIPs are packet switches extended with the hardware and software necessary to support the multiplexing of a large number of slow-speed terminals, thus allowing cost-effective terminal access to networks.

From the cost viewpoint, the use of identical packet switches at each node imposed the unreasonable constraint of having identical throughput capabilities at each site in spite of the fact that the traffic requirements at the various nodes might be quite different. Recognition of this fact has led to the design of multiprocessor packet switches termed the *Pluribus IMP* [18].

Numerous good surveys relating to the responsibilities and tradeoffs inherent in packet-switch design have appeared in the literature, among them Newport and Ryzlak [25]; Feinroth, Franceschini, and Goldstein [26]; and the recent Kimbleton and Schneider survey [5]. They all describe a set of communication responsibilities which lead to an organization similar to the structure of most current packet switches such as the ARPANET IMP, the communication computer of the MERIT network, or TAC in TELENET.

The communication subsystems of the packet switch which have the specific responsibility of handling the various communication problems are usually termed the *communications protocols*. For reasons very similar to those cited in the context of structured programming, communication protocols are almost always multilayered, with the lower layer being entirely opaque to all higher-level layers. Figure 1-1 gives a general organizational diagram of the relationship between these multiple levels of protocol. Figure 3-3 details the general communication protocol model given in chapter 1. The lowest-level protocols are related to supporting direct switch-to-switch communication along a physical circuit. These protocols are usually termed *data-link controls* (DLCs). The DLC addresses itself to the problems of handshaking, message and field synchronization, character versus binary transmission, error detection, and error correction. Attempts have been made to standardize the data-link controls, but there is no single industrywide standard in use. Currently popular DLCs include IBM's BISYNC and SDLC [27], ANSI DLC, and Digitals Equipment's DDCMP. Two excellent overviews of the entire area of data-link controls can be found in references 27 and 28. This level of protocol is analogous to communication on a path.

The next level of protocol is concerned with establishing a logical (that is, virtual) channel between the source and destination packet switches. This now involves us in the areas of routing, message assembly and disassembly, end-to-end acknowledgments, and deadlock recovery procedures. These protocols have been termed the *transmission protocols*, or link management, and are described in Stutzman [29]. These protocols, along with the necessary conventions for handling the host-packet-switch link, allow us to create a virtual channel between any pair of hosts. The level of protocol resulting from the complexity of routing functions is a network of switches. This level of protocol is the highest level usually associated entirely with the communication problem.

The *interprocess communication (IPC) protocols* are "the entire set of conventions whereby host operating systems establish, maintain, and terminate connections between user processes running on remote computers" [29]. The IPC protocol originally used by the ARPA network is described in Stutzman [29]. A summary of other approaches to implement IPC protocols can be found in references 30, 31, and 32.

Finally the highest-level protocols, or *user-level protocols*, are concerned with such job-oriented directives as file transfers, remote job initiation, or the requesting of a network service. These last two levels of protocol are essentially independent of physical-interconnection issues and are really the "logical" interconnection levels of the system. The remainder of this chapter concentrates on the design issues primarily associated with level 1 protocols. Level 0 design issues and concepts are primarily discussed in chapter 6.

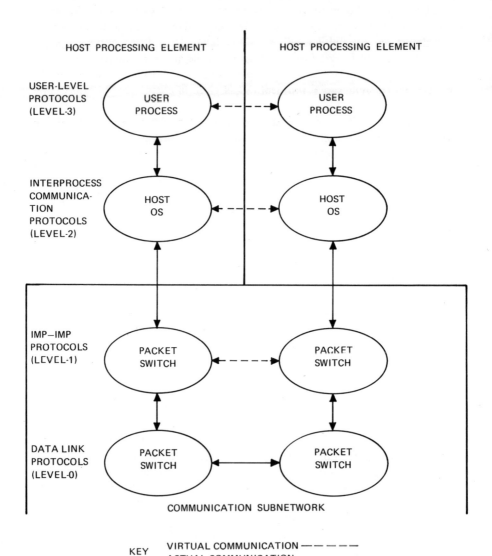

**Figure 3-3.** Packet-Switched Network Communication System Model. Reprinted with permission from K.J. Thurber, "Computer Communications Techniques," COMPSAC, IEEE Computer Society, 1978, pp. 589-594.

For information entirely on the subject of packet switches and their incorporation into the design of distributed networks, refer to the enormously informative and descriptive treatments of the subject by Davies and Barber [33], Abramson [7], Schwartz [34], Kleinrock [11, 12], or a special issue of the *IEEE Transactions on Communications* [2].

**Summary of Design Considerations for a Packet-Switch Communication Subnetwork**

The PS performs two major functions—source-destination functions and store-and-forward functions [5]. Source-destination functions include error control, end/end acknowledgment, segmentation and segmentation and addressing, and flow control. End/end acknowledgment is an alternative to store-and-forward functions. There are two primary store-and-forward operations—routing and error control. These functions are discussed in detail.

*Level 0: Data-link Protocols*

This is the lowest-level protocol, and it involves the support communication procedures necessary to communicate between switches on a physical circuit. Current important protocols are SDLC, BISYNC, and DDCMP. These are described in chapter 6. Theoretical properties of various DLC protocols may be found in references 26, 27, and 33.

*Level 1: Link-Management Protocols*

The major design issues are discussed.

**Error Control**. The packet switch is responsible for accumulation of error-checking information to be transmitted with the packet. Further, the switch is required to check incoming packets to see that they are correctly received. The most basic error control concepts are:

1.  VRC (vertical-redundancy checks)
2.  LRC (longitudinal-redundancy checks)
3.  $M$-out-of-$N$ codes
4.  Check-sum procedures (cyclic error checking or polynomial codes)

In the VRC technique, parity bits are added to each transmitted character. The LRC technique adds parity bits on a per message basis. The $M$-out-of-$N$

code technique uses a code set in which characters are mapped onto the code assignments such that all $N$-bit characters contain exactly $M$ bits set to the value 1. Check-sum techniques compute a correctness value based on either a cyclic error code or a polynomial error code. Combinations of these techniques could also be used.

Since some techniques (polynomial codes) provide for not only error-detection but also error-correction capabilities, two different strategies could be developed—error correcting and error detecting. Some researchers refer to these as static and dynamic techniques, respectively [5]. If an error-correcting technique is selected, enough redundant information is added to each packet that not only can transmission errors be detected, but they can also automatically be corrected at the destination without the source being involved after the initial transmission. This approach is very expensive because the encoding of redundant data can require complex computational capabilities along with using up significant transmission bandwidth for the redundant information. Therefore, static techniques are generally not used.

The error-detecting, or dynamic, approach is potentially quite a bit more efficient from the viewpoint of channel utilization than the error-correcting approach. The basic concept is to require retransmission of any incoming packet which contains an error. Typically, the destination must return an acknowledgment (ACK) signal to the source before some specified event occurs at the source (for example, a time-out period is exceeded), or else the packet is retransmitted. If a specified number of transmissions fail to complete (that is, generate an ACK within the allowable time), then the line and/or destination packet switch must be declared inoperable.

One dynamic approach could be:

1. Each packet-switch source generates an error-detection field at the hardware interface for each packet to check for line errors.
2. Each packet-switch destination checks the incoming packet for correctness based on the error-detection field.

This procedure would be implemented on a node-to-node basis. Thus, as the packet goes between each pair of source-destination switches (on its way from its initial source to its final destination), line errors are checked. An error notification strategy must also be selected. Basically the choice is (1) explicit negative acknowledgment (NAK) or (2) explicit positive acknowledgment (ACK). In the case of an explicit NAK, if a destination packet switch detects an error, a NAK message is sent to the source packet switch. In this case unless an NAK is received, the packet is assumed properly transmitted. This solution, however, has the disadvantage that we are not sure that the packet was ever received. This problem could be solved by requiring that the destination sent an ACK, in addition to an explicit NAK, for every correctly received packet. However, a simpler procedure which accomplishes the same effect is discussed later. Another consideration is whether to embed (by software) an error-detection sequence into the packet itself at the initial source for checking at the final destination in an end-to-end error-checking procedure.

The basic technique involving an explicit ACK assumes that the source packet switch has a time-out mechanism. This could be a time-out counter or some other form of event timer. Also, packets must have a field in their control bits into which the ACK message can be encoded. The procedure would work as follows:

1.  If the destination packet switch (upon examination of the source-generated error-detection field) receives a correct packet, an ACK is sent to the source "piggybacked" into the ACK field of any outgoing packet; otherwise, no action is taken.
2.  Receipt of an ACK before time-out inhibits retransmission of the packet.

To avoid having to acknowledge an ACK (thus generating an infinite sequence of ACKs to complete a transmission), any reception of a damage ACK causes retransmission of the packet just as a time-out would cause retransmission.

The explicit ACK approach can also be applied to the problem of ensuring that a correct message is received at the final destination from the initial source. End-to-end flow-control techniques (in particular the isarithmic concept discussed later) may also be able to perform the message-level error-control function. At one time the ARPANET used a strategy in which once a complete message was received, a special packet (a ready-for-next-message packet or RFNM packet) was sent from the final destination to the initial source [35].

**Segmentation and Addressing.** Each message received from the host by the source packet switch is segmented into a set of independent packets which can be individually transferred from source to destination. The process of breaking the message into packets is called *segmentation*. Basically, the message is sequentially broken into packets, and each packet is assigned its appropriate sequential identifier in the packet header so that the message can be reconstructed at the destination. Header and trailer control fields for error control, message identification, final destination addressing, and so on are added to the packet. The packet is then stored in memory, and pointers to it are queued into a data structure for appropriate retrieval for later transmission.

In order for the message to be transmitted, system addresses must be generated; however, since we are interested only in how the communication occurs, we tend to see only the need for addresses associated with the message name, packet number, initial source, and final-destination packet switches. However, many hierarchies of addressing are required to support the total system model of the system hierarchy given in figure 3-3. Each of the virtual communication links shown requires a level of addressing. For example, the user must establish "connections" between logical ports, message identifications must be generated, and translation of these logical addresses onto real hardware and memory resources must occur. Only then can the actual communication take place. A good example of the complexity of the problems associated with addressing, part-connection establishment, and so on can be found in chapter 7 in the description of the IBM system network architecture.

**Flow Control**. Congestion (blockage, slow down, or excessive traffic delays) can occur within the communication subnetwork. The function of *flow-control* algorithms is to prevent and relieve congestion and ensure that information transfers between hosts are maximized.

The basic flow-control techniques can be classified as either local or global procedures. Some local procedures are sometimes viewed as providing end-to-end acknowledgment capabilities.

There are at least three local techniques: (1) user allocation, ARPANET [35], (2) node allocation, and (3) special routing techniques [3]. The basic concept of local algorithms is to prevent packet transmission unless specific conditions can be met. Typically, these algorithms attempt to establish a maximum on the number of packets which can be outstanding between any source-destination pairs of hosts.

Typical algorithms could limit the number of packets allowed to be outstanding on a user or on a node (use of the RFNM packet) basis. Another algorithm concept may require that all buffers necessary to reassemble a message at the destination be available and reserved before the transmission could begin. This would relieve the condition known as "reassembly lockup." A further modification of the buffer preallocation concept is the establishment of special routes for messages. A general set of rules for determining how to set up a special route can be enumerated [4]. The global-algorithm concepts are basically attempts to control the total number of packets outstanding in the system regardless of the number of packets outstanding between any set of pairs of hosts. Such procedures are sometimes denoted isarithmic algorithms [36]. Ring networks can essentially be viewed as a set of circulating packet frames whose number has been fixed by the system. The only way a node can enter a packet into the communication subnetwork is for an empty frame to become available at the node. Thus, some ring networks use isarithmic algorithms.

One technique to implement an isarithmic algorithm is to develop a set of "dummy" packets or tokens which are placed into the communication subnetwork when the system is initialized. Each time a packet arrives at a node, the node transmits a packet; that is, when a node receives a packet, either it transmits a real packet (if it has a message desiring to be transmitted) or it transmits a dummy packet. The dummy packet can be transmitted randomly around the subnetwork if desired. A dummy packet can be viewed as a transmission permit which is circulating in the subnetwork looking for a node desiring transmission privileges. A variation on this concept is to assign each node a pool of permits. This would tend to reduce time delays due to waiting for the randomly circulating permits to arrive at a particular node.

**Routing.** In a packet-switched network, it is possible to send many packets of a message simultaneously because they are independent. These packets, when in transmission, are controlled by an algorithm which determines their route of travel from the source to the destination, called the *routing algorithm*. Not all packets of a message are necessarily transmitted through the same set of intermediate nodes in traversing the "path" of travel between source and destination. Generally, each packet is routed individually. Thus, the basic function of the routing algorithm is to minimize delay and maximize throughput in the subnetwork while being simple to compute. Routing can be implemented as a process in which each packet switch contains a routing table. When a packet is to be routed, the most efficient route is selected from the table, and the packet is transmitted. This section discusses how such "tables" are computed, used, and updated.

In the following discussion we assume that we are attempting to minimize the transmission time of a packet from the source node to the destination node as the basic algorithm-efficiency criteria. An alternative would be to develop algorithms which attempt to minimize the number of links traversed or which use other more complex cost measures. We also ignore the possibility of packets having a priority and assume that a packet is given and we are solely responsible for selecting the optimal route. In reality, we may have had to first select packets for transmission, and this may have involved knowing about the relative priority of packets.

There are three main categories of routing algorithms in which the authors attempted to form a taxonomy: Kimbleton and Schneider [5], Fultz and Kleinrock [37], and Rudin [38]. In addition, Greene and Pooch [4] provide a good overview of the basic algorithms; Schwartz [34] provides interesting overviews, mathematical analysis, and simulation results; and Rudin [38] provides interesting simulation and comparison results of four major algorithms compared to his "Delta routing" algorithm. Further analysis is available in many articles, but the basis analytic techniques are based on queuing theory analysis [11, 12, 13].

Kimbleton and Schneider break the algorithm taxonomy into the generic techniques listed in figure 3-4. They concentrate their analysis on the adaptive distributed algorithm because of its ARPANET implications. Fultz and Kleinrock developed the taxonomy pictured in figure 3-5. However, since Rudin's categorization encompasses most of the algorithms categorized by Fultz and Kleinrock, we base our discussion of routing on the extension of his development shown in figure 3-6. Each algorithm in figure 3-7 is discussed briefly.

```
                    DETERMINISTIC

                    ADAPTIVE
                      LOCAL
                      GLOBAL
                      DISTRIBUTED
```

**Figure 3-4.** Kimbleton and Schneider's Routing-Algorithm Taxonomy.

```
              DETERMINISTIC
                FLOODING
                  ALL LINKS
                    SELECTIVE LINKS
                FIXED
                SPLIT TRAFFIC
                  OPTIMUM
                  SUBOPTIMUM
                IDEAL OBSERVER

              STOCHASTIC
                RANDOM
                ISOLATED
                  LOCAL DELAY ESTIMATE
                  SHORTEST QUEUE
                DISTRIBUTED
                  PERIODIC UPDATE
                  ASYNCHRONOUS UPDATE
```

**Figure 3-5.** Fultz and Kleinrock's Routing-Algorithm Taxonomy.

```
          CENTRALIZED
            FIXED
            NETWORK ROUTING CENTER
              FIXED BETWEEN UPDATES
              PROPORTIONAL
            IDEAL OBSERVER (PRESENT)
            IDEAL OBSERVER (FUTURE)

          DISTRIBUTED
            COOPERATIVE, PERIODIC OR ASYNCHRONOUS UPDATE
            ISOLATED, LOCAL DELAY ESTIMATE
            ISOLATED, SHORTEST QUEUE AND BIAS
            RANDOM
            FLOODING

          DELTA
```

**Figure 3-6.** Rudin's Routing-Algorithm Taxonomy.

```
DISTRIBUTED
   FLOODING
   RANDOM
   ISOLATED
      LOCAL DELAY ESTIMATE
      SHORTEST QUEUE AND BIAS
         ZERO
         NONZERO
   COOPERATIVE UPDATED ROUTING TABLE
      PERIODIC
         MINIMUM DELAY
         AREA
      ASYNCHRONOUS
         MINIMUM DELAY
         AREA

CENTRALIZED
   FIXED
   NETWORK ROUTING CENTER
      FIXED BETWEEN UPDATES
      PROPORTIONAL OR SPLIT TRAFFIC
   IDEAL OBSERVER
      PRESENT
      FUTURE

DELTA
   SYNCHRONOUS
   ASYNCHRONOUS
```

**Figure 3-7.** Summary of the Routing-Algorithm Taxonomy.

*Distributed Flooding.* There are two basic forms of the distributed-flooding concept—all links or selected links only. The all-link algorithm operates as follows: no routing table per se is required for the all-link flooding concept; rather, the following procedure is used. When a packet is received by a node, the packet is retransmitted immediately over every link connected to the node with the exception of the link on which the packet was originally received. After a specified period a message is returned to the initial source node to confirm that the flooding has occurred. This algorithm is computationally simple, requires no routing table or state information about the network, produces a loop-free routing path so that messages do not get trapped in closed paths, and does not attempt to base its decision of route on the current state of the network. Unfortunately, this algorithm quickly generates many duplicate packets, thereby causing excessive traffic and network congestion. Further, it routes a given packet from initial source to final destination with minimum delay. Efficiency considerations effectively eliminate flooding all links as a practical algorithm in most situations.

A modification of all-link flooding is known as selective link flooding. In this algorithm a node retransmits the packet only over certain selected links, rather than over all links. Otherwise, the algorithm operates the same as the all-link flooding algorithm.

*Distributed Random Algorithm.* The concept of the random algorithm is that when a packet enters a node which is an intermediate node (not the final destination), the link on which the packet is retransmitted is selected at random. Eventually, the packet arrives at its destination. One could bias the "random" selection so that the packet was traveling, in some sense, in the "right direction." However, one of the major advantages of a random algorithm is that it easily copes with node or link failures. This ability to operate in failure-prone networks may override the inefficiency of the algorithm. Biasing the algorithm tends to reduce the ability of the random algorithm to cope with failures so that even biased algorithms should attempt to retain a large degree of randomness.

*Distributed Isolated Techniques.* There are two primary techniques using isolated routing—local-delay estimate and shortest queue.

Isolated routing using local-delay estimates assumes that traffic delays between any pair of nodes are symmetrical. Thus, the delay *to* a particular node can be measured by observing the delay from the node. This technique is sometimes called *backward learning*. At each node of the network, a table is constructed. The table is organized by destination node and transmission link and contains the observed delay from that node via that link. To determine a route, the destination is located in the table, and the link with the least delay is selected. Each time a packet arrives over a link from a destination, the table is updated so that the routing table contains the most recent delay information to every node. Obviously, there must exist in the network a time standard so that packet transit time can be measured.

There are two forms of the isolated routing with the shortest queue technique—zero bias and nonzero bias. Generally, the procedure works as follows. When a packet arrives at a node, a "handover" number is incremented. A ranked list of neighbor nodes which connect most directly to each destination is available in the routing table. The packet is sent to the "highest-ranked" available neighbor or to the first available neighbor if currently none is available (that is, the packet exits via the shortest queue or the highest-ranked neighbor. In the case with zero bias the packet is simply sent to the neighbor who ranks highest in the queue. In the nonzero-bias case, the handover number is multiplied by a constant (the bias) and added to the queue length of each neighbor. The queue length is measured in terms of time required to transmit the currently queued messages. Routing decisions then choose the minimal sum value which, in effect, is the shortest queue with a nonzero bias.

*Distributed Cooperative Updated Routing Table.* The cooperative techniques essentially operate on the basis that each node maintains in the packet switch a matrix which specifies the observed delays between nodes. This information can be provided on either a periodic or an asynchronous basis depending on implementation. Here we discuss the algorithm concepts and leave the details of periodic or asynchronous updating to the implementer to ponder and resolve.

If the nodes were all to exchange information on all delays observed, the distributed cooperative updated routing concept would use a large amount of network communication capacity simply to transmit measurement information. Thus, two techniques to reduce information flow are common. First is the concept of a "minimum delay vector." In this approach nodes exchange only a list of estimated minimum delays to all other nodes in the network. A receiving node can add to each received vector its know delays and thus compute the route and the delay to any destination via the set of all paths it has available. Therefore, a node can determine what it views as the shortest path between nodes and pass this information on to other nodes.

The area concept is to partition the network into a hierarchical collection of nodes. All nodes in a group exchange information with one another, all groups of nodes exchange information with other groups of nodes, and so on. Thus the amount of information transfer is reduced, as is the amount of retained information. In the area concept it is conceivable to exchange minimum-delay vectors between nodes in a group, groups of nodes, and so forth until the highest-level areas have exchanged delay vectors.

Because of the importance of the minimum-delay vector concept we discuss more of its theory later [39] . The problem of determining an optimal path through a set of interconnected nodes with only local information is well known in optimization theory. Such problems can be formulated as a $K$-step decision process, and the solution of such problems is governed by a well-known theory— Bellman's principle of optimality. The principle of optimality basically states that in a problem involving multiple possible states in which you have limited knowledge to determine the optimal solution, an optimal policy has the property that whatever the initial state and initial decision are, the remaining decisions (of the $K$-step process) must constitute an optimal policy with regard to the state of the system resulting from the first decision. Therefore, if we have a network which has a set of distributed routing tables based on the minimum-delay vector concept, we can describe an optimal policy to route a packet from node $i$ to node $j$. The policy is simply to select at node $i$ and at every intermediate node between $i$ and $j$ the route which claims to have the minimum delay. Further, by Bellman's principle of optimality, we know that this gives an optimal routing policy. Regardless of information changes encountered during the routing process, the policy remains optimal because we have made the best decision possible at each stage of the process.

The extension of this concept to other areas will also make it possible to create algorithms which represent optimal policies, since the process is really to make at each stage of the routing process the best decision possible based on the available information.

The remaining major algorithms are considered to be centralized; however, under proper circumstances, such as sufficient storage and instantaneous copying or updating to every node, the algorithms could be distributed because every node could be furnished a copy for use.

*Centralized Fixed Routing.* The simplest centralized algorithm can be derived by assuming that the network has a fixed known topology with known traffic patterns. Then, a priori, the best route (set of routes) between any two nodes can be computed. When a packet is to be routed, the route is simply retrieved from the directory. Obviously, one centralized system or many (distributed system) directories can be provided. ARPANET experience has shown that more than one route per source-destination pair is required to ensure good performance. The major problem with this concept is its lack of dynamic adaptibility to changing real-time system demands.

*Centralized Network Routing Center.* A modification of the fixed routing concept is to establish a network routing center (NRC). At some time (periodic or nonperiodic) the NRC recomputes the set of routes to be used in the routing algorithm. These routes then remain fixed until the next update of the routing table. This algorithm is called the *fixed-between-update algorithm.*
    An extension of the concept of fixed multiple routes is to determine fixed routes between each set of source-destination pairs and then associate a probability with each route. Then the routing algorithm routes a packet over a route based on a probability distribution. This algorithm is termed *split traffic,* or *proportional routing.*

*Centralized Ideal Observer.* The last two centralized algorithm concepts are essentially only useful to bound traffic. These are the present ideal observer and the future ideal observer. In the case of the present ideal observer, it is assumed that the route of a new packet is based on total continuous knowledge of the entire network of all present routes. Generally, this is not practical. The concept of the future ideal observer assumes knowledge of not only the total state of the present system but also packets which will arrive for routing in the future. Clearly, such algorithms can be used only to develop performance limits.

*Delta Routing.* The concept of delta routing [38] is to note that global (centralized) strategies have advantages because of their ability to use information on past overall average performance to make decisions; local (distributed) strategies, however, have advantages because in total they know the current instantaneous detailed state of the network since all nodes know their neighbors' states. The delta concept tries to combine the advantages of both concepts by developing a strategy which implements a global strategy modified by local decisions when necessary for efficiency. The value which regulates the relative amount of decision-making authority delegated to the node is $\delta$ (delta). The delta approach makes a centralized decision which is transmitted to the nodes and is valid for a period of time. During the validity interval, when appropriate, the nodes can modify or select a detailed route.

The centralized decisionmaker provides the node with multiple route choices for all appropriate links, and the node selects the detailed link. In this sense, the split-traffic algorithms are very similar to the delta concept. Simulation results of the delta algorithm indicate its utility. By adjusting δ the algorithm can be biased toward centralized or fully distributed algorithms. Tables for such algorithms may be synchronously or asynchronously updated.

**Typical Packet-Switch Software and Buffer Requirements.** Typically a packet switch has a set of buffers, processing routines, and an ordering scheme for packet transmission. An example of these features is briefly listed for completeness. The information is derived from considering the IMP of ARPANET [9] and illustrates some of the detailed issues that would have to be considered in designing an actual packet switch.

Packets tend to be prioritized for transmission by the following priority division scheme:

Priority 1. Previously transmitted unacknowledged packets
Priority 2. Priority packets to be transmitted
Priority 3. Regular packets to be transmitted

Priority 1 is the highest priority, and priority 3 is the lowest.

There are three primary categories of buffers in a packet switch: (1) line buffers—one output and two input per line (link); (2) a store-and-forward pool of buffers; and (3) message-reassembly storage buffers.

There are essentially seven processing routines: (1) host to IMP, (2) task, (3) IMP to modem, (4) modem to IMP, (5) IMP to host, (6) background, and (7) Time-out.

*Gateways and Supernetworks*

The following discussion is based primarily on Sunshine's thesis [40] which details the techniques for interconnection of networks. This definition is necessary for understanding purposes: A *gateway* is an interface between two networks.

Gateways may be viewed as supernodes in a supernetwork. Individual networks (local networks) would be the links that connect hosts to supernodes and supernodes to one another. Since typically each link has a different set of communication protocols (based on the protocols in the individual networks), it is the function of the gateway to implement the correct network protocols for the networks to be interfaced. Further it is important for the designers to attempt to preserve the independence of each of the individual networks [40].

One of the basic issues is the question of addressing. This problem can be solved by using addresses of the form (net, local address). The problem then becomes how to manipulate the packet for transmission. One concept (which preserves individual network independence) is to *embed* an internetwork header and trailer into the data field of the local network packet [41]. The alternative is to develop a packet in which the internetwork header and trailer are also used as the header and trailer in the local network (the overlapped-header concept). However, this latter technique would not necessarily provide local network independence. The main problem with the embedded approach is that source hosts must generate the local network address of the first gateway. Then, each gateway must choose the next local network and the next gateway and specify the local network address of that gateway, until the packet reaches its destination. The local network header also adds overhead. The concept of overlapped header/trailer avoids these disadvantages if local network operation is altered so that the internetwork header and address can be directly interpreted. Because of the changes necessary to current systems, the overlapped concept is probably unacceptable unless new systems are designed to process hierarchical addresses or new networks are designed to handle multiple-packet types.

Supernetworks can be implemented with either a single gateway per independent network or multiple gateways per local network. If the single-gateway concept is used, routing consists of a reasonably simple concept, that is, the central-office concept can be used. All internetwork traffic is routed to the local central office, then the traffic is routed between the central offices of different networks, and finally the packet is routed from the destination central office to the destination host.

In the case of multiple gateways per local network, the independence of local networks may have to be compromised because to provide effective routing between the source and destination, the optimal local gateway choice must be made. However, this requires knowledge of the cost of routes outside the current local network. Thus the local network would be involved in the problem of internetwork routing. A number of routing algorithms have been suggested for such concepts. One important internetwork routing concept which does not appear to have an analog in the set of routing algorithms discussed earlier in this chapter is called *source routing*. This concept works as follows. The source packet specifies the complete internetwork route. This requires that a packet be able to carry a variable-length route description, but the concept eliminates tho nood for routing docisions at intormodiato points [40].

Basically a gateway can be implemented as a packet switch or as a host. In the former case it uses the packet switch-packet switch protocol level for local network communication. In the latter case the host-packet switch communication protocols are used. Implementation of the gateway as a packet switch-packet switch interface appears difficult (if not impossible). Use of a packet switch-packet switch interface makes the resultant system appear to be one large network, but protocol differences and addressing problems make such a solution highly doubtful. If the gateway is implemented as a host-packet switch interface, then service levels such as datagram, virtual call, bulk data transfer, and interactive terminal service can be implemented. Further, the implementation approach in a host-packet switch implementation can be in terms of either end-to-end or source-destination techniques. Importantly, local network independence can be preserved under a host-packet switch interface. For implementation, the gateway could be viewed as consisting of two halves. A gateway half is associated with a local network and implements all local network protocols. A gateway could then consist of two physical devices (one unique to each of the connected local networks) with their internetwork interface being a simple communication link for exchange of internetwork packets and routing data. Sunshine provides an extensive discussion of whether the gateway implementation concepts should be end-to-end or source-destination oriented, which is far beyond the scope of this discussion [40].

Three major problems that the gateway must deal with need to be mentioned for completeness' fragmentation, accounting, and system status [40]. Packet sizes are not standardized. Therefore the gateway has to convert (fragment packets) between different packet sizes. The alternative is some standardization in packet size which is probably disadvantageous since the packet size of each local network was chosen for efficiency reasons and a standard size is probably not cost-effective. There is a problem of accounting for internetwork charges because the local network administration has to collect and correctly allocate both local and internetwork fees. However, post offices and telephone networks are good examples of solutions to this problem. Attempting to establish routing on a minimum-cost basis could complicate the system design. System status becomes more complex in a supernetwork because local-network status may be required to achieve overall system efficiency. Further, additional services may be required at the gateway interface.

*Random-Access (Aloha) Algorithms*

In general, the techniques in this chapter and the majority of this book are based on point-to-point and multipoint communication systems. The bus discussions in chapter 5 are mainly applicable to such system types. However, in chapter 5 we discuss some implicit allocation algorithms which are quite analogous to the concept of broadcast systems. In this chapter for completeness we provide a brief summary of current broadcast-system concepts since they have appeared mainly in the network context.

The basic idea of broadcast-type systems is that devices may have random access to the data channels [7]. Arbitration of user access to the channel is implicit based on an agreement for retransmission if a collision (that is, simultaneous transmission of two packets) occurs. If the application involves bursty messages infrequently transmitted, it is appropriate to have data sources transmit at will (randomly). The basic Aloha procedure [7] works as follows. First, a packet switch desiring to transmit a packet transmits whenever it is ready. Second, if no acknowledgment is received within a designated time-out period, the packet switch concludes that a collision has occurred and retransmits the packet.

The main design decision is when to retransmit the packet to stagger the retransmission of the colliding packets. Probably the simplest approach is to allow the packet switch to retransmit the packet at some random time after the time-out. The major assumption of the broadcast concept is that the reason no acknowledgment is received after a transmission is that a collision of two packets resulted in the garbled message and therefore simple retransmission of the packets in a staggered time sequence will avoid further collisions. On the average, assuming a large number of identical users, this pure random-access transmission scheme allows utilization of at most 18 percent of the system transmission capacity. In some special situations, channel usage can exceed 18 percent as discussed later [34].

One suggestion to increase utilization is to establish a system time base and use it to delimit time slots. Each packet switch would then be required to transmit only during a time slot. This technique is typically referred to as slotted aloha [42]. Slotted aloha can double the maximum used bandwidth in comparison to a pure random-access scheme. Further, concepts include techniques in which a reservation is made and the user then requests a time slot in advance of transmission. Typical arbitration techniques for devices requesting transmission rights are discussed in detail in chapter 5. The carrier-sense concept requires that each packet switch monitor other packet-switch transmissions and transmit only if no other transmission is occurring [43]. Additional work on random-access systems has included techniques to provide immediate acknowledgment of a transmitted message [8].

## Summary and Conclusion

This chapter discussed issues associated with the level 1 protocols of a packet-switched computer network. Level 0 protocol issues for data-link controls are discussed in chapter 6. The design of a packet-switch subnetwork is one technique to implement a computer communication subnetwork. The general techniques discussed in this chapter are applicable to both message- and packet-switching systems. A packet switch may be viewed as a special case of a more general concept, the message switch; that is, a packet switch contains fixed-size packet frames in the packet-switch memory and causes a message to be transmitted as a set of independent packets. Other techniques—circuit switches and bus structures—could be used to implement a communication subnetwork. These techniques are discussed in later chapters.

Networks may be categorized in terms of their function—remote-access networks, value-added networks, and mission-oriented networks. Remote-access networks are primarily designed to support host-user interaction. Value-added networks are primarily oriented toward host-host communication. In value-added networks, the hosts may be administratively independent of the communication subnetwork. Mission-oriented networks are value added networks in which the hosts and communication subnetwork are controlled under the same administration.

The main issues discussed in this chapter include techniques for routing, flow control, and error control. The key design decision is to select algorithms so that cost effectiveness is achieved in the network while allowing for support of varying traffic types. Further problems discussed in the chapter included gateways between independent networks and random-access communication techniques.

The application of the approaches and concepts discussed in this chapter can have a dramatic impact on system performance. Thus, we suggest that any system design be extensively analyzed before development and suggest as good analysis studies the books by Schwartz [34] and Kleinrock [13], and extremely important references 5, 27, 28, 30, 31, 32, 37, 38, 40, 41, and 44 to 51.

Lastly, the view of flow control taken in this chapter is one of managing buffer space rather than link bandwidth. A link-oriented concept sometimes known as "speed control" or "isoflow control" may be found in reference 52.

## Exercises

1. Develop a routing table and detail an algorithm for the following types of routing: centralized fixed and isolated routing shortest queue. Compare the potential performance of these algorithms on an irregular network with five nodes containing the following bidirectional connection pairs:(1, 2), (1, 3), (1, 4), (1, 5), (2, 3), (3, 4), (3, 5), (4, 5).

2. Repeat exercise 1 for a random algorithm and a minimum-delay-vector distributed algorithm.

3. Given two local networks A and B, assume that network A has a line protocol as follows: bit serial; 27-bit header containing the packet number (3 bits), destination address (12 bits), and source address (12 bits); an information field of 128 bits; and no trailer. Assume that network B has a line protocol as follows: byte parallel (8 bits per byte); VRC; header consisting of packet number (8 bits), destination address (16 bits), source address (16 bits), and parity field (8 bits); 64-bit information field; and source transmission time (16 bits). Design a gateway to allow these networks to be connected.

Document any assumptions you make.

4. For network A of exercise 3 lay out the interface message-processor software necessary to build a packet switch. Assume a minimum-delay-vector distributed routing algorithm and a maximum message size of 16 packets from the host. Document all assumptions.

5. Repeat exercise 4 for network A of exercise 3.

## References

[ 1] *Proceedings of the IEEE*, Special issue on packet communication networks, November 1978.

[ 2] *IEEE Transactions on Communications*, Special issue on computer communications, January 1977.

[ 3] *Computer*, Special issue on computer networks, November 1977.

[ 4] W. Greene and U.W. Pooch, "A Review of Classification Schemes for Computer Communication Networks," *Computer* 10 (November 1977), pp. 12-21.

[ 5] S.R. Kimbleton and G.M. Schneider, "Computer Communication Networks: Approach, Objectives, and Performance Consdierations," *ACM Computing Surveys*, September 1975, pp. 129-173.

[ 6] W.W. Chu, "Asynchronous Time-Division Multiplexing Systems," in *Computer-Communication Networks*, eds. Norman Abramson and Franklin Kuo (Englewood Cliffs, N.J.: Prentice-Hall, Inc., 1973), pp. 236-268.

[ 7] N. Abramson, "The Aloha System," in *Computer-Communication Networks*, eds. Norman Abramson and Franklin Kuo (Englewood Cliffs, N.J.: Prentice-Hall, Inc., 1973), pp. 501-518.

[ 8] M. Tokoro and K. Tamaru, "Acknowledging Ethernet," *COMPCON*, Fall 1977, pp. 320-325.

[ 9] LeRoy Tymes, "Tymnet—A Terminal-Oriented Communication Network," *SJCC* 38 (1971), pp. 211-216.

[10] F.E. Heart et al., "The Interface Message Processor for the ARPA Computer Network," *SJCC* 36 (1970), pp. 551-567.

[11] L. Kleinrock, *Communication Nets: Stochastic Message Flow and Delay* (New York: McGraw-Hill, 1964).

[12] L. Kleinrock, "Analytic and Simulation Methods in Computer Network Design," *SJCC* 36 (1970), pp. 569-579.

[13] L. Kleinrock, *Queuing Systems*, vol. 1: *Theory and Queuing Systems*, vol. 2: *Computer Applications* (New York: John Wiley & Sons, 1975).

[14] D.J. Farber et al., "The Distributed Computing System," *COMPCON*, 1973, pp. 31-34.

[15] H. Frank, I.T. Frisch, and W. Chou, "Topological Considerations in the Design of the ARPA Computer Network," *SJCC* 36 (1970), pp. 581-587.

[16] D. Karp and S. Seroussi, "A Communications Interface for Computer Networks," ACM/IEEE Second Symposium on Problems in the Optimization of Data Communication Systems, Palo Alto, Calif., October 1971.

[17] W.D. Becher and E. Aupperle, "The Communications Computer Hardware of the MERIT Network," *IEEE Transactions on Communications* 20 (June 1972), pp. 516-526.

[18] L.G. Roberts and B.D. Wessler, "Computer Network Development to Achieve Resource Sharing," *SJCC*, 1970, pp. 543-549.

[19] F.E. Heart et al., "A New Minicomputer/Multiprocessor for the ARPA Network," *NCC* 42 (1973), pp. 529-537.

[20] W.J. Luther, "The Conceptual Basis of Cybernet," *Computer Networks*, ed. Randall Rustin (Englewood Cliffs, Prentice-Hall, Inc. N.J.: 1973).

[21] S.M. Ornstein, et al., "The Terminal IMP for the ARPA Computer Network," *SJCC* 40 (1972), pp. 243-254.

[22] H. Opderbeck and R.B. Hovey, "TELENET—Network Features and Interface Protocols," *Proceedings NTG—Conference on Data Networks,* Baden, West Germany, February 1976.

[23] H. Opderbeck and L. Kleinrock, "The Influence of Control Procedures on the Performance of Packet-Switched Networks," in *IEEE 1974 National Telecommunications Conference Record* (New York: IEEE, 1974), pp. 810-817.

[24] H. Frank, R.E. Kahn, and L. Kleinrock, "Computer Communication Network Design—Experiment with Theory and Practice," *SJCC* 40 (1972): 255-270.

[25] C.B. Newport and J. Ryzlack, "Communication Processor," *Proceedings of the IEEE* 60 (November 1972), pp. 1321-1332.

[26] Y. Feinroth, E. Franceschini, and M. Goldstein, "Telecommunication Using a Front End Computer," *CACM* 16 (March 1973), pp. 153-160.

[27] R.A. Donnan and J.R. Kersey, "Synchronous Data Link Control: A Perspective," *IBM Systems Journal* 13, no. 2 (1974), pp. 140-160.

[28] J.P. Gray, "Line Control Procedures," *Proceedings of the IEEE* 60 (November 1972), pp. 1301-1312.

[29] B.W. Stutzman, "Data Communication Control Procedures," *ACM Computing Surveys* 4 (December 1972), pp. 197-220.

[30] S.D. Crocker, J.F. Heafner, and J.B. Postel, "Function Oriented Protocols for the ARPA Computer Network," *SJCC* 40 (1972), pp. 271-279.

[31] David Walden, "A System for Interprocess Communication in Resource Sharing Computer Networks, *CACM* 15 (April 1972), pp. 221-230.

[32] E. Akkoyunlu, A. Bernstein, and R. Shantz, "Interprocess communication Facilities for Network Operating Systems," *Computer* 17 (June 1974), 46-55.

[33] D.W. Davies and D.L.A. Barber, *Communication Networks for Computers* (New York: John Wiley & Sons, Inc., 1975).

[34] M. Schwartz, *Computer-Communication Network Design and Analysis* (New York: Prentice-Hall, Inc., 1977).

[35] L. Kleinrock et al., "A Study of Line Overhead in the ARPANET," *CACM* 19 (January 1976), pp. 3-13.

[36] D.W. Davis, "The Control of Congestion in Packet-Switching Networks," *IEEE Transactions on Communications* 20 (June 1972), pp. 546-550.

[37] G.L. Fultz and L. Kleinrock, "Adaptive Routing Techniques for Store-and-Forward Computer Communication Networks," AD727989, National Technical Information Center, July 1972.

[38] H. Rudin, "On Routing and 'Delta Routing': A Taxonomy and Performance Comparison of Techniques for Packet Switched Networks," *IEEE Transactions on Communications* 24 (January 1976), pp. 43-59.

[39] R. Bellman, *Dynamic Programming* (Princeton, N.J.: Princeton University Press, 1957).

[40] C.A. Sunshine, "Interprocess Communication Protocols for Computer Networks," Contract no. MDA 903-76C-0093, National Technical Information Center, December 1975.

[41] V.G. Cerf and C. Sunshine, "Protocols and Gateways for the Interconnection of Packet Switching Networks," ALOHA System Technical Report CN 74-22, January 1974.

[42] L. Kleinrock and S.S. Lam, "Packet-Switching in a Slotted Satellite Channel," *NCC* 42 (1973), pp. 703-710.

[43] L. Kleinrock and F.A. Tobagi, "Packet-Switching in Radio Channels: Part I—Carrier Sense Multiple-Access Modes and Their Throughput-Delay Characteristics," *IEEE Transactions on Communications* 23 (December 1975), pp. 1400-1416.

[44] V.G. Cerf and R.E. Kahn, "A Protocol for Network Intercommunication," *IEEE Transactions on Communications* 22 (May 1974), pp. 637-648.

[45] J.M. McQuillan, Adaptive Routing Algorithms for Distributed Computer Networks," AD 781467, National Technical Information Center, May 1974.

[46] B. Cosell, A. Nemeth, and D. Walden, "X.25 Link Access Procedures," *Computer-Communication Review*, October 1977.

[47] ACM, *Proceedings of the ACM SIGCOMM/SIGOPS Interprocess Communications Workshop*, March 1975 [also known as *ACM Operating System Review* 9, no. 3 (July 1975)].

[48] L.G. Roberts, "The Evolution of Packet Switching," *Proceedings of the IEEE* 66 (November 1978), pp. 1307-1313.

[49] L. Kleinrock, "Principles and Lessons in Packet Communications," *Proceedings of the IEEE* 66 (November 1978), pp. 1320-1329.

[50] L. Pouzin and H. Zimmermann, "A Tutorial on Protocols," *Proceedings of the IEEE* 66 (November 1978), pp. 1346-1370.

[51] V.G. Cerf and P.T. Kirstein, "Issues in Packet-Network Interconnection," *Proceedings of the IEEE* 66 (November 1978), pp. 1386-1408.

[52] M. Irland, "Simulation of CIGALE 1974," *Proceedings of the Fourth Data Communications Symposium*, 7-9 October, 1975, Quebec City, Canada, pp. 5-13 to 5-19, IEEE Catalog No. 75CH1001-7 Data.

# 4

# Interconnection Networks and Circuit-Switching Techniques

## Introduction

This chapter develops a constructive design concept for the creation of an interconnection network.[1] From this chapter, a designer can develop interconnection networks of all sizes from very small to very large. The design strategy is based on space-division multiplacer concepts developed for telephone switching networks but is amenable to the application of time-division multiplexing (TDM) techniques. This chapter deals with the functional aspects of interconnection switch design. The techniques to transmit the information over the circuits would either be the communication techniques discussed in the latter sections of chapter 5 or the appropriate transmission techniques selected from chapter 6.

Figure 4-1 indicates the application of interconnection networks into a general distributed processor as defined in chapters 3 and 1, respectively [1]. This chapter primarily concentrates on routing and construction techniques for circuit switches (level 1 in figure 4-1). The higher-level design issues could be developed as described by references given in chapter 3. The design strategy is developed inductively, and thus the connection algorithms are described constructively and a switch of any arbitrary size can be constructed.

First, we describe how to build elementary circuit switches using TDM techniques. Second, we describe how to build large interconnection networks which are composed of stages of cascaded elementary circuit switches. These elementary circuit switches could be conventional crossbar switches or TDM circuit switches. The reason that one eventually cascades such elementary circuit switches to form an interconnection networks is that a single circuit switch would eventually possess insufficient transmission bandwidth to adequately serve a channel as more and more channels are connected to a fixed-bandwidth switch. The reason that one eventually cascades crossbar switches to form interconnection network is that crossbar switches grow as $n^2$, where $n$ is the number of input lines. In some cases where speed is a major factor, designers have utilized interconnection networks based on multilevel crossbar switches for small systems AN/USQ-67 [2]. The AN/USQ-67 system is a 640 device by 640 device interconnection network designed to connect high-speed digital computers. The Bell Telephone System uses multistage interconnection networks that contain both crossbar switches and TDM-based circuit switches as elemental switches. C. mmp and some Burroughs multiprocessor systems also utilize circuit-switch interconnection techniques.

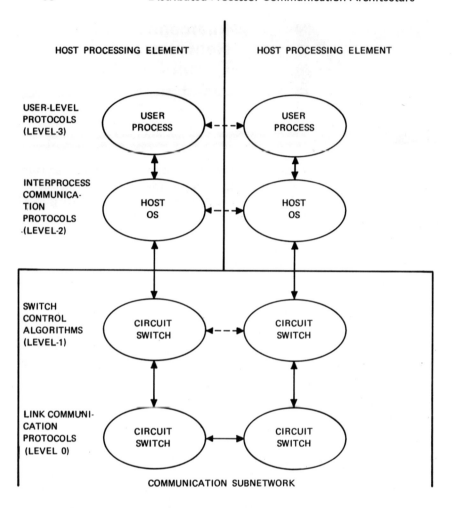

HOST PROCESSING ELEMENT            HOST PROCESSING ELEMENT

USER-LEVEL
PROTOCOLS          USER                USER
(LEVEL-3)         PROCESS             PROCESS

INTERPROCESS
COMMUNICA-
TION              HOST                HOST
PROTOCOLS         OS                  OS
(LEVEL-2)

SWITCH
CONTROL
ALGORITHMS      CIRCUIT             CIRCUIT
(LEVEL-1)       SWITCH              SWITCH

LINK COMMUNI-
CATION
PROTOCOLS       CIRCUIT             CIRCUIT
(LEVEL 0)       SWITCH              SWITCH

COMMUNICATION SUBNETWORK

KEY     VIRTUAL COMMUNICATION — — — ——
        ACTUAL COMMUNICATION  —————

**Figure 4-1.** Circuit-Switch Hierarchical Communication System Model.
Reprinted with permission from K.J. Thurber, "Computer
Communication Techniques," COMPSAC, IEEE Computer
Society, 589-594.

An interconnection network is an arrangement of circuit switches that
allows sets of terminals (input/output parts) to be interconnected. Most large-
scale communication systems contain interconnection networks [3]. Realization of the advantages of distributed processing and networking may require a
high degree of interconnection capability which can be provided by different
types of interconnection networks [4], message switches, or buses. The design

of restructurable buses in large systems may require that a large number of signals be steered by an interconnection network from their input point to their destination at very high speeds [5, 6, 7, 8]. The development of an automatically programmed hybrid computer system would require highly flexible interconnection networks [9, 10, 11].

The three main components of an interconnection network are (1) circuits over which communication can take place, (2) input and output terminals to which devices are attached, and (3) crossbar switches or time-division multiplexer circuit switches which can be "programmed" to interconnect the input and output terminals (in various specific connection conditions). While such factors as the number of memory elements, the amount and spacing of hardware, and the complexity of control are all relevant considerations in the design of an interconnection network, the number of crossbar switches and circuit switches is, in most cases, of overriding significance. This important variable is considered as the key design tradeoff in the remainder of this chapter.

The capability of an interconnection network to connect input terminals to output terminals is determined by the network structure. This structure can be described as one in which terminals have switches between them and terminals can be connected by closing these switches.

## Multiplexing

Multiplexing is the technique used to alternate signals from a group of lines onto a single line. There are two forms of multiplexing—time-division multiplexing (TDM) and frequency-division multiplexing (FDM). Time multiplexing divides the transmitted signal into discrete time slots. Typically, several lines supply inputs to the TDM system. The system then samples the inputs and composes a single output message for transmission. If every channel is sampled sequentially $(1, 2, \ldots, n, 1, 2, \ldots, n, 1, 2, \ldots)$ in round robin fashion and the data on each channel are sent, no identifier is necessary with the data. If, however, every channel is not sent every time it has a slot available to it, then an identifier must be provided so that the multiplexer at the other end can unscramble the received data. Which type of TDM is designed depends on the complexity allowed for the multiplexer and a tradeoff between the bandwidth needed for the identifier and the bandwidth wasted by transmitting unnecessary information.

Constructing a switch based on TDM techniques may require buffer memories for data storage at the inputs and outputs of the switch. If, instead, a switch is constructed using crossbar switch techniques (sometimes called static switching), the crosspoints in the crossbar are set so that the circuits are actually physically connected. This is discussed in more detail later in this chapter.

Also FDM techniques use a single line to transmit multiple channels. Typically, each channel is assigned its own separate baseband frequency. Then several channels may be simultaneously transmitted on a single line. The base-band and sideband frequencies must be chosen so that they do not overlap into other channels that are assigned frequencies.

## Crossbar Switches

Figure 4-2 shows a typical crossbar switch. This switch has $N$ input terminals and $M$ output terminals. At the intersection of each input and output line is a crosspoint circuit. Each crosspoint circuit has two conditions—the on, or closed, condition and the off, or open, condition. In the on condition, the two terminals are connected and communication can pass from one to the other; in the off condition, the terminals are disconnected and no information can pass through. Because of the defined operation of a crosspoint, the crossbar switch can be viewed as a device capable of static connection of $N$ input terminals onto $M$ output terminals in an arbitrary manner.

TDM circuit switches and crossbar switches of equal size are architecturally equivalent.

## Time Division Multiplex Circuit Switches

TDM circuit switches differ from crossbar circuit switches in that they sample inputs, store the samples in memory, and transmit the sample to the output terminals rather than providing a continuous connection between input and

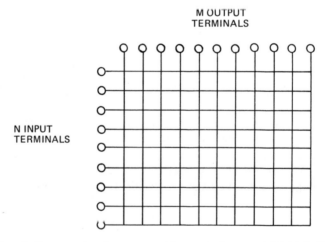

**Figure 4-2.** A Rectangular Connection Network, Denoted $R(N,M)$. Reprinted with permission from K.J. Thurber, "Circuit Switching Technology: A State-of-the-Art Survey," COMPCON, IEEE Computer Society, Fall, 1978.

output terminals. Each TDM switch is time-shared among several channels. The primary disadvantages of TDM circuit switches are (1) Complex control (2) Large high-speed memories may be required as buffers (3) High speed switching logic may be required. One of the major advantages of TDM circuit switches is the flexibility that results from the ability to reconfigure the switch every bit period. This eliminates the need for a great deal of redundant hardware to prevent blocking inability to make a circuit connection, as in the crossbar switch case. Further, if the logic is fast enough, and the memories are of sufficient size and speed, then a TDM circuit switch of very large size can be built quite simply.

A simple four input-four output TDM switch is illustrated in figure 4-3. It is functionally equivalent to a unidirectional four input-four output crossbar switch. The numbers of the inputs and outputs to be connected are loaded into the circular shift registers. The top number in each register drives a decoder and enables the desired input-to-output connection for one clock period. The clock shifts the connection pairs in the registers. The signal data on the input is stored in the appropriate output buffer for the remainder of the switch cycle (that is, four clock periods). In this simple case, the shift register, associated with the inputs, could be replaced with the counter if sequential sampling of the inputs is satisfactory.

Figure 4-4 is another implementation of a TDM switch. A slightly different approach is to use a fixed sequential multiplexer (serializer) and route the data stream through a time-slot interchanger and then into a sequential demultiplexer [12]. A switch like that in figure 4-4 could be used as a building block for larger matrices. However, the uncertainty in propagation time through the switch could be a problem, and the efficiencies of TDM switching would not be realized using this configuration.

The major advantage TDM circuit switches have over crossbar switches is that the number of switch points is proportional to the number of inputs; with crossbar switches, however, the number of switch points is proportional to the square of the number of inputs. Any technique to build large TDM switches which does not retain this advantage is probably less cost-effective than use of crossbar switches since crossbar switches can be decomposed so that their cost is on the order of $n \log n$.

In building TDM circuit switches with large numbers of inputs and outputs, one quickly runs out of sampling time. For example, if a TDM switch had 100 inputs and outputs and each input changed every 200 nanoseconds, then each sample period would have to be only 2 nanoseconds or less. If the selected technology cannot sample and set the buffer memory bit within that time, some kind of staging is necessary.

One technique is to add another bank of demultiplexers as shown in figure 4-4. A variation of this method would use additional multiplexers in the second bank. In both cases, the purpose is to provide signal paths between bank 1

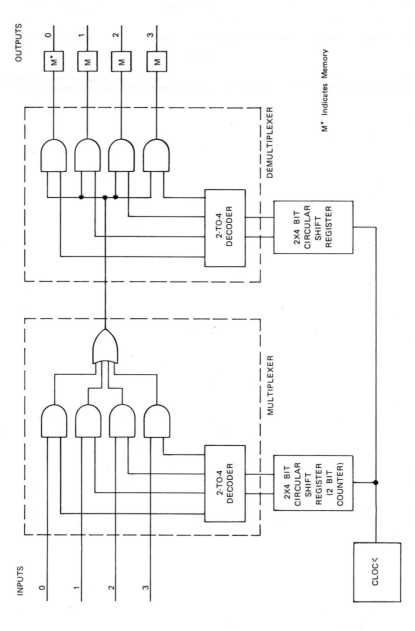

**Figure 4-3.** Four Input-Four Output TDM Switch. Reprinted with permission from K.J. Thurber, "Circuit Switching Technology: A State-of-the-Art Survey," COMPCON, IEEE Computer Society, Fall, 1978.

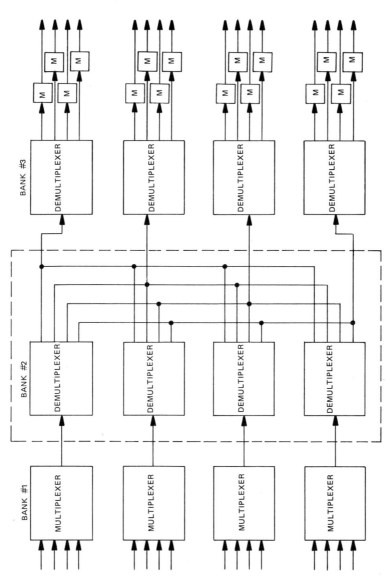

**Figure 4-4.** Three-Bank TDM Switch. Reprinted with permission from K.J. Thurber, "Circuit Switching Technology: A State-of-the-Art Survey," COMPCON, IEEE Computer Society, Fall, 1978.

multiplexers and bank 3 demultiplexers at different levels (for example, between the top multiplexer in bank 1 and the third demultiplexer in bank 3). The bank 2 demultiplexers, along with the interconnections of their outputs, can be considered as a 4 X 4 coordinate switch, which is reconfigured every sample period. The reconfigurations are cyclical, and decoders could be driven by end-around shift registers as before. The broken line in figure 4-4 encloses that switch. This observation leads to one technique to further expand the matrix. A large number (perhaps hundreds) of multiplexers could be connected to an equally large number of demultiplexers using a staged matrix capable of being reconfigured in a cyclical manner, as before. One problem with this three-bank TDM switch is that two or more signals sampled simultaneously in different multiplexers in bank 1 may have to be routed to the same demultiplexer in bank 3. This requires two or more signals on the same line at the same time. A possible solution to this problem uses special signal memory elements between banks or stages of a TDM switch. This approach, in addition to requiring significantly more hardware, may cause additional propagation delay between the input and the output terminals of a switch. The blocking problem could also be solved by proper programming of the switch.

Serializing a parallel channel eliminates the need to duplicate the switch forty times (for a 40-parallel-signal channel), but the bandwidth of the matrix components must be forty times that required for a parallel matrix. For the same overall data transmission rate and the same bandwidth switching components, a TDM matrix might multiplex forty channels into a serial bit stream, but all forty parallel lines in each channel must be switched; therefore, forty such TDM switches would be required.

Successive decomposition of crossbar switches using a three-stage switch model is the technique employed to reduce the crosspoint count from $n^2$ to $n$ log $n$. Thus to develop the theory of staged interconnection networks, we use crossbar switch techniques; however, since functionally TDM and crossbar systems are identical, the designer could use either TDM or crossbar-based basic building blocks.

## Nomenclature

Figure 4-2 shows a rectangular interconnection network denoted $R(N, M)$. There are $N$ input terminals, $M$ output terminals, and $NM$ crosspoints. This network has the property of being able to connect any output terminal to any input terminal. $NM$ crosspoints is the upper bound on the number of crosspoints necessary to realize $R(N, M)$.

Figure 4-5 shows an asymmetrical three-stage interconnection network. This network consists of two outside stages of rectangular networks called *input switches* and *output switches* and an inner stage of rectangular networks

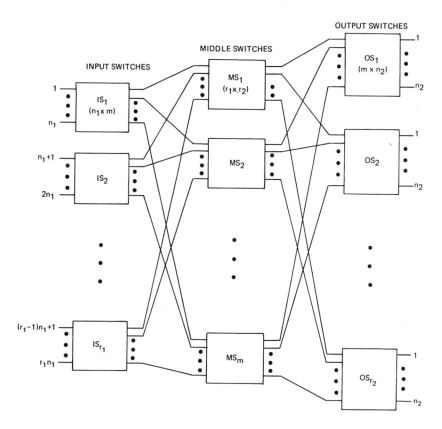

**Figure 4-5.** An Asymmetrical Three-Stage Network, Denoted $(m, n_1,$ $r_1, n_2, r_2)$. Reprinted with permission from K.J. Thurber, "Computer Communication Techniques," COMPSAC, IEEE Computer Society, 1978: 589-594.

called *middle switches*. The input stage contains $r_1$ rectangular ($r_1 \times m$) input switches; the output stage contains $r_2$ rectangular ($m \times n_2$) output switches; and the middle stage contains $m$ rectangular ($r_1 \times r_2$) middle switches. The switches of the input and output stages are connected to the middle stages by links. There is exactly one link connecting each middle switch to each input switch, and there is one link connecting each middle switch to each output switch. The $r_1 n_1$ inlets to the input switches are called *input terminals*, and the $r_2 n_2$ outlets from the output switches are called *output terminals*. This interconnection network is denoted $\nu(m, n_1, r_1, n_2, r_2)$, where $m, n_1, r_1, n_2$, and $r_2$ are defined relative to figure 4-5. If $n_1 = n_2$ and $r_1 = r_2$, the network is called a *symmetrical* three-stage interconnection network.

*Fan-out* is defined as the internal connection of a switch inlet to more than one switch outlet. The *degree* of fan-out is defined to be the total number of outlets connected to inlets minus the total number of inlets connected to outlets on a specific switch. The degree of fan-out of an interconnection network stage is the sum of the degrees of fan-out of each switch in the stage.

Any combination of open and closed switches is called a *state* of the network. If a specified connection between an input terminal and an output terminal cannot be made, the network is said to be in a *blocked state* relative to the desired connection. A specification of input-terminal connections to output terminals (regardless of the possible paths that the actual connections might take through the network) is called an *assignment*. If some network state could connect the specified input and output terminals, the connection assignment is said to be *realizable* by that interconnection network. An assignment may be realizable by more than one state of a particular network. The most common type of assignment has a one-to-one, input-output relationship. In a more general type of assignment (a multiple-connection assignment) each input terminal can be connected to more than one output terminal. A general multiple connection assignment is an assignment in which there are no restrictions on the number of output terminals that can be connected to any input terminal. All assignments considered are restricted so that each output terminal can be connected to a maximum of one input terminal.

An interconnection network is strictly *nonblocking* if any input terminal can be connected to any unconnected output terminal within the restrictions of the class of assignments being considered, regardless of the state of the network, without changing any of the existing connections. This is the strongest of all connecting properties. A network with this property has no blocking states. A rectangular interconnection network is strictly nonblocking. An interconnection network for which blocking states exist, but for which there exists a connection algorithm such that all blocking states can be avoided, is called a nonblocking interconnection network.

An interconnection network for which, in any given state, an input terminal can be connected to any unconnected output terminal, within the restrictions of the class of assignments being considered (perhaps at the expense of rearranging some of the existing connections), is called a *rearrangeable* interconnection network. For a network with this property, connections can be made until a blocked state is reached. A rearrangement algorithm is then needed to change the paths through the network of some of the existing connections and provide an open path for the blocked connection.

There exist three main classes of interconnection networks—concentration, connection, and expansion. In a concentration network, specific idle inputs request arbitrary idle outputs. A connection network allows specific idle inputs to request specific idle outputs. Finally, in an expansion network, specific (not necessarily idle) inputs request specific idle outputs (in other words, fan-out is allowed). In the next section the previous work on connection networks is considered. Later, a more general overview is given.

## Survey of Previous Results for Connection Networks

The most frequently considered structures for connection networks are those corresponding to rectangular interconnection networks, $R(N, M)$, and symmetrical three-stage interconnection networks, $\nu(m, n_1, r_1, n_1, r_1)$.

Clos [13] has shown that for one-to-one connection assignments a $\nu(m, n_1, r_1, n_1, r_1)$ interconnection network is strictly nonblocking if $m \geqslant 2n_1 - 1$. In comparing the number of crosspoints of $R(N, M)$ networks with that of $\nu(2n_1 - 1, n_1, r_1, n_1, r_1)$ networks, Clos showed that the number of crosspoints of the latter was less than that of the former for all values of $N \geqslant 36$. Clos also investigated multistage networks of more than three stages, for one-to-one assignments, and suggested methods of determining values of $n_1$ and $r_1$ which result in three- and five-stage networks with a minimum number of crosspoints.

The property of rearrangeability of $\nu(m, n_1, r_1, n_2, r_2)$ in the realization of one-to-one assignments has been considered by Duguid [14] and Slepian [15]. Using an inductive proof based on a combinatorial theorem of Hall [16] on distinct representatives of subsets, Duguid and Slepian showed that a $\nu(m, n_1, r_1, n_1, r_1)$ is rearrangeable if and only if $m \geqslant n_1$.

Bounds on the number of connections which must be rearranged in order to alleviate a block condition in a $\nu(n_1, n_1, r_1, n_1, r_1)$ network realizing one-to-one assignments were first given by Slepian [15]. Slepian's original upper bound was restricted to $\nu(n_1, n_1, n_1, n_1, n_1)$ networks and was set at $2n_1 - 2$. Paull [17] halved this result, and his method of doing so yielded a rearrangement algorithm. He showed that for a $\nu(n_1, n_1, n_1, n_1, n_1)$ network, the maximum number of connections that must be rearranged in order to alleviate a blocked condition is $n_1 - 1$. Benes [18] offered a simpler inductive proof, extended Paull's results to $\nu(n_1, n_1, r_1, n_1, r_1)$ networks, and gave a rearrangement algorithm. Benes proved that for such a network realizing one-to-one assignments, the maximum number of connections which must be rearranged to alleviate a blocked condition is $r_1 - 1$.

Cellular connection networks have been considered by Waksman [19]. He has shown the construction of such networks capable of $n$ permutations of $n$ input terminals. The building blocks for these networks are binary cells capable of permuting their two input terminals to their two output terminals. A more complete study of cellular interconnection networks has been made by Kautz, Levitt, and Waksman [4].

Applications of graph theory to interconnection networks have been made by Paull [20] and Aggarwal, Mayeda, and Ramamoorthy [21]. Paull established a relation between setting up connections in an interconnection network designed to connect any set of pairs of input terminals and a problem in graph theory. The main result showed that a particular class of multistage triangular networks is rearrangeable and gave a rearrangement algorithm for changing any existing connections. Aggarwal, Mayeda, and Ramamoorthy developed theoretical procedures for the design of minimal multitransmission networks and described techniques for making such networks survivable under component failure.

Designing interconnection networks is a very difficult job. Little real design theory exists. Many significant detailed design tradeoffs must be made to design an interconnection network. The major problem is realizing a design while trying to minimize the number of crosspoints. Many researchers give different bounds on the number of crosspoints, yet it is often found that no way is truly available to construct the network and trade off the amount of required control logic.

Realizable designs can best be described by considering constructive system designs based on set theory and math induction concepts. Because of the complexity of this subject we provide the following summary of the crosspoint complexity for the most important of the previously defined networks. For the advanced reader, we then provide the detailed analysis necessary to prove the bounds presented from a constructive point of view. Thus, by studying the theorem proofs, the reader could inductively construct networks which meet the minimum values along with appropriate control strategies.

## Crosspoint Bounds

The number of crosspoints has been determined by a series of searches over the range of possible values of the switch parameters. Although these values cannot be proved to be the absolute minimum, the extensiveness of the search ensures that these values are certainly near minimal and allows conclusions to be drawn in the comparison of different networks for the realization of common types of assignments. To appreciate these results, the following notation is necessary.

## Notation

Figure 4-5 shows an asymmetrical three-stage interconnection network. The $r_1$ input switches of an asymmetrical three-stage interconnection network are denoted by

$$\left\{ IS_j \right\} = \left\{ IS_1, \ldots, IS_{r_1} \right\}$$

the $r_2$ output switches are denoted by

$$\left\{ OS_i \right\} = \left\{ OS_1, \ldots, OS_{r_2} \right\}$$

and the $m$ middle switches are denoted by

$$\{MS_k\} = \{MS_1, \ldots, MS_m\}$$

The $r_1 n_1$ input terminals of an asymmetrical three-stage connection network form the set

$$I = \{1, \ldots, n_1, n_1 + 1, \ldots, (r_1 - 1)n_1, (r_1 - 1)n_1 + 1, \ldots, r_1 n_1\}$$

The input terminals connected to each of the $r_1$ input switches are denoted by the $r_1$ disjoint subsets of $I$

$$\{I_j\} = \{I_1, \ldots, I_{r_1}\}$$

where

$$I_j = \{(j - 1)n_1 + 1, \ldots, jn_1\}$$

In realizing any assignment, it is necessary to consider only input terminals being connected to output switches, rather than output terminals, since once an input terminal is connected to an output switch, the fan-out capability of that rectangular output switch can connect it to the proper output terminal(s). Therefore, the set

$$\{O_i\} = \{O_1, \ldots, O_{r_2}\}$$

where

$$O_i \subset I \quad i = 1, \ldots, r_2$$

and

$$|O_i| \leqslant n_2$$

where $|\ |$ denotes cardinality of a set, defines an assignment in which $O_i$, $i = 1, \ldots, r_2$, corresponds to the input terminals assigned to output switch $OS_i$.

There is exactly one link from every input switch to every middle switch, and one from every middle switch to every output switch. This means that every middle switch can connect to each output switch exactly one input terminal from each input switch. The set

$$\{M_k\} = \{M_1, \ldots, M_m\}$$

is a set of subsets of $I$ where $M_k$, $k = 1, \ldots, m$, contains one integer from each

$I_j$, $j = 1, \ldots, r_1$, corresponding to the input terminal of $I_j$ connected to $\text{MS}_k$. Thus,

$$M_k \in I_1 \times \cdots \times I_{r_1} \qquad k = 1, \ldots, m$$

### $C(n_1, n_2)$ Connection Assignments

A $C(n_1, \dot{n}_2)$ assignment is one in which the $n_1$ input terminals on any input switch are assigned to a maximum of $n_2$ output terminals. If under this restruction $|O_i| = n_2$, $i = 1, \ldots, r_2$, and no input terminal is connected to more than one output terminal on any output switch, then the corresponding assignment is called a *maximal* $C(n_1, n_2)$ assignment. If all maximal $C(n_1, n_2)$ assignments are realizable by an interconnection network, then all $C(n_1, n_2)$ assignments are realizable. If some output switch were assigned to less than $n_2$ input terminals, this would obviously be a subassignment of some maximal $C(n_1, n_2)$ assignment and, therefore, it would be realizable. If some input terminal were assigned to more than one output terminal on the same output switch, by means of the connecting capability of that rectangular output switch, it would be necessary to make only one connection between that input terminal and that output switch, and the actual assignment would be a subassignment of some maximal $C(n_1, n_2)$ assignment and, therefore, would be realizable.

### Strictly Nonblocking Three-Stage Interconnection Networks and Rectangular Interconnection Networks for the Realization of $C(n_1, n_2)$ Assignments

A sufficient number of middle switches in a three-stage network such that the network has the property of being strictly nonblocking in the realization of $C(n_1, n_2)$ assignments is $2n_2 - 1$. Let $\text{N3SC}_s$ be the number of crosspoints in a $\nu(2n_2 - 1, n_1, r_1, n_2, r_2)$ network, and let $NR$ be the number of crosspoints in a rectangular network. Then for given values of $N$ and $M$,

$$NR = N \cdot n$$

and

$$\text{N3SC}_s = (2n_2 - 1)(N + M + r_1 r_2)$$

**Table 4-1**

**Number of Crosspoints of Strictly Nonblocking Three-Stage Networks and Rectangular Networks Used for the Realization of $C(n_1,n_2)$ Assignments**

| N | $n_1$ | M | $n_2$ | $N3SC_s$ | NR |
|---|---|---|---|---|---|
|    |    | 32 | 8 | 1,200 | 768 |
| 24 | 4 | 64 | 16 | 3,472 | 1,536 |
|    |    | 96 | 24 | 6,768 | 2,304 |
|    |    | 288 | 24 | 29,328 | 48,384 |
| 168 | 12 | 576 | 48 | 86,640 | 96,768 |
|    |    | 864 | 72 | 171,600 | 145,152 |
|    |    | 1,152 | 48 | 228,000 | 718,848 |
| 624 | 24 | 2,304 | 96 | 678,432 | 1,437,696 |
|    |    | 3,456 | 144 | 1,350,048 | 2,156,544 |
|    |    | 3,200 | 80 | 1,043,040 | 5,376,000 |
| 1,680 | 40 | 6,400 | 160 | 3,133,440 | 10,752,000 |
|    |    | 9,600 | 240 | 6,207,840 | 16,128,000 |
|    |    | 4,608 | 96 | 1,796,928 | 11,059,200 |
| 2,400 | 48 | 9,216 | 192 | 5,368,128 | 22,118,400 |
|    |    | 13,824 | 288 | 10,708,800 | 33,177,600 |

For given values of $n_1$, $n_2$, $N$, and $M$, table 4-1 compares the number of crosspoints of rectangular and $v(2n_2-1,n_1,r_1,n_2,r_2)$ networks.

**Rearrangeable Three-Stage Interconnection Networks and Rectangular Interconnection Networks in the Realization of $C(n_1,n_2)$ Assignments**

A necessary and sufficient number of middle switches such that a $v(m,n_1,r_1, n_2,r_2)$ network has the property of being rearrangeable in the realization of $C(n_1,n_2)$ assignments is given as $n_2$. Let $N3SC_r$ be the number of crosspoints of a $v(n_2,n_1,r_1,n_2,r_2)$ network. Then for given values of $N$ and $M$,

$$N3SC_r = n_2(N + M + r_1r_2)$$

Table 4-2 compares the number of crosspoints of rectangular and $v(n_2,n_1, r_1,n_2,r_2)$ networks for given values of $n_1$, $n_2$, $N$, and $M$.

**Table 4-2**
**Number of Crosspoints of Rearrangeable Three-Stage Networks and Rectangular**
**Networks for the Realization of $C(n_1, n_2)$ Assignments**

| N | $n_1$ | M | $n_2$ | N3SC$_r$ | NR |
|---|---|---|---|---|---|
| 24 | 4 | 32 | 8 | 640 | 680 |
|    |   | 64 | 16 | 1,792 | 1,536 |
|    |   | 96 | 24 | 3,456 | 2,304 |
| 80 | 8 | 128 | 16 | 4,608 | 10,240 |
|    |   | 256 | 32 | 13,312 | 20,480 |
|    |   | 384 | 48 | 26,112 | 30,720 |
| 168 | 12 | 288 | 24 | 14,976 | 48,384 |
|    |   | 576 | 48 | 43,776 | 96,768 |
|    |   | 864 | 72 | 86,400 | 145,152 |
| 440 | 20 | 800 | 40 | 67,200 | 352,000 |
|    |   | 1,600 | 80 | 198,400 | 704,000 |
|    |   | 2,400 | 120 | 393,600 | 1,056,000 |
| 624 | 24 | 1,152 | 48 | 115,200 | 718,848 |
|    |   | 2,304 | 96 | 340,992 | 1,437,696 |
|    |   | 3,456 | 144 | 677,376 | 2,156,544 |

### $G(N,M)$ Connection Assignments

A $G(N,M)$ connection assignment is an assignment in which there is no restriction on the number of output terminals that can be connected to any input terminal. If

$$|O_i| = n_2 \qquad K = 1, \ldots, r_2$$

and no input terminal is connected to more than one output terminal on any output switch, the corresponding connection assignment is called a *maximal* $G(N,M)$ assignment. If all maximal $G(N,M)$ assignments are realizable by a connection network, then all $G(N,M)$ assignments are realizable. If some output switch were assigned to less than $n_2$ input terminals, this would obviously be a subassignment of some maximal $G(N,M)$ assignment and would therefore be realizable. Similarly, if some input terminal were assigned to more than one output terminal on the same output switch, because of the fan-out capability of that rectangular output switch, it would be necessary to make only one connection between that input terminal and that output switch. Thus the actual assignment would be some subassignment of a maximal $G(N,M)$ assignment and would also be realizable.

## Strictly Nonblocking Three-Stage Connection Networks and Rectangular Networks in the Realization of $G(N,M)$ Assignments

A sufficient condition on the number of middle switches of a $\nu(m,n_1,r_1,n_2,r_2)$ network such that the network has the property of being strictly nonblocking in the realization of $G(N,M)$ assignments is that $m = r_2 n_1 + n_2 - 1$. Let $\text{N3SG}_s$ be the number of crosspoints in a three-stage network meeting these conditions. For given values of $N$ and $M$,

$$\text{N3SG}_s = (r_2 n_1 + n_2 - 1)(N + M + r_1 r_2)$$

The switch parameters $n_1$ and $n_2$ of the three-stage strictly nonblocking network with the minimum number of crosspoints are the values of $n_1$ and $n_2$ which minimize the above equation for given values of $N$ and $M$, where

$$r_1 = \left\lceil \frac{N}{n_2} \right\rceil \quad \text{and} \quad r_2 = \left\lceil \frac{M}{n_2} \right\rceil$$

where $\lceil a \rceil$ denotes the smallest integer greater than or equal to $a$. This network will have $r_1 - 1 = \lfloor N/n_1 \rfloor$ input switches, each with $n_1$ input terminals, where $\lfloor a \rfloor$ denotes the greatest integer less than or equal to $a$, and one input switch with $n - \lfloor N/n_1 \rfloor n_1$ input terminals; and this network will have $r_2 - 1 = \lfloor M/n_2 \rfloor$ output switches, each with $n_2$ output terminals, and one output switch with $M - \lfloor M/n_2 \rfloor n_2$ output terminals. The equation for $\text{N3SG}_s$ can then be rewritten as

$$\text{N3SG}_s = \left( n_1 \left\lceil \frac{M}{n_2} \right\rceil + n_2 - 1 \right) \left[ n_1 \left\lfloor \frac{N}{n_1} \right\rfloor + \left\lceil \frac{N}{n_1} \right\rceil \left\lceil \frac{M}{n_2} \right\rceil + \left\lfloor \frac{M}{n_2} \right\rfloor n_2 \right.$$
$$\left. + \left( N - \left\lfloor \frac{N}{n_1} \right\rfloor n_1 \right) + \left( M - \left\lfloor \frac{M}{n_2} \right\rfloor n_2 \right) \right]$$

Figures 4-6 to 4-9 compare the number of crosspoints of $\nu(r_2 n_1 + n_2 - 1, n_1, r_1, n_2, r_2)$ networks for which the switch parameters $n_1$ and $n_2$ minimize, or nearly minimize, $\text{N3SG}_s$ with the number of crosspoints of rectangular networks for given values of $N$ and $M$ equal to $kN$.

The crossover point for two such networks and a given value of $k$, where $M = kN$, is defined to be the value of $N$ corresponding to the number of input terminals such that for all values of $N$ greater than this crossover value, switch

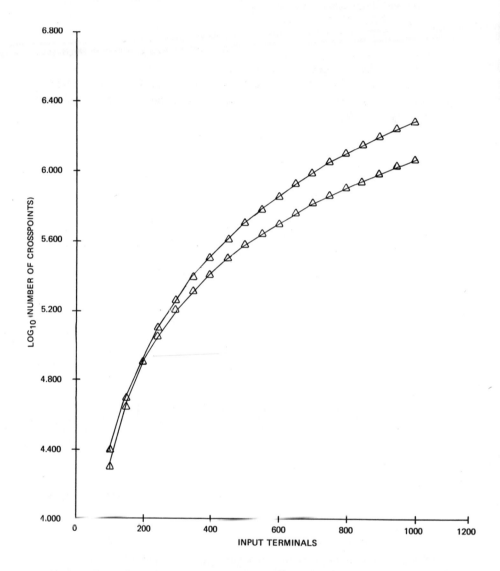

**Figure 4-6.** Graph of Crosspoint Requirements for Rectangular Strictly Nonblocking Three-Stage Connection Networks with $k = 2$.

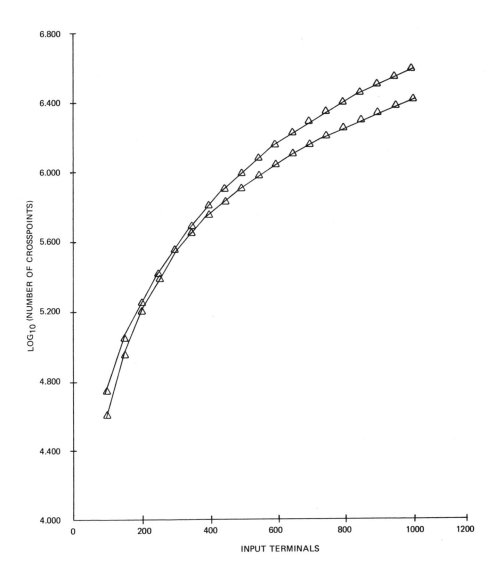

**Figure 4-7.** Graph of Crosspoint Requirements for Rectangular Strictly Non-blocking Three-Stage Connection Networks with $k = 4$.

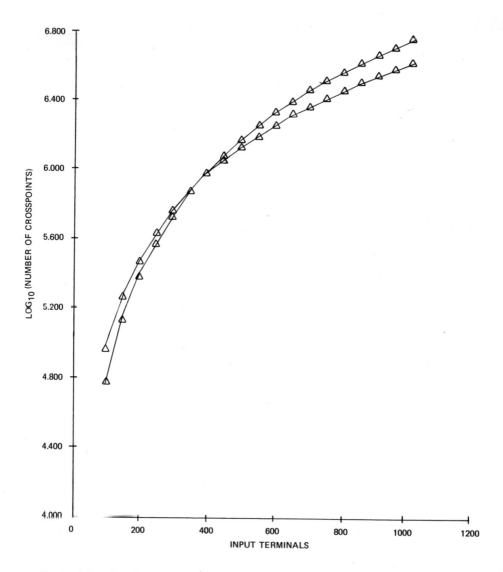

**Figure 4-8.** Graph of Crosspoint Requirements for Rectangular Strictly Non-blocking Three-Stage Connection Networks with $k = 6$.

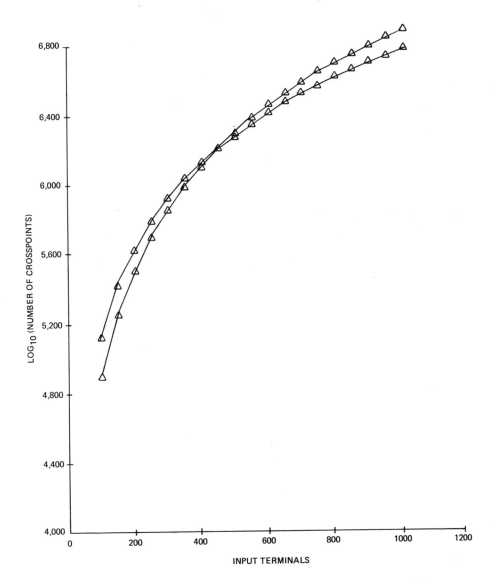

**Figure 4-9.**   Graph of Crosspoint Requirements for Rectangular Strictly Non-blocking Three-Stage Connection Networks with $k = 8$.

parameters $n_1$ and $n_2$ can be found such that

$$\text{N3SG}_s \leqslant NR$$

Table 4-3 shows approximate values of crossover points for $\nu(r_2 n_1 + n_2 - 1, n_1, r_1, n_2, r_2)$ networks and rectangular networks for a range of values of $k$.

**Rearrangeable Three-Stage Connection Networks and Rectangular Connection Networks for the Realization of $G(N,M)$ Assignments**

A sufficient condition for the number of middle switches of a $\nu(m, n_1, r_1, n_2, r_2)$ network such that the network has the property of being rearrangeable for the realization of $G(N,M)$ assignments is $m = \max(r_2, n_1, r_2)$. Let N3SG$_r$ be the number of crosspoints of a three-stage network meeting these conditions. Then for given values of $N$ and $M$,

$$\text{N3SG}_r = [\max(r_2 n_1, n_2)] \, (N + M + r_1 r_2)$$

**Table 4-3**
**Crossover Points of Rearrangeable Three-Stage and Rectangular Networks, and Strictly Nonblocking Three-Stage and Rectangular Networks Used for the Realization of $G(N,kN)$ Assignments**

| k | Crossover Point | |
|---|---|---|
| | Rearrangeable | Strictly Nonblocking |
| 1 | 27 | 180 |
| 2 | 32 | 203 |
| 3 | 42 | 240 |
| 4 | 47 | 284 |
| 5 | 54 | 329 |
| 6 | 60 | 370 |
| 7 | 68 | 418 |
| 8 | 72 | 460 |
| 9 | 83 | 508 |
| 10 | 86 | 552 |

The switch parameters $n_1$ and $n_2$ of the minimal, or near-minimal, rearrange-able three-stage connection network for given values of $N$ and $M$ are the values of $n_1$ and $n_2$ which minimize, or nearly minimize, the following equation:

$$N3SG_r = \left[ \max\left( \left\lceil \frac{M}{n_2} \right\rceil n_1, n_2 \right) \right] \left[ n_1 \left\lfloor \frac{N}{n_1} \right\rfloor + \left\lceil \frac{N}{n_1} \right\rceil \left\lceil \frac{M}{n_2} \right\rceil + \left\lfloor \frac{M}{n_2} \right\rfloor n_2 \right.$$
$$\left. + \left( N - \left\lfloor \frac{N}{n_1} \right\rfloor n_1 \right) + \left( M - \left\lfloor \frac{M}{n_2} \right\rfloor n_2 \right) \right]$$

Figures 4-10 to 4-13 compare the number of crosspoints of minimal, or near-minimal, three-stage rearrangeable connection networks with the number of crosspoints of rectangular connection networks for given values of $N$ and $M = kN$. Table 4-4 gives approximate crossover points of such networks for a range of values of $k$.

## Strictly Nonblocking Five-Stage and Three-Stage Connection Networks for the Realization of $G(N,M)$ Assignments

A $j$-stage connection network, where $j$ is an odd number, can be considered to be a three-stage connection network, where each middle stage is a $(j-2)$-stage connection network. A five-stage strictly nonblocking network can be considered an outside three-stage connection network consisting of $r_1 - 1 = \lfloor N/n_1 \rfloor$ input switches, each with $n_1$ input terminals, and one input switch with $N - \lfloor N/n_1 \rfloor n_1$ input terminals; $r_2 - 1 = \lfloor M/n_2 \rfloor$ output switches, each with $n_2$ output terminals, and one output switch with $M - \lfloor M/n_2 \rfloor n_2$ output terminals; and $m$ middle switches, $m = \lceil M/n_2 \rceil n_1 + n_2 - 1$, where each middle switch is a three-stage network with

$$r_1' - 1 = \left\lfloor \frac{r_1}{n_1'} \right\rfloor = \left\lfloor \frac{\lceil N/n_1 \rceil}{n_1'} \right\rfloor$$

input switches, each with $n_1'$ input terminals, and one input switch with

$$\left\lceil \frac{N}{n_1} \right\rceil - \left\lfloor \frac{\lceil N/n_1 \rceil}{n_1'} \right\rfloor n_1'$$

input terminals, and

$$r_2' - 1 = \left\lfloor \frac{\lceil M/n_2 \rceil}{n_2'} \right\rfloor$$

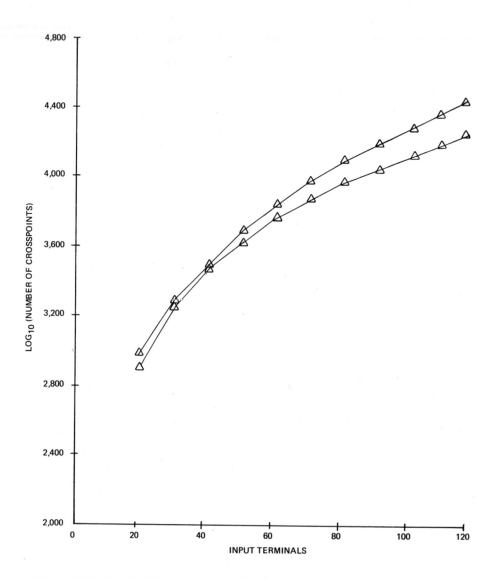

**Figure 4-10**. Graph of Crosspoint Requirements for Rectangular Three-stage
Rearrangeable Connection Networks with $k = 2$.

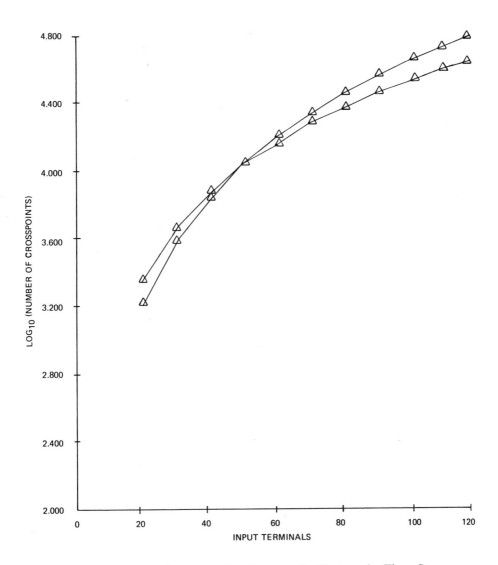

**Figure 4-11.** Graph of Crosspoint Requirements for Rectangular Three-Stage Rearrangeable Connection Networks with $k = 4$.

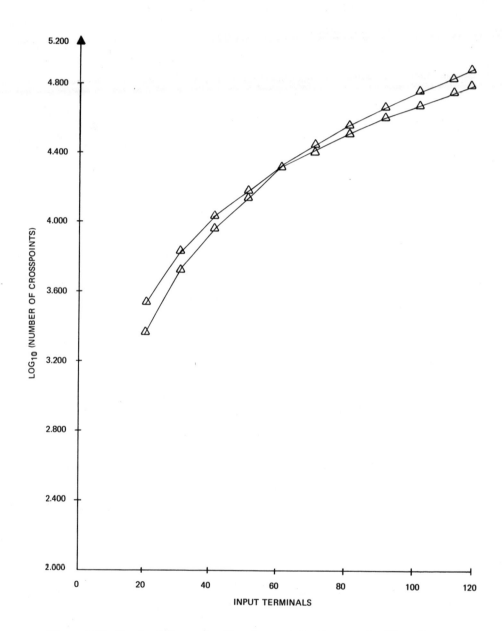

**Figure 4-12.** Graph of Crosspoint Requirements for Rectangular Three-Stage Rearrangeable Connection Networks with $k = 6$.

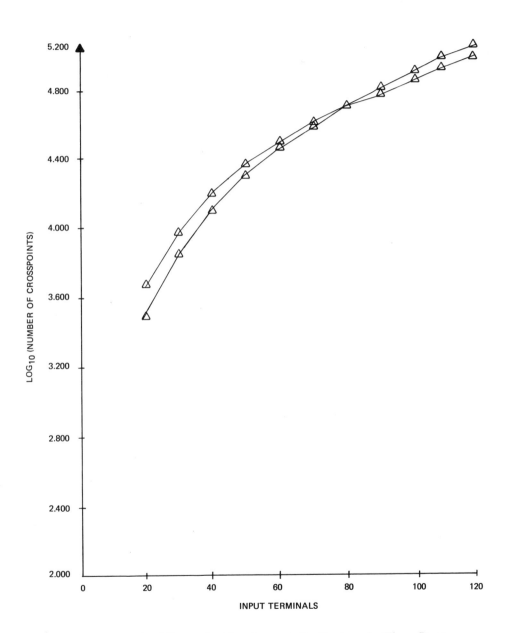

**Figure 4-13.** Graph of Crosspoint Requirements for Rectangular Three-Stage Rearrangeable Connection Networks with $k = 8$.

**Table 4-4**
**Comparison of the Number of Crosspoints of Strictly Nonblocking Five-Stage, Strictly Nonblocking Three-Stage and Rectangular Connection Networks Used for the Realization of $G(N,M)$ Assignments**

| N | M | N5SG$_s$ | N3SG$_s$ | NR |
|---|---|---|---|---|
| 10,000 | 20,000<br>40,000<br>60,000 | 58,422,760<br>124,799,509<br>200,906,934 | 54,704,375<br>122,537,400<br>200,336,080 | 200,000,000<br>400,000,000<br>600,000,000 |
| 30,000 | 60,000<br>120,000<br>180,000 | 348,100,038<br>748,503,392<br>1,184,241,600 | 341,550,000<br>767,760,000<br>1,249,968,969 | 1,800,000,000<br>3,600,000,000<br>5,400,000,000 |
| 50,000 | 100,000<br>200,000<br>300,000 | 800,999,472<br>1,703,155,913<br>2,711,719,724 | 800,711,662<br>1,786,716,000<br>2,928,188,880 | 5,000,000,000<br>10,000,000,000<br>15,000,000,000 |
| 70,000 | 140,000<br>280,000<br>420,000 | 1,386,504,000<br>2,939,301,680<br>4,681,635,840 | 1,402,374,528<br>3,154,552,960<br>5,131,818,341 | 9,800,000,000<br>19,600,000,000<br>29,400,000,000 |

output switches, each with $n_2'$ output terminals, and one output switch with

$$\left\lceil \frac{M}{n_2} \right\rceil - \left\lfloor \frac{\lceil M/n_2 \rceil}{n_2'} \right\rfloor n_2'$$

output terminals, and $m'$ rectangular middle switches, where

$$m' = \left\lceil \frac{\lceil M/n_2 \rceil}{n_2'} \right\rceil n_1' + n_2' - 1$$

Let N5SG$_s$ be the number of crosspoints of such a network. The optional five-stage network with the minimum number of crosspoints for given values of $N$ and $M$ is the network for which the switch parameters $n_1$, $n_2$, $n_1'$, and $n_2'$ minimize the following:

$$
\text{N5SG}_s = \left(\left\lceil \frac{M}{n_2} \right\rceil n_1 + n_2 - 1\right)\left\{\left\lfloor \frac{N}{n_1} \right\rfloor n_1 + \left(\left\lceil \frac{\lceil M/n_2 \rceil}{n_2'} \right\rceil n_1' + n_2' - 1\right)\left[\left\lfloor \frac{\lceil N/n_1 \rceil}{n_1'} \right\rfloor n_1'\right.\right.
$$

$$
+ \left\lceil \frac{\lceil N/n_1 \rceil}{n_1'} \right\rceil\left\lceil \frac{\lceil M/n_2 \rceil}{n_2'} \right\rceil + \left\lfloor \frac{\lceil M/n_2 \rceil}{n_2'} \right\rfloor n_2' + \left(\left\lceil \frac{N}{n_1} \right\rceil - \left\lfloor \frac{\lceil N/n_1 \rceil}{n_1'} \right\rfloor n_1'\right)
$$

$$
+ \left.\left(\left\lceil \frac{M}{n_2} \right\rceil - \left\lfloor \frac{\lceil M/n_2 \rceil}{n_2'} \right\rfloor n_2'\right)\right] + \left\lfloor \frac{M}{n_2} \right\rfloor n_2 + \left(N - \left\lfloor \frac{N}{n_1} \right\rfloor n_1\right)
$$

$$
+ \left.\left(M - \left\lfloor \frac{M}{n_2} \right\rfloor n_2\right)\right\}
$$

Table 4-4 compares the number of crosspoints of five-stage connection networks for which the switch parameters $n_1, n_2, n_1'$, and $n_2'$ give near-minimal solutions of $\text{N5SG}_s$ with the number of crosspoints of three-stage connection networks for which the switch parameters $n_1$ and $n_2$ give near-minimal solutions of $\text{N3SG}_s$ for given values of $N$ and $M$.

## Rearrangeable Five-Stage and Three-Stage Connection Networks for the Realization of $G(N,M)$ Assignments

Let $\text{N5SG}_r$ be the number of crosspoints in a rearrangeable five-stage connection network used fo the realization of $G(N,M)$ assignments. For given values of $N$ and $M$, the minimum number of crosspoints of such a network is the network with switch parameters $n_1, n_2, n_1'$, and $n_2'$ which minimize the following:

$$
\text{N5SG}_r = \left[\max\left(\left\lceil \frac{M}{n_2} \right\rceil n_1, n_2\right)\right]\left\{\left\lfloor \frac{M}{n_1} \right\rfloor n_1 + \left[\max\left(\left\lceil \frac{\lceil M/n_2 \rceil}{n_2'} \right\rceil n_1', n_2'\right)\right]\left[\left\lfloor \frac{\lceil N/n_1 \rceil}{n_1'} \right\rfloor n_1'\right.\right.
$$

$$
+ \left\lceil \frac{\lceil N/n_1 \rceil}{n_1'} \right\rceil\left\lceil \frac{\lceil M/n_2 \rceil}{n_2'} \right\rceil + \left\lfloor \frac{\lceil M/n_2 \rceil}{n_2'} \right\rfloor n_2' + \left(\left\lceil \frac{N}{n_1} \right\rceil - \left\lfloor \frac{\lceil N/n_1 \rceil}{n_1'} \right\rfloor n_1'\right)
$$

$$
+ \left.\left(\left\lceil \frac{M}{n_2} \right\rceil - \left\lfloor \frac{\lceil M/n_2 \rceil}{n_2'} \right\rfloor n_2'\right)\right] + \left\lfloor \frac{M}{n_2} \right\rfloor n_2 + \left(N - \left\lfloor \frac{N}{n_1} \right\rfloor n_1\right)
$$

$$
+ \left.\left(M - \left\lfloor \frac{M}{n_2} \right\rfloor n_2\right)\right\}
$$

Table 4-5 compares the number of crosspoints of five-stage rearrangeable networks for which the switch parameters $n_1, n_2, n_1'$, and $n_2'$ give near minima of $\text{N5SG}_r$ with the number of crosspoints of three-stage connection networks

**Table 4-5**
**Number of Crosspoints of Rearrangeable Five-Stage, Rearrangeable Three-Stage and Rectangular Connection Networks Used for the Realization of $G(N,M)$ Connection Assignments**

| N | M | N5SG$_r$ | N3SG$_r$ | NR |
|---|---|---|---|---|
| 100 | 200 | 16,456 | 13,775 | 20,000 |
|  | 400 | 32,200 | 30,000 | 40,000 |
|  | 600 | 51,500 | 50,000 | 60,000 |
| 200 | 400 | 45,200 | 43,600 | 80,000 |
|  | 800 | 96,800 | 98,600 | 160,000 |
|  | 1,200 | 153,000 | 160,000 | 240,000 |
| 300 | 600 | 86,100 | 84,000 | 180,000 |
|  | 1,200 | 187,840 | 189,200 | 360,000 |
|  | 1,800 | 301,500 | 307,800 | 540,000 |
| 400 | 800 | 140,000 | 136,000 | 320,000 |
|  | 1,600 | 293,600 | 307,090 | 640,000 |
|  | 2,400 | 469,600 | 496,800 | 960,000 |
| 500 | 1,000 | 192,528 | 198,576 | 500,000 |
|  | 2,000 | 433,664 | 446,880 | 1,000,000 |
|  | 3,000 | 672,224 | 736,764 | 1,500,000 |

for which the switch parameters $n_1$ and $n_2$ give near-minimal values of N3SG$_r$ for given values of $N$ and $M$.

The following sections discuss the construction concepts necessary to build the multistage interconnection networks.

## Strictly Nonblocking Interconnection Networks for $(n_1, n_2)$ Assignments

An interconnection network is strictly nonblocking if any unconnected output terminal can be connected to any input terminal regardless of the state of the network without rearranging any previously made connections. A network with this property has no blocking states. A rectangular interconnection network is strictly nonblocking.

A straightforward extension of the work of Clos [13] proves the following theorem.

**Theorem 4.1.** A $v(m,n_1,r_1,n_2,r_2)$ network is strictly nonblocking for $C(n_1,n_2)$ assignments if $m \geqslant 2n_2 - 1$.

**Proof.** A sufficient number of middle switches is required to permit the connection of any input terminal to any output terminal. Consider any arbitrary input terminal and any output terminal. This input terminal is a member of an input switch which can be assigned to as many as $n_2 - 1$ other output terminals. The chosen output terminal is a member of an output switch having $n_2 - 1$ other output terminals. Thus, $n_2 - 1 + n_2 - 1 = 2n_2 - 2$ middle switches are needed for the input and output switches of which the input and output terminals are members, plus one more for the chosen connection. Hence, $m \geqslant 2n_2 - 1$.

## Rearrangeable Interconnection Networks for $(n_1,n_2)$ Assignments

An interconnection network for which in any given state an input terminal can be connected to any unconnected output terminal at, perhaps the expense of rearranging some of the existing connections, is called a *rearrangeable interconnection network*. Two theorems [16, 22] concerning sets of distinct representatives find applications in rearrangeability considerations of $v(m,n_1,r_1,n_2,r_2)$ networks.

**Hall's Theorem.** Let $\{S_i\} = \{S_1, \ldots, S_{r_2}\}$ be any $r_2$ subsets for the set $\{IS_1, \ldots, IS_{r_1}\}$. A necessary and sufficient condition for the existence of a set of distinct representatives (SDR) is $\{S_i\}$. For any $t$, $1 \leqslant t \leqslant r_2$, the union of any $t$ of the sets $S_1, \ldots, S_{r_2}$ has at least $t$ elements.

**Hoffman and Kuhn's Theorem.** For the above sets $\{S_i\}$ and $\{IS_1, \ldots, IS_{r_1}\}$, A necessary and sufficient condition for the existence of an SDR for $\{S_i\}$ containing a prescribed set of elements $\{S_i'\} = \{IS_{i(1)}, \ldots, IS_{i(q)}\}$, $0 \leqslant q \leqslant r_2$, is that (1) there exists an SDR, (2) for each $q'$, $0 \leqslant q' \leqslant q$, any $q'$ subset of $\{S_i'\}$ is intersected by at least $q'$ of the $S_i$, $i = 1, \ldots, r_2$.

These two theorems can be used to prove the following.

**Theorem 4.2.** A $v(m,n_1,r_1,n_2,r_2)$ network is rearrangeable for $C(n_1,n_2)$ assignments if and only if $m \geqslant n_2$.

The proof of theorem 4.2 gives a construction technique for a rearrangeable network[2] and provides a technique to construct and control such networks.

The proof of theorem 4.2 leads to two interesting observations concerning the design of the connections made through the middle switches. Fan-out of a switch is defined to be the connection of an inlet on that switch to more than one outlet on that switch. First the inductive construction method used to connect the maximal $C(n_1,n_2)$ assignments in the proof of theorem 4.2 showed the following.

An $C(n_1,n_2)$ assignment is realizable with a $\nu(n_2,n_1,r_1,n_2,r_2)$ network using no middle stage fan-out.

The design relationship between the sets $M_k$, $k = 1,\ldots,n_2$, and $O_i$, $i = 1,\ldots,r_2$, in the realization of maximal $C(n_1,n_2)$ assignments with $\nu(n_2,n_1,r_1,n_2,r_2)$ networks was also given in the proof of the theorem. Each output switch was assigned to $n_2$ distinct input terminals and therefore used all $n_2$ links from the middle switches. The set $M_k$ is the set of input terminals connected to $MS_k$. Therefore, to realize a maximal $C(n_1,n_2)$ assignment, each $O_i$, the set of input terminals connected to $OS_i$, must be an SDR of $\{M_k\}$. This is stated as follows: A maximal $C(n_1,n_2)$ assignment, $\{O_i\} = \{O_1,\ldots,O_{r_2}\}$, is realizable by a $\nu(n_2,n_1,r_1,n_2,r_2)$ connection network if and only if there exists a set $\{M_k\} = \{M_1,\ldots,M_{n_2}\}$, $M_k \in \{I_1 \times \cdots \times I_{r_1}\}$, $k = 1,\ldots,n_2$, such that each $O_i \in \{O_i\}$ is a set of distinct representatives of $\{M_k\}$.

Although a $\nu(n_2,n_1,r_1,n_2,r_2)$ network can realize any $C(n_1,n_2)$ assignment, it is possible that while the assignment is implemented a blocked state can occur in which some specific connection of the $C(n_1,n_2)$ assignment cannot be made. That is, in the existing state of the network, an input terminal on some input switch, say $IS_j$, cannot be connected through any of the $n_2$ middle switches to an output terminal on some output switch, say $OS_i$. To alleviate a blocked condition, it is necessary to rearrange existing connections through the middle switches such that the resulting state of the network can accommodate this specific connection along with all previously made connections. Since there is at least one unconnected output terminal on $OS_i$, it follows that there is at least one middle switch, call it $MS_k$, with an unused link to $OS_i$. Similarly, since input switch $IS_j$ has been connected to at most $n_2 - 1$ output terminals, there is at least one middle switch, call it $MS_k'$, with an unused link to $IS_j$. Thus the blocked conditions can be alleviated as follows.

From observation one, all $C(n_1,n_2)$ assignments can be realized without any middle stage or output-stage fan-out. Suppose that prior to this blocked condition only input-stage fan-out had been used. Then the connections through the middle switches can be represented as follows. Let the set $\{C_k\}$, $k = 1, 2, \ldots, n_2$, be the set of ordered pairs

$$\{C_k\} = \left\{ \left( IS_{j(k(1))}, OS_{i(k(1))} \right), \ldots, \left( IS_{j(k(s))}, OS_{i(k(s))} \right) \right\}$$

where for each pair the first element denotes an input switch, the second element denotes an output switch, and each pair corresponds to a connection made between the denoted input and output switches made through middle switch $MS_k$. For the blocked connection and middle switches $MS_k$ and $MS_{k'}$, $\{C_k\}$ contains at most $r_2 - 1$ pairs, and $\{C_{k'}\}$ contains at most $r_2$ pairs. $OS_i$ is not an element of any pair contained in $\{C_k\}$; $IS_j$ is not an element of any pair contained in $\{C_{k'}\}$. Since no middle-stage fan-out has been used to make any of the existing connections, no pairs in $\{C_k\}$ have the same first element. Likewise, no pairs of $\{C_{k'}\}$ have the same first element.

Two rearrangement procedures are considered to alleviate the blocked condition—rearrangement procedure one, RP1, and rearrangement procedure two, RP2. Both procedures involve moving some connections previously made through $MS_k$ to $MS_{k'}$ and some connections which were previously made through $MS_{k'}$ to $MS_k$. RP1 results in $MS_k$ having unused links to both $IS_j$ and $OS_i$, and $MS_{k'}$ having used links to both these switches. RP2 results in $MS_{k'}$ having unused links to both $IS_j$ and $OS_i$, and $MS_k$ having used links to both these switches. When RP1 is completed, $MS_k$ can be used to make the specified connection; when RP2 is completed, $MS_{k'}$ can be used to make the blocked connection.

The RP1 algorithm can be designed as follows. For middle switches $MS_k$ and $MS_{k'}$ determine $\{C_k\}$ and $\{C_{k'}\}$. Move the pair in $\{C_k\}$ containing $OS_i$, say $(IS_{j'}, OS_i)$, into $\{C_{k'}\}$. If there exists a pair in $\{C_k\}$ which has the same first element, say $(IS_{j'}, OS_{i'})$, move this into $\{C_k\}$. If there exists a pair in $\{C_k\}$ with the same second element, say $(IS_{j''}, OS_{i'})$, move this into $\{C_{k'}\}$. Continue this procedure until $\{C_{k'}\}$ contains no pairs with the same first element and $\{C_k\}$ contains no pairs with the same second element. This completes the RP1 algorithm.

The RP2 algorithm can be described similarly. Move the pair in $\{C_{k'}\}$ containing $IS_j$, say $(IS_j, OS_{i'})$, into $\{C_k\}$. If there exists a pair in $\{C_k\}$ having the same second element, say $(IS_{j'}, OS_{i'})$, move this into $\{C_{k'}\}$. Continue this procedure until $\{C_k\}$ contains no pairs with the same second elements and $\{C_{k'}\}$ contains no pairs with the same first elements. This completes the RP2 algorithm.

In addition to the two algorithms which describe procedures for unblocking a network, we can derive bounds on the number of connections which must be rearranged to realize a $C(n_1, n_2)$ assignment with a $\nu(n_2, n_1, r_1, n_2, r_2)$ network.

**Lemma 4.1.** The first move in RP1 is not contained in RP2; the first move in RP2 is not contained in RP1.

**Proof.** The first move in RP1 is to move the pair containing $OS_i$ from $\{C_k\}$ to $\{C_{k'}\}$. This move could be contained in RP2 only if some pair in $\{C_{k'}\}$ contained $OS_i$ and the move was initiated by the preceding move in which this pair was moved to $\{C_k\}$. By definition of $\{C_{k'}\}$, no such pair containing $OS_i$ exists. Thus, the first move of RP1 is not contained in RP2. Similarly, the first move in RP2 is to move the pair containing $IS_j$ from $\{C_{k'}\}$ to $\{C_k\}$. This move could be contained in RP1 only if some pair in $\{C_k\}$ contained $IS_j$. By definition of $\{C_k\}$, no such pair exists. Thus, the first move of RP2 is not contained in RP1.

By lemma 4.1 RP1 results in a state of the network in which $MS_k$ has unused links to $IS_j$ and $OS_i$, which can now be used to make the previously blocked connection. RP2 results in a state of the network in which $MS_{k'}$ has unused links to $IS_j$ and $OS_i$, which can now be used to make the previously blocked connection.

**Lemma 4.2.** RP1 and RP2 have no moves in common.

**Proof.** By lemma 4.1 the first move in RP1 is not contained in RP2. Suppose that the $k$th move of RP1 is not contained in RP2. To show that this implies that the $(k + 1)$st move of RP1 is not contained in RP2, assume otherwise. Then the $(k + 1)$st move of RP1 is contained in RP2. But this move is initiated by the $k$th move of RP1, which implies that the $k$th move of RP1 is also contained in RP2. This contradicts the assumption. Thus RP1 and RP2 have no moves in common.

We can then calculate that there are a total of $2r_2 - 1$ possible moves. If one of the rearrangement procedures involves $j$ moves, then the other rearrangement procedures involve at most $2r_2 - 1 - j$ moves. Using this knowledge, we can show the following result.

**Theorem 4.3.** The maximum number of connections which must be rearranged in order to realize a particular connection of a $C(n_1, n_2)$ assignment with a $\nu(n_2, n_1, r_1, n_2, r_2)$ network is $r_2 - 1$.


## Strictly Nonblocking Interconnection Networks for $G(N,n)$ Assignments

An interconnection network is strictly nonblocking if any unconnected output terminal can be connected to any input terminal regardless of the state of the network without rearranging any previously made connections. The following theorem shows us how to design a nonblocking network.

**Theorem 4.4.** A $\nu(m, n_1, r_1, n_2, r_2)$ network is strictly nonblocking for $G(N,M)$ assignments if $m \geqslant r_2 n_1 + n_2 - 1$.

**Proof.** A sufficient number of middle switches is required to permit the connection of any input terminal to any output terminal. Consider any input terminal and output terminal. It is never necessary to make more than $r_2 n_1$

connections between an input switch and the output switches. The input terminal is a member of an input switch which needs at most $r_2 n_1 - 1$ other connections to the output switches. The chosen output terminal is a member of an output switch having $n_2 - 1$ other output terminals. Thus, $r_2 n_1 + n - 2$ middle switches are needed for the input and output switches of which the chosen input and output terminals are members, plus one more for the chosen connection. Hence, $m \geqslant r_2 n_1 - n_2 - 1$.

## Rearrangeable Interconnection Networks for $G(N,n)$ Assignments

An interconnection network for which in any given state an input terminal can be connected to any unconnected output terminal at, perhaps, the expense of rearranging some of the existing connections is called a *rearrangeable interconnection network*.

Theorem 4.5 describes the conditions necessary to develop a rearrangeable network. The proof of this theorem provides an algorithm for construction of rearrangeable networks.[3]

**Theorem 4.5.** A $v(m,n_1,r_1,n_2,r_2)$ network is rearrangeable for $G(N,M)$ assignments if $m \geqslant \max(n_2, r_2 n_1)$.

The proof of the theorem leads to two interesting corollaries concerning the connections made through middle switches in the realization of $G(N,M)$ assignments. The inductive method used to connect the maximal $G(N,M)$ assignments in the proof of theorem showed the following corollary.

**Corollary.** Any $G(N,M)$ assignment is realizable with a $v(m,n_1,r_1,n_2,r_2)$ network where $m > \max(n_2, r_2 n_1)$, using no middle-stage fan-out.

The relationship between the sets $M_k$, $k = 1, \ldots, m$, where $m \geqslant \max$ $(n_2, r_2 n_1)$, and $O_i$, $i = 1, \ldots, r_2$, in the realization of maximal $G(N,M)$ assignments with $v(m,n_1,r_1,n_2,r_2)$ networks was also given in the proof of the theorem. Each output switch was assigned to $n_2$ distinct input terminals and therefore used all the links from the middle switches. The set $\{M_k\}$ is the set of input terminals connected to $MS_k$. To realize a maximal $G(N,M)$ assignment, each $O_i$, the set of input terminals connected to $OS_i$, must be an SDR of $\{M_k\}$. This is stated in the following corollary.

**Corollary.** A maximal $G(N,M)$ assignment $\{O_i\}$ is realizable by $v(m,n_1,r_1,n_2,r_2)$ connection network if and only if there exists a set $\{M_k\} = \{M_1, \ldots, M_m\}$, $M_k \in \{I_1 \times \cdots \times I_{r_1}\}$, $k = 1, \ldots, m$, such that each $O_i \in \{O_i\}$ is a set of distinct representatives of $n_2$ of the $M_k \in \{M_k\}$.

This corollary gives precisely the relationship which must exist among the sets $\{I_j\}$, $\{M_k\}$, and $\{O_i\}$ such that the relationship between $\{I\}$ and $\{O_i\}$ is realizable.

Although a $\nu(m,n_1,r_1,n_2,r_2)$ network, where $m \geqslant \max(n_2, r_2 n_1)$, can realize any $G(N,M)$ assignment, it is possible that while the assignment is implemented a blocked state can occur in which some specific connection of the $G(N,M)$ assignment cannot be made. To alleviate this blocked condition, it is necessary to rearrange some of the existing connections made through the middle switches such that the resulting state of the network can make the blocked connection along with all the previously made connections. Since there is at least one unconnected output terminal on $OS_i$, it follows that there is at least one middle switch, call it $MS_k$, with an unused link to $OS_i$; similarly, since input switch $IS_j$ has been connected to at most $n_1 r_2 - 1$ output switches, there is at least one middle switch, call it $MS_{k'}$ with an unused link to $IS_j$.

Let the set $\{C_k\}$, $k = 1, 2, \ldots, m$, be the set of ordered pairs

$$\{C_k\} = \left\{\left(IS_{j(k(1))}, OS_{i(k(1))}\right), \ldots, \left(IS_{j(k(s))}, OS_{i(k(s))}\right)\right\}$$

where for each pair the first element denotes an input switch, the second element denotes an output switch, and each pair corresponds to a connection between the denoted input and output switches made through middle switch $MS_k$. For the blocked connection described and middle switches $MS_k$ and $MS_{k'}$, $\{C_k\}$ contains at most $r_2 - 1$ pairs, $\{C_{k'}\}$ contains at most $r_2$ pairs, and

$$(IS_j, OS_q) \in \{C_k\} \qquad \text{for at least one } q \in \{1, \ldots, r_2\}$$

$$(IS_r, OS_i) \in \{C_{k'}\} \qquad \text{for some } r \in \{1, \ldots, r_1\}$$

and

$$(IS_j, OS_s) \notin \{C_{k'}\} \qquad \text{for all } s \in \{1, \ldots, r_2\}$$

$$(IS_t, OS_i) \notin \{C_k\} \qquad \text{for all } t \in \{1, \ldots, r_1\}$$

Since there is only one link from each middle switch to each output switch, no two pairs in any set can have the same output-switch entries. However, middle-stage fan-out is denoted by two or more pairs in a set having the same input switch entry. Each such input-switch entry represents a connection from the same input terminal on that input switch.

Two rearrangement procedures can be algorithmically described which can alleviate this blocked condition. Rearrangement procedure one (RP1) involves moving pairs between $\{C_k\}$ and $\{C_{k'}\}$ until $\{C_k\}$ contains all the pairs in which $OS_i$ and $IS_j$ are entries, thereby allowing $\{C_{k'}\}$ to accept the blocked pair

$(IS_j, OS_i)$. Rearrangement procedure two (RP2) involves moving pairs between $\{C_k\}$ and $\{C_{k'}\}$ until $\{C_{k'}\}$ contains all the pairs in which $OS_i$ and $IS_j$ are entries, thereby allowing $\{C_k\}$ to accept the blocked pair. In both procedures the moving of pairs from one set to the other can cause input-switch and output-switch conflicts, which must be resolved in order for the network to realize all the previously made connections together with the blocked connection. An input-switch conflict occurs when two or more pairs in the same set have the same input-switch entry, and these entries denote different input terminals on the denoted input switch. This corresponds to a middle switch being required to make two or more connections from two or more different input terminals on the same input switch. An output-switch conflict occurs when two or more pairs in a set have the same output-switch entry. This corresponds to a middle switch being required to make connections from different input terminals to the same output switch.

The initial move of RP1 is to move the pair in $\{C_{k'}\}$ containing $OS_i$ to $\{C_k\}$; the initial move of RP2 is to move all the pairs in $\{C_k\}$ containing $IS_j$ to $\{C_{k'}\}$. Each of these moves is the initiating move of a primary sequence of moves which can be described as follows: if pairs moved from $\{C_k\}$ to $\{C_{k'}\}$ in the primary sequence cause conflicts, then the conflicts can be only output-switch conflicts, and they are resolved by moving the conflicting pairs which were members of $\{C_{k'}\}$ previous to this last move to $\{C_k\}$. If pairs moved from $\{C_{k'}\}$ to $\{C_k\}$ in the primary sequence cause a conflict, then the conflicts can be only input-switch conflicts, and they are resolved by moving the conflicting pairs which were members of $\{C_k\}$ previous to this last move to $\{C_{k'}\}$. Again by considering relationships between RP1 and RP2 we can determine a bound on the number of connections which must be rearranged.

**Lemma 4.3.** The initial move in the primary sequence of RP1 is not contained in the primary sequence of RP2; the initial move in the primary sequence of RP2 is not contained in the primary sequence of RP1.

By the previous lemma, the primary sequence of RP1 results in a state of the network in which $MS_{k'}$ has unused links to $IS_j$ and $OS_i$ and can now be used to make the previously blocked connection. The primary sequence of RP2 results in a state of the network in which $MS_k$ has unused links to $IS_j$ and $OS_i$ and can now be used to make the previously blocked connection.

**Lemma 4.4.** The primary sequences of RP1 and RP2 have no moves in common.

Since the proofs of these lemmas are similar to those of previous lemmas, their proofs are left to the reader.

There are a total of $2r_2 - 1$ possible primary-sequence moves. If one of the rearrangement procedures involves $j$ primary-sequence moves between two sets $\{C_k\}$ and $\{C_{k'}\}$, then the other rearrangement procedure involves at most $2r_2 - 1 - j$ primary-sequence moves between these sets. Thus, the maximum number of primary-sequence moves necessary between two sets to allow one set to accept a particular pair is $r_2 - 1$.

However, besides this primary sequence of moves, middle-stage fan-out in the middle switch with the used link to $OS_i$, that is, $MS_{k'}$, can result in a secondary sequence of moves which can be described as follows: pairs moved from $\{C_k\}$ to $\{C_{k'}\}$ can cause both input- and output-stage conflicts; likewise, pairs moved from $\{C_{k'}\}$ to $\{C_k\}$ can cause both input- and output-stage conflicts. The first such move which causes this change in the order of the conflicts represents the first move of the secondary sequence. The previous move is considered to have terminated the primary sequence and initiated the secondary sequence, and is referred to as the initiating move of the secondary sequence. Such a secondary sequence occurs when one of two or more fanned-out pairs is moved from $\{C_{k'}\}$ to $\{C_k\}$ in the primary sequence because of an output-switch conflict. A subsequent input-switch conflict in $\{C_k\}$ results in a move of the conflicting pair to $\{C_{k'}\}$. This, however, causes an input-switch conflict with the remaining fanned-out pairs with the same input-switch entry, as well as a possible output-switch conflict with some other pair. Thus, the move of this first fanned-out pair to $\{C_k\}$ was the initiating move of this secondary sequence.

In the case of RP1, it is possible that pairs in $\{C_k\}$ which contain $IS_j$ can be moved to $\{C_{k'}\}$ because of output-switch conflicts in this secondary sequence. In the case of RP2, it is possible that the pair in $\{C_{k'}\}$ which contains $\{OS_i\}$ can be moved to $\{C_k\}$ because of input-switch conflicts in the secondary sequence. In both cases, when the procedures have been completed, neither $\{C_k\}$ nor $\{C_{k'}\}$ could accept the blocked pair. Thus, this secondary sequence has nullified the rearrangement procedures. To prevent this situation from occurring, the pair moved in the initiating move of the secondary sequence or the other fanned-out pairs with the same input-switch entry in $\{C_{k'}\}$ can be moved to a set other than $\{C_{k'}\}$. There must exist at least one set, call it $\{C_{k''}\}$, which has no pairs with the same input-switch entry as the initiating pair. This is due to the fan-out in $\{C_{k'}\}$. At least two of the maximum of $n_1 r_2$ connections to the output switches required by this input switch are provided by $MS_{k'}$. Thus, there is a maximum of $n_1 r_2 - 2$ paths which must be provided by the remaining $m - 1 \geqslant n_1 r_2 - 1$ middle switches. At least one middle switch, say $MS_{k''}$, has an idle link to this input switch. The rearrangement procedures can now be performed on $\{C_{k'}\}$ and $\{C_{k''}\}$ to move this initiating pair of the secondary sequence to $\{C_{k''}\}$, or to move all the other fanned out pairs in $\{C_{k'}\}$ with this same input-switch entry to $\{C_{k''}\}$. Both moves prevent the initiating of the secondary sequence. It is possible that the rearrangement procedures performed on $\{C_{k'}\}$ and $\{C_{k''}\}$ can also result in a similar nullifying sequence. Again, the initiating fanned-out pair, or the other fanned-out pairs with the same input-switch entry, can be moved to a different set. This situation can continue to occur as long as middle-stage fan-out is present in the network. From the lemmas it was seen that if no secondary sequences develop during the rearrangement procedures, the maximum number of moves necessary to alleviate a blocked condition is $r_2 - 1$. Since it may be necessary to move all but one of each fanned-out connection in order to prevent nullifying secondary sequences, the following theorem has been proved and we know how to alleviate blocking and the maximum number of connections that must be moved.

**Theorem 4.6.** Let $d$ be the degree of middle-stage fan-out present in a state of a $v(m, n_1, r_1, n_2, r_2)$ network, where $m \geqslant \max(n_2, r_2 n_1)$. The maximum number of connections which must be moved in order to alleviate a blocked condition is $(d + 1)(r_2 - 1)$.

**Multistage Interconnection Networks**

The conditions previously presented can also be used for the analysis and design of connection networks of more than three stages. For example, five-stage connection network can be considered to be a three-stage connection network where each middle switch is a three-stage network. In general, a $j$-stage network, where $j$ is an odd number, can be considered to be a three-stage network, where each middle switch is actually a $(j - 2)$-stage network.

**Further Results**

Interconnection network design is a very fruitful area of current research. There are many concepts and theories which can be applied to the design of such systems. Several of these concepts are discussed in the following subsections.

*Data Alignment Networks*

One way to increase the speed of a wide class of computational procedures is to arrange such procedures so that many intermediate results can be computed simultaneously. Highly redundant computations such as those involving vectors or arrays of numbers lend themselves readily to this type of analysis [23, 24]. However, it is not enough merely to provide several processing units to perform computations simultaneously, since conflicts resulting from many processors accessing the same memory elements can wipe out any increase in speed obtained from the additional processors.

Clearly, in order to add two rows of a matrix, the data fetched from the memories must be aligned so that the proper column elements of each of the rows end up being added. It would seem that a network which provides a way to implement these functions would find use in this type of application. A rectangular interconnection network can certainly produce the necessary rearrangements. However, if $N$ is the number of processors, the number of crosspoints required increases on the order of $N^2$. Lawrie [25] has proposed what is called an omega network to solve this problem in applications involving the processing of arrays.

An omega network is composed of $N/2$ stages of $\log_2 N$ switching elements which are connected by what is known as a perfect shuffle connection [26]. The defining property of the perfect shuffle connection can be given in terms of the binary representations of the indices of the input and output connections. If $s_1 s_2 \cdots s_1$ is the binary representation of the index number of the input to the shuffle connection, after passing through the connection, the signal appears at the output terminal with the index given by the binary representation $s_2 s_3 \cdots s_1 s_1$. Thus the binary representation of the index has simply been shifted one place to the left, with the original leftmost digit carried around and placed on the right. An $8 \times 8$ omega network is shown in figure 4-14. Note the rearrangement of the eight input lires before they enter the first switching stage. Input 0, with binary representation 000, is sent to the 000th input of the first switching stage. Input 1, whose binary representation is 001, is sent to the 010th or second input of the switching stage.

The switching elements in the omega network have the property at any given time that they may be in any one of four states. In one state, the inputs are simply transmitted to the corresponding outputs. In the second state, inputs are transmitted to the opposite output. In the third and fourth states, one of the inputs is broadcast to both outputs simultaneously.

It is clear that there is one and only one path from each input terminal to each output terminal. In addition, some of the unique paths overlap. Although the omega connection network only requires on the order of $(N/2)$ $\log_2 N$ switching elements, a considerable improvement over the $N^2$ elements of a crossbar switch, versatility has been lost in that not all possible interconnections of inputs and outputs can be realized. Lawrie [25] has shown that the rearrangements of interest in aligning data stored using the generalized skewing scheme outlined in figure 4-14 can indeed be performed by the omega network, and Lawrie gives a simple algorithm for setting up the switching elements to perform the desired connection.

Besides providing properties which prove to be useful for accessing skewed data stored in separate memory segments, the omega network is practical in the sense that it can be partitioned into segments composed of larger switching elements. For example, an $8 \times 8$ omega network can be built using basic $4 \times 4$ circuit-switch elements in two stages, as shown in figure 4-15. The properties of the perfect shuffle connection [26] between the switching stages are largely responsible for this added feature, which can facilitate the construction of large omega networks composed of optimally packaged smaller units.

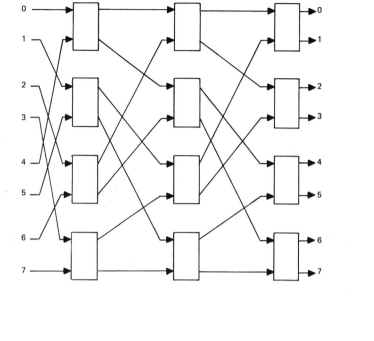

STRAIGHT                INTERCHANGE            LOWER BROADCAST        UPPER BROADCAST

**Figure 4-14.** An 8 × 8 Omega Network and Allowed States of the
Switching Elements.

Some of the details associated with the omega network are as follows. Let the
array $A$ have $K$ dimensions, and let $M$ be the number of memories. $A$ is said to be
stored using a $(d_1, d_2, \ldots, d_k)$ *skewing scheme* if the element of $A$ with coordinates
$(i_1, i_2, \ldots, i_k)$ is stored in memory unit $i_1 \cdot d_1 + i_2 \cdot d_2 + \cdots i_k \cdot d_k \pmod{M}$.
A *d-ordered* vector is a vector of $N$ elements whose $i$th logical element is stored
in memory unit $di + c \pmod{M}$, where $c$ is an arbitrary constant. With the
above, we can now prove the following theorem.

**Theorem 4.7.** If $M$ is greater than or equal to $N[\text{Gcd}(d,M)]$, then a $d$-ordered
$N$ vector is accessible without conflicts. $\text{Gcd}(d,M)$ denotes the greatest common
divisor of $d$ and $M$.

**Proof.** Suppose it is not possible to access the $d$-ordered vector without conflicts. That is, there exist $i$ and $j$, both less than $N$, such that the $i$th and $j$th
elements of the vector are both stored in the same memory element. Then by

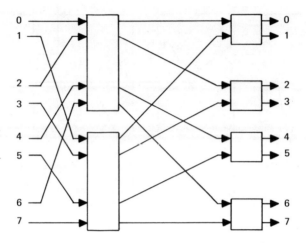

**Figure 4-15.** An 8 × 8 Omega Network Composed of 4 × 4 and 2 ×2 Switching Elements.

the definition of a $d$-ordered vector, $i$ and $j$ must satisfy $di + c = dj + c$ (mod $M$), which implies that $di = dj$ (mod $M$). Now form $d'$ and $M'$ by dividing $d$ and $M$, respectively, by $\gcd(d,M)$. Then $i$ and $j$ satisfy $d'i = d'j$ (mod $M'$) with $\gcd(d',M') = 1$. But this means that $i = j$ (mod $M'$). This is true if and only if $i = j$ or at least one of $i$ and $j$ is greater than or equal to $M'$. But, by hypothesis, $i$ and $j$ are both less than $N$, and $M'$ is greater than or equal to $N$. Hence $i = j$. Thus different elements of the array are stored in different memory units.

If an array is stored using a $(d_1,d_2)$ skewing scheme, then the following statements are true:

1. Rows of the matrix are $d_2$-ordered.
2. Columns of the matrix are $d_1$-ordered.
3. Forward diagonals are $d_1 + d_2$-ordered.
4. Backward diagonals are $d_1 - d_2$-ordered.

The proof of these statements is obvious upon writing general expressions for elements of a row, column, and diagonal and examining the expressions for the memory unit in which each element is stored.

Thus, if the number of processors $N$ is an even power of 2 and $M$, the number of memories, is chosen to be $2N$, the use of $(N^{1/2} + 1, 2)$ skewing makes it possible to access rows, columns, and diagonals without conflict. This is true since $N^{1/2} + 1, N^{1/2} + 3, N^{1/2} - 1$ are all odd and therefore prime to $M$.

Figure 4-16 shows a 4 × 4 array stored in five memories using a (2,3) skewing scheme. For the types of data alignment procedures needed for the efficient parallel processing of skew-stored arrays, the omega network provides a much more attractive method of rearranging data than do other circuit-switch

MEMORY

| $a_{00}$ | $a_{02}$ | X | $a_{01}$ | $a_{03}$ |  |
|---|---|---|---|---|---|
| $a_{11}$ | $a_{13}$ | $a_{10}$ | $a_{12}$ | X |  |
| $a_{22}$ | X | $a_{21}$ | $a_{23}$ | $a_{20}$ |  |
| $a_{33}$ | $a_{30}$ | $a_{32}$ | X | $a_{31}$ |  |

**Figure 4-16.** A $(2,3)$ Skewing Scheme with Five Memories.

concepts. Networks similar to the omega network have been developed, but these suffer from excessively long setup times and/or long propagation times through the network. For other types of data alignment problems, or other storage schemes, however, the omega network may not prove to be optimal since only a subset of all possible input-output connections can be made using this network.

In addition to the important work of Lawrie [25], Kuck and Sameh [24], and Stone [26], fixed-structure or limited-capability structure networks for data alignment have been applied in STARAN [27] and in a STARAN application at RADC [28]. Data are stored in a "skewed" fashion internal to STARAN and are unscrambled by the "flip" network [27]. Feng [28] has designed a data alignment network to interface STARAN to a mass memory.

*Banyans as Partitioning Networks*

In recent implementations of multiple-processor computing systems it has been found useful to interconnect the processors and associated peripherals via a single, common bus structure. A bus-switching system provides for dynamic reconfiguration of the interconnections, depending on system requirements. At any instant of time, it may be desirable for a group of resource modules, either processors or peripherals, to have their buses connected in order to exchange data. Thus the idea of a partitioning network becomes important, that is, a switching network designed to provide interconnections between elements within partition sets of the set of resource modules. For example, it may be necessary for a processor to transfer data to memory unit A at the same time as data are being transferred from a disk drive to memory B. The role of the partitioning network would be to provide simultaneous, separate bus connections between the processor and memory A and between the disk drive and memory B. Of course, the number of resource modules in a given interconnection is not limited to 2. In general, any number of modules could be connected to a common bus at the same time.

For systems using a small number of resource modules, probably the simplest interconnection network which provides the partitioning desired is the basic crossbar switch. However, the cost of a crossbar network increases as the square of the number of modules it connects. A network proposed by Goke and Lipovski [29] as a partitioning network which proves less expensive than the crossbar for connecting a large number of modules is the banyan network.

A *banyan* network is defined in terms of a graph representation, where vertices represent data buses and edges represent switching elements connecting the buses. In this representation, a banyan network is a Hasse diagram of a partial ordering in which there is one and only one connection between any base and any apex. A *base* is a vertex having no arcs incident into it, and an *apex* is a vertex having no arcs incident out from it. When viewed as a partitioning network, resource modules are connected to the bases, and all other vertices form the interior of the network. The term *banyan network* therefore encompasses a fairly large variety of switching networks, whose interconnection geometries may either be highly regular or almost random, subject to the defining conditions. A somewhat general banyan network is depicted in figure 4-17.

The connection of some subset of bases in a banyan network is achieved by providing a connection path from each of the bases in the subset to a common apex. Connection of each of the sets of bases in a partition involves the use of one apex for each partition set. An example of an interconnection is shown in figure 4-18. An algorithm for closing connections from a set of bases to an apex can be based on the banyan property that there is a unique path from any given base to a given apex. Goke and Lipovski describe a scheme where each switching element has control logic used to determine the switching elements along the unique path.

Banyan networks have a certain modularity in their construction in that replacement of vertices in a banyan graph with other banyan networks results in a larger banyan network if the replacement is made subject to some constraints. The network replacing the vertex in the original graph must have the same number of bases, since arcs incident into the vertex are being replaced, and the same number of apexes, since arcs incident out from the vertex are

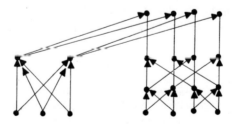

**Figure 4-17.** A Banyan Network.

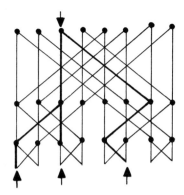

**Figure 4-18.** Connection of Three Bases through a Single Apex.

being replaced. In addition, each of the arcs incident into the vertex must connect directly to a distinct base of the replacing network, and each of the apexes in the replacing network must connect to a distinct arc incident out from the vertex.

Since the structure of a banyan network can be rather general, in order to study the usefulness of banyans as partitioning networks it is convenient to study the properties of more regular types of banyan networks. An $L$-level banyan is a banyan in which arcs of the graph connect only vertices in adjacent subsets, or levels. An example of an $L$-level banyan is shown in figure 4-19. An SW banyan with $M$ levels is defined recursively by expanding a crossbar switch into a set of SW banyans with $M - 1$ levels. A CC network is a rectangular network in which connections between levels are such that a configuration of input signals applied to the bases is shifted circularly an arbitrary number of places before appearing at the apexes. A crossbar switch may also be viewed as a banyan network, as shown in figure 4-20.

When partitions of resource modules are implemented using banyans, it is seen that because there is only one connection between any given base and apex, it may not be possible to provide connections for any partition of bases in a single banyan network. This difficulty can be circumvented by providing several identical networks, termed *layers*. As many connections as possible are made in the first layer, and then connections which cannot be made in the first layer are made in subsequent layers. Goke and Lipovski [29] have used computer simulations to determine approximate numbers of layers needed to implement randomly devised partitions.

Besides their uses as partitioning networks, banyans can have applications in other types of switching systems, for example, as permutation networks. There is a good deal of room for analytical results pertaining to the properties and performance of banyans in any system to which they might be applied.

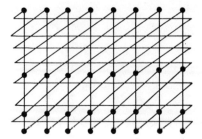

**Figure 4-19**. An $L$-Level Banyan.

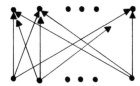

**Figure 4-20**. The Crossbar as a Banyan.

Banyan theory could provide a general framework for analyzing different types of connection networks, since several commonly discussed networks are included as special cases of banyans.

## Asymptotic Considerations

The numerical results presented indicate that for sufficiently large values of $N$ and $M$, multistage networks can be designed with less crosspoints than rectangular networks and, as illustrated using five-stage networks, with less crosspoints than multistage networks with fewer stages. Networks of more than three stages, of course, require more control. In a real application, the relative cost of each must be taken into account.

Each generalization which provides a reduction in the number of crosspoints can be expected to be accompanied by an increase in the corresponding complexity of the control algorithm. Both networks of figures 4-2 and 4-5 are *uniform* in the sense that they have the same number of closed crosspoints involved in any connection of inputs to outputs. We could also consider *nonuniform* interconnection networks where different connections involve different numbers of closed crosspoints. A further control complication results if, upon noting that the networks thus far described do not involve connecting paths which are fed back or iterate through previously passed stages of cross-points, we consider *feedback* interconnection networks. Such interrelationships and engineering tradeoffs between control complexity and the number of cross-points provide some of the main preoccupations of the applications of inter-connection network theory. Define the *capacity* of an interconnection network to be the maximal number of interconnections which it must ever simultane-ously realize.

The following results are either constructive or nonconstructive. *Construc-tive results* are those which explicitly lead to interconnection network construc-tions (such as those discussed previously). *Nonconstructive results* are those which indicate the existence of interconnection network constructions but can-not be used to actually construct such a network. Previously we discussed only constructive results. As we will see, there are situations in which there is a significant gap between what we know exists and what we can actually build. Regarding the complexity of the control algorithm, our results are in the form of the number of operations to determine a path to satisfy a new request for incremental assignments, or to determine a state to realize a total assignment. For each of these issues, we will see more specifically the conflicting situation described regarding the number of crosspoints and the control algorithm; a hierarchy of difficulty will also become apparent.

The means which we use to describe some of the following results are asymptotic bounds on the growth of the number of crosspoints or the number of operations to obtain a desired result as the number of inputs (or the number of outputs) increases. This type of description is often used because explicit formulas or tables not only are cumbersome but also usually give little insight into the effect of the various associated parameters of the network which they are meant to describe. It should be pointed out, however, that constructive results which are asymptotically optimal might not, indeed, be the most practi-cal for certain applications; and when possible, explicit implementations should always be considered within the ranges of interest.

In a concentration network we have specific, idle inputs requesting paths to arbitrary, idle outputs. In the following, we assume that there are $N$ inputs and $M$ outputs and $N > M$ (since any other case clearly would not be of inter-est). It is convenient to describe some notation within this section for concen-tration networks which can be easily modified for use in the following two sections on connection and expansion networks. Accordingly, we refer to an $N$-input, $M$-output, concentration network when it has a capacity of $C$ as an $(N, M, C)_\chi$-*concentrator*, where $\chi \in \{r,n\}$ depending on whether the concen-trator is rearrangeable or strictly nonblocking. (In the following we refer to "strictly nonblocking" simply as "nonblocking.") Furthermore, we let $\{(N,M,\overline{C})_\chi$-concentrator$\}$ denote the set of all such networks for a given $N$, $M$, and $C$, and $Q(N,M,C)_\chi$-concentrator denote the number of crosspoints in an $(N,M,C)_\chi$-concentrator. Then $Q_{\min}((N,M,C)_\chi$-concentrator) is the minimum number of crosspoints in any concentration network which is a member of $\{(N,M,C)_x\text{-concentrator})\}$.

It is clear that in any single-stage network in which there were crosspoints between each of the $N$ inputs and any choice of $C$ of the $M$ outputs, any concentration assignment (of capacity less than or equal to $C$) could be obviously realized. We therefore have a benchmark with which to compare subsequent results of $Q_{\min}((N,M,C)_x\text{-concentrator}) \leqslant CN$. (If $C = M$, this benchmark corresponds to a rectangular network.) Moreover, since there must clearly be at least one crosspoint between each input and some output, it is easily seen that the asymptotic lower bound on the growth of the number of crosspoints as $N$, the number of inputs, is increased is proportional to $N$. We describe this more succinctly by writing that the information-theoretic lower bound is $O(N)$ crosspoints. Hence, we immediately have a straightforward, constructive result and a nonconstructive, optimal guideline.

Alternative forms of rearrangeable concentration networks having less than $CN$ crosspoints were first presented in the literature independently by Pinsker [22] and Pippenger [30].

Pinsker showed that $Q_{min}((N,M,M)_r\text{-concentrator}) < 29N$. Moreover, under the condition that $M/N \rightarrow 0$ as $N \rightarrow \infty$, it is shown that $Q_{min}((N,M,M)_r\text{-concentrator}) < 3N$; and under the condition that $M/N \rightarrow 1$ as $N \rightarrow \infty$, it was shown that $Q_{\min}((N,M,M)_r\text{-concentrator}) < 4N$. Two particularly interesting aspects to these results should be noted here. First, there is the recursive use of the nonuniform network structure shown in figure 4-21 for $(N,M,M)_r$-concentrators where $2M \geqslant N$. This idea of recursively using a structural concept by starting with the complete problem and then using some insightful observation to form subproblems, which can also then be decomposed into further subproblems,

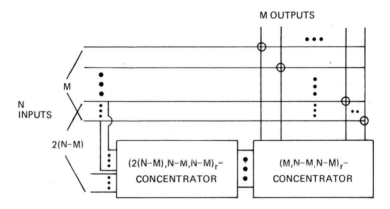

**Figure 4-21.** Pinsker's $(N,M,M)_r$-concentrator, $2M \geqslant N$. Reprinted with permission, from K.J. Thurber, "Circuit Switching Technology: A State-of-the-Art Survey," COMPCON, IEEE Computer Society, Fall, 1978.

is common. The key is to determine the structural concept which provides some reduction in, for this case, the number of crosspoints relative to a benchmark and perhaps is even asymptotically in agreement with the information-theoretic optimum.

The other interesting aspect of Pinsker's approach is the use of a coding information theory result [31, 32] which can be used with Hall's Theorem to show that there exists a sparse rectangular network construction having exactly $s$ crosspoints between each input and the set of $M$ outputs which is an $(N,M,C)_r$-concentrator $C < N,M$. More specifically, $Q_{min}((N,M,C)_r$-concentrator) $\leq sN$, $C < N,M$, for any $s$ satisfying the following condition [31, 32]:

$$\frac{H\,C/N + (M/N)\,HC/M + (1/N) \log \left\{ M(C-s)/[2\pi(M-C)^2] \right\}}{-(C/N) \log (C/M)} < s < \frac{(M/N)(s-1)/(M-1)}{(cN)^{1/s}}$$

where for $0 < t < 1$

$$H(t) = -t \log t - (1 - t) \log (1 - t)$$

The use of this condition is basically the foundation of Pippenger's argument [30] as well, where it was shown that for all $N$ and all $b > a > 1$, there exists a $(bN,aN,N)_r$-concentrator with $sN$ crosspoints where $s$ is $O(b \log b/\log a)$ as either $a \to 1$ with $b$ constant or $b \to \infty$ with $a$ constant.

In each case we clearly have an upper bound on the asymptotic growth of the number of crosspoints in the network as the number of inputs $N$ grows which is $O(N)$ crosspoints and is, by the information-theoretic bound, the best order of growth possible. Note, however, that these results are nonconstructive in that they do not lead, in general, to explicit constructions because they are based on a proof of the existence of the needed $(N,M,C)_r$-concentrator, and there does not exist a method at present (other than a consideration of all possibilities) to obtain it for a general $N$.

Some recent contributions have been made along the lines of this latter point, however. Margulis [33], on the basis of a quite complex argument involving the theory of group representations, has given a straightforward construction technique which results in a concentrator of predetermined capacity with $k$ stages, each stage requiring at most $5N$ crosspoints. Presently, however, it is very difficult to determine a bound for $k$, which unfortunately jeopardizes the applicability of the results. Further research might rectify this problem. Another constructive result, much closer to the surface, is the binomial concentrator of Masson [34, 35]. Figure 4-22 shows a $(15,6,4)_4$-concentrator cascaded with a $(6,4,4)_r$-concentrator. The result is a $(15,4,4)_r$-concentrator with 42 crosspoints (as opposed to the 60 crosspoints which would be required in the rectangular benchmark). The underlying theory of such binomial concentrators is based on Hall's theorem (as are the $(N,M,C)_r$-concentrators discussed earlier).

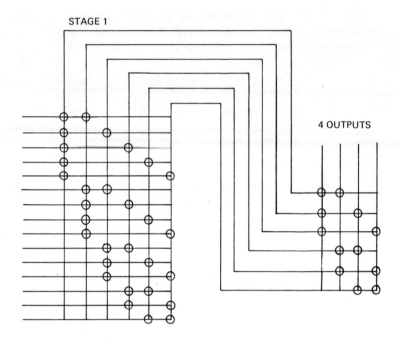

**Figure 4-22.** $(15,4,4)_r$-Binomial Concentrator. Reprinted with permission from K.J. Thurber, "Circuit Switching Technology: A State-of-the-Art Survey," COMPCON, IEEE Computer Society, Fall, 1978.

This theorem is used in a straightforward manner to construct multistage $(N,M,M)_r$-concentrators having less than $NM$ crosspoints. By formulating the concentration network problem to be one of constructing the $p$ subsets $I_1, \ldots, I_p$, such that any $i_1, \ldots, i_{p'}$, $p' \leqslant p$, is a set of distinct representatives of some $p'$ of these subsets. A practical aspect of the binomial network is that an upper bound of 1 plus the number of stages can be shown for the number of existing paths which must be rearranged to satisfy a new request [35].

Regarding nonblocking concentration networks realizing incremental assignments, Pippenger [36] has proved the unexpected and insightful result that $Q_{\min}((N,M,M)_n$-concentrator) must have $O(N \log N)$ crosspoints. This is remarkable because, as will be seen, asymptotically this is the same as the result which will be obtained for nonblocking connection networks realizing incremental assignments, although (at least intuitively) the incremental connection problem seems more complex. Thus, the information-theoretic lower bound cannot, in this case, be constructed. If there existed a construction of a $O(N \log N)$ nonblocking connection network for incremental assignments, it could, of course, be used in this case. Unfortunately, although its existence can be proved, the best known construction is $0[N(\log N)^2]$, and then this leads us to our next consideration.

In a connection network, specific, idle inputs request interconnecting paths to specific, idle outputs. Because of the affinity of such networks with telephone systems, one finds a significant and impressive amount of published work regarding this subject. Furthermore if $N = M$, then any connection assignment involving all $N$ inputs and all $N$ outputs can be represented by what is known as a *bijective mapping* of the inputs onto the outputs. In other words, the assignment is a permutation of the inputs, and this observation permits the application of a broad range of mathematical theory. Since results for other situations follow from the results for the case where $N = M = C$, we discuss this case only.

It is clear that since a rectangular switching network has one crosspoint between every input and output, such a network will operate as a connection network. Hence, if we refer to an $N$-input, $N$-output, connection network of capacity $N$ as an $(N,N,N)_\chi$-connector, we know, recalling the notation of the previous section, that $Q_{min}((N,N,N)_\chi$-connector$) < N^2$. This, then, is a benchmark with which to compare our subsequent reported results. To get an information-theoretic lower bound on the order of growth of the number of crosspoints, we can use an argument given by Shannon [37]. Since there are effectively $N!$ assignments which must be realized by an $(N,N,N)_\chi$-connector, and since each crosspoint in such a network effectively has two states (opened or closed), we have that $2^{Q\min(N,N,N)_\chi\text{-connector})} \geqslant N!$. By Stirlings' well-known formula for the approximation of a factorial [38], we have that the asymptotic growth of $Q_{min}((N,N,N)_\chi$-connector$)$ is $0(N \log N)$.

We first consider rearrangeable connection networks. In his classic book Benes [3] described a constructive technique which is based on Hall's theorem for distinct representatives. For a three-stage network, the approach uses Hall's theorem to decompose the original assignment into $n$ subassignments. Repeating this decomposition on the subassignments now associated with each of the $n$ middle switches leads to a multistage connection network. Joel [39], Waksman [19], and Opferman and Tsao-Wu [40] have further cultivated Benes' approach by incorporating a two input-two output switching cell as the basic element of their network, as illustrated in figure 4-23. The result in all three networks is a construction whose number of crosspoints has $0(N \log N)$ growth with $N$, which, by our earlier discussion, is the best order of growth possible. It should be clear that for these networks the number of stages, and therefore the number of crosspoints involved in any path, is $0(\log_2 N)$. This means, of course, that in response to either total or incremental assignments, determining a realizing state can be quite complex.

Regarding this latter point somewhat more specifically, given a total assignment to be realized by one of the above $0(N \log N)$ connection networks, Waksman [19] gives a straightforward algorithm which requires $0[N(\log N)^2]$

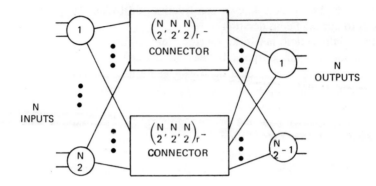

**Figure 4-23.**   $(N,N,N)_r$-Connector of Two Input-Two Output Cells. Reprinted with permission from K.J. Thurber, "Circuit Switching Technology: A State-of-the-Art Survey" COMPCON, IEEE Computer Society, Fall, 1978.

operation while Tsao-Wu and Opferman [41] give a $0(N \log N)$ operation algorithm. For rearrangeable connection networks and incremental assignments, the measure of interest becomes the complexity of rearranging existing interconnecting paths to satisfy the new request. Paull [17] has shown that for a Benes rearrangeable three-stage network if $m = n$, at most $n - 1$ of the existing paths must be rearranged. For the networks composed of two input–two output cells, this means there can be $0(N/2)$ rearrangements just involving the outer stages; the inner stages could potentially require still further rearrangements. Such extensive rearrangements might prohibit the use of such networks for various applications. Other than this work, however, and some modest further refinements [42, 43], little is known in general about the complexity of this issue.

We consider nonblocking connection networks next. The first published work retarding the construction of such networks for the realization of incremental assignments is due to Clos [13]. He showed by means of a straightforward argument that the structure of figure 4-5, if $m = 2n - 1$ middle stations, results in nonblocking capability for a three-stage network. By repeatedly decomposing the resulting stations (which are rectangular networks), the number of crosspoints can be shown to grow asymptotically with $N$ at a rate of $0\left(N\epsilon^{2\sqrt{\log_2 N}}\right)$. Clos' results might be the best known in interconnection network theory; regardless of whether they actually suit the applications, they are surely the most often used.

Recently, Bassalygo and M. Pinsker [44] have shown that, indeed, constructions for $(N,N,N)_n$-connectors do exist for which $Q_{min}((N,N,N)_n$-connector) is $0(N \log N)$. This makes the earlier cited results of Pippenger [36] for $(N,N,N)_n$-concentrators somewhat more remarkable. However, similar to the results obtained for rearrangeable concentrators [22], the proof is only of the existence, as it requires a one-stage switching network for which, in general, no explicit construction technique is known.

The best known construction of an $(N,N,N)_n$-connector has been provided by Cantor [45, 46]. The construction of one-half of the network is illustrated in figure 4-24. Note that we again see the use of two input-two output switching cells. The subnetworks $S$ are not necessarily nonblocking, but are constructed such that each input of $S$ has access to at least one-half the outputs of $S$ regardless of the existing interconnecting paths through it. Figure 4-24, therefore, shows the decomposition which would be appropriate until the resulting $S$ networks had only two inputs. At this point a two-input, $2r$-output rectangular network would be used $(n = 2^h)$. If one input of the total network and all the paths to it were now removed, we would have that, regardless of the state, any input of the resulting network could be connected to more than one-half the outputs. Clearly, if this network were reversed and the two networks cascaded, the result would be an $(N-1,N-1,N-1)_n$-connector, Cantor has shown that such a network has $0[N (\log N)^2]$ crosspoints, and at present this is the best known construction available.

It should be expected that algorithms to provide interconnecting paths should be less complex for nonblocking networks. Indeed, it can be seen that in a Cantor network the number of complete paths satisfying any request is $0(N \log N)$. Pippenger [30] has exploited this to give an insightful algorithm for Cantor networks requiring only $0[(\log N)^2]$ operations to determine a state which will satisfy a new request.

We have not considered sorting networks in this section, although they are certainly a very important aspect of switching network theory. Briefly, a sorting network permutes its inputs (as does a connection network) but uses only interconnected binary comparators. Hence the control can be considered to be distributed, as opposed to the centralized control we have considered thus far. This requires a somewhat different approach, the results of which are not detailed here except to say that a great deal of attention has been given to this

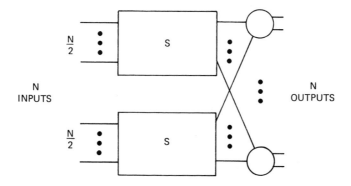

**Figure 4-24.** Construction Technique for One-Half of an $(N-1,N-1,N-1)_n$-Cantor Connector.

important area, with Batcher [47], Marcus [48], Van Voorhis [49], and Bose and Nelson [50] perhaps making the most notable contributions.

Finally, a summary of the connection network theory area which would be of interest is that of Thurber [51]. We now proceed to the consideration of expansion switching networks.

In an expansion network, a specific, not necessarily idle, input requests an interconnecting path to a specific, idle output. It is easily seen that the bench-mark number of crosspoints and the information-theoretic lower bound on the number of crosspoints of an $(N,N,N)_\chi$-expander are the same as those for a connection network. However, the similarities stop here, and there is no reason to expect that a network designed to handle connection assignments should be capable, in general, of handling expansion assignments. This has been shown by Masson [52].

The first published work concerning expansion switching networks is by Masson and Jordan [53, 54] where conditions on the parameters of multistage structures, as shown in figure 4-5, were given which were sufficient, and some-times necessary and sufficient, for the capability of realizing expansion assign-ments in both rearrangeable and nonblocking manners. Asymptotically, the number of crosspoints of such networks for the general multistage case can be seen

to be $0\left(N^{\frac{3}{2}} \log N\right)$ for the rearrangeable case and $0\left(N^{\frac{3}{2}}(\log N)^{(\log 3)/(\log 2)}\right)$

for the nonblocking case. For the rearrangeable case and incremental assign-ments, it is shown that the number of interconnecting paths which must be rearranged in order to satisfy a new request is dependent on the number of exist-ing paths which utilize middle-stage fan-out (that is, where the input is to be con-nected to more than one output, but where there is only one path from the input stage to the middle stage and the fan-out originates at the middle stage).

Pippenger [30] gives a nonuniform rearrangeable expansion network using feedback. It is simply constructed from two $(N,N,N)_r$-connectors, one used specifically for feedback. Hence, an interconnecting path involving one input and many (perhaps all) outputs can iterate through the network $0(N \log N)$ times. Clearly, the paths through such a network are nonuniform, but by the work of Tsao-Wu and Opferman [41] a state realizing a total assignment can be determined with $0(N \log N)$ operations.

A binomial expansion network which is rearrangeable for incremental assignments has been developed by Masson [35]. It is developed upon the observation that, as shown in figure 4-25, if concentrators are cascaded and then followed by an expander, the resulting network operates as an expander. The binomial expanders are, therefore, cascaded binomial concentrators, followed by a rectangular switching network.

Pippenger [30] used this same observation to show that $0[N(\log N)^{\nu+1}]$ crosspoint expanders can be constructed if $0[N(\log N)^{\nu}]$ crosspoint concentra-tors are used. Since a connection network certainly operates as a concentration

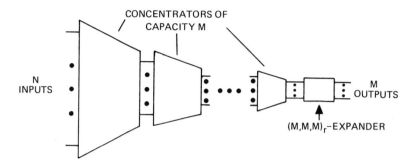

**Figure 4-25.** $(N,M,M)_r$-Expander Composed of Cascaded Concentrators of Capacity $M$ and an $(M,M,M)_r$-Expander. Reprinted with permission from K.J. Thurber, "Circuit Switching Technology: A State-of-the-Art Survey," COMPCON, IEEE Computer Society, Fall, 1978.

network, we can use this technique to construct a $O[N(\log N)^3]$ crosspoint expander by using Cantor's $O[N(\log N)^2]$ crosspoint connectors. Similarly, this approach shows that if a state satisfying a new request can be determined with $O[(\log N)^w]$ operations for the concentrators, then the resulting expander requires $O[(\log N)^{w+1}]$ operations to do the same.

Many open questions remain concerning expansion networks, particularly regarding their construction. At the same time, for a wide variety of reasons, expansion capability is emerging as one of the principal switching network requirements in modern applications.

**Summary**

In this chapter we briefly surveyed the three classes of networks which seem to enter most often into various applications—concentration, connection, and expansion. Indeed, it should be clear that a wide assortment of hybrid types of capabilities would be obtainable by simply combining the appropriate results for these three types of networks. Our approach has been to illustrate the constructive and nonconstructive optimal results concerning such interconnection networks by using the asymptotic bounds on the growth of either the number of crosspoints or the number of elemental switch operations required to obtain a desired result. In addition, it has been possible to compare each result with an asymptotic, information-theoretic lower bound and a straightforward, benchmark alternative. In all cases it was seen that, assuming that the network was of sufficient size (that is, what is commonly referred to as "large-scale"), there existed constructive alternatives to the benchmark network which had less crosspoints, and for which at least some appreciation could be had for the associated increase in control complexity. It was also seen, however, that in many cases while the existence of still better alternatives can be proved, there presently exists no known realistic way of constructing them in general.

Further, we discussed TDM circuit switches, and because of the constructive concepts used to develop the interconnection networks, it is possible to build multistage TDM switches or switches composed of a combination of smaller crossbar and TDM switches.

## Notes

1. There is a terminology problem in this chapter. Generally in this book, *network* means a geographically distributed packet-switched system. However, in the context of circuit switching, the circuit switch is usually referred to as a switching network, interconnection network, network, and so forth. This is due to terminology which originally was developed in telephone contexts. Further, terminals refer to the input and output ports of the network (circuit switch) rather than to printers, plotters, and so on. In this chapter, rather than develop new terminology we have chosen to utilize standard terms associated with circuit-switching contexts. The context in which the terminology appears should make its meaning readily apparent.

2. **Proof of Theorem 4.2.** The necessity of this condition can be seen in the realization of any $C(n_1,n_2)$ assignment in which at least one output switch is assigned to $n_2$ distinct input terminals. The subassignment to be connected to this switch can be realized only with $n_2$ separate connections made through the middle switches to the assigned $n_2$ input terminals. Since a middle switch can provide only one such connection, $n_2$ middle switches are necessary.

For the sufficiency of this theorem, it is necessary to consider only maximal $C(n_1,n_2)$ assignments since if all maximal $C(n_1,n_2)$ assignments are realizable, then all subassignments are also realizable. Consider any maximal $C(n_1,n_2)$ assignment $\{O_i\}$. Each output switch is assigned to $n_2$ input terminals. Let $S_i$, $i = 1, 2, \ldots, r_2$, be the set of input switches having input terminals assigned to output switch $OS_i$. Since a $C(n_1,n_2)$ assignment allows each input switch to be assigned to a maximum of $n_2$ output terminals, for any $t$ output switches, $\{OS_{i(1)}, \ldots, OS_{i(t)}\}$, $t = 1, 2, \ldots, r_2$,

$$\left| \bigcup_{p=1}^{t} S_{i(p)} \right| > t$$

By Hall's theorem this implies that there exists an SDR for the set

$$\{S_i\} = \{S_1, \ldots, S_{r_2}\}.$$

Consider each of the input switches which are assigned to exactly $n_2$ output terminals. Call this set of input switches

$$\left\{S_{i'}\right\} = \left\{\text{IS}_{i(1)}, \ldots, \text{IS}_{i(q)}\right\} \qquad 0 \leqslant q \leqslant r_2$$

Since each output switch is assigned to $n_2$ input terminals, any $q'$ subset of $\left\{S_{i'}\right\}$, where $q' \leqslant q$, is intersected by at least $q'$ of the members of $\left\{S_i\right\}$. Thus, by Hoffman and Kuhn's theorem, there exists an SDR for $\left\{S_i\right\}$ which contains $\left\{S_{i'}\right\}$. This SDR represents a subassignment of $\left\{O_i\right\}$ involving one output terminal on each output switch, and one input terminal on $r_2$ of the $r_1$ input switches; and in particular, $q$ or those $r_2$ input switches are input switches which, for the assignment $\left\{O_i\right\}$, are assigned to $n_2$ output terminals. Such a subassignment can be realized by middle switch $\text{MS}_1$. The specific input terminals on the $r_2$ input switches which middle switch $\text{MS}_1$ connects to the $r_2$ output switches, together with one input terminal chosen from each of remaining $r_1 - r_2$ input switches, form the set $\left\{M_1\right\}$.

The remaining unconnected subassignment of $\left\{O_i\right\}$ has each output switch assigned to $n_2 - 1$ input terminals and each input switch assigned to a maximum of $n_2 - 1$ output terminals.

Assume that this argument is repeated $j$ times. The remaining unconnected subassignment of $\left\{O_i\right\}$ would have each output switch assigned to $n_2 - j$ output terminals and each input switch assigned to a maximum of $n_2 - j$ output terminals. Let $S_i$, $i = 1, 2, \ldots, r_2$, now be the set of input switches having input terminals assigned to output switch $\text{OS}_i$ in the remaining unconnected subassignment of $\left\{O_i\right\}$. Consider any $t$ output switches, $\left\{\text{OS}_{i(1)}, \ldots, \text{OS}_{i(t)}\right\}$, $t = 1, \ldots, r_2$. Since no input switch in this unconnected subassignment is assigned to more than $n_2 - j$ output terminals,

$$\left| \bigcup_{p=1}^{t} S_{i(p)} \right| \geqslant t$$

By Hall's theorem this implies that there exists an SDR for the sets $\left\{S_i\right\} = \left\{S_1, \ldots, S_{r_2}\right\}$. If $q$ of the input switches are assigned to exactly $n_2 - j$ output terminals, any $q'$ subset of this $q$ subset of $\left\{\text{IS}_1, \ldots, \text{IS}_{r_1}\right\}$

$$\left\{S'\right\} = \left\{\text{IS}_{i(1)}, \ldots, \text{IS}_{i(q)}\right\} \qquad 0 \leqslant q \leqslant r_2$$

is intersected by at least $q'$ of the $S_i$, since each output switch is assigned to $n_2 - j$ input terminals. By Hoffman and Kuhn's theorem, there exists an SDR for $\left\{S_i\right\}$ which contains $\left\{S_{i'}\right\}$. This SDR represents a subassignment of $\left\{O_i\right\}$ involving one output terminal on every output switch and one input terminal on $r_2$ of the $r_1$ input switches; and, in particular, $q$ of those $r_2$ input switches are input switches for which the remaining unconnected subassignment of $\left\{O_i\right\}$ are assigned to $n_2 - j$ output terminals. This subassignment can be realized by middle switch $MS_{j+1}$. The specific input terminals of the $r_2$ input switches which middle switch $MS_{j+1}$ connects to the $r_2$ output switches, together with one input terminal from each of the remaining $r_1 - r_2$ input switches, form the set $\{M_{j+1}\}$.

The remaining unconnected subassignment of $\{O_i\}$ has each output switch assigned to $n_2 - j - 1$ input terminals and each input switch assigned to a maximum of $n_2 - j - 1$ output terminals. If $j$ is set equal to $n_2 - 1$, then all $n_2$ output terminals on each output switch have been connected to their assigned input terminals with $n_2$ middle switches, and $n_2$ middle switches are sufficient.

3. **Proof of Theorem 4.5.** Suppose that $n_2 = r_2 n_1$. The necessity of this condition can be seen in the realization of any $G(N,M)$ assignment in which at least one output switch is assigned to $n_2 = r_2 n_1$ distinct input terminals. The subassignment to be connected to this output switch can be realized only with $r_2 n_1$ separate connections made through the middle switches to the assigned $n_2 = r_2 n_1$ input terminals. Since a middle switch can provide only one such connection, $n_2 = r_2 n_1$ middle switches are necessary.

For the sufficiency of this theorem in the case where $n_2 = r_2 n_1$, it is necessary to consider only maximal $G(N,M)$ assignments since, as explained previously, if all maximal $G(N,M)$ assignments are realizable, then all $G(N,M)$ assignments are also realizable. Consider any maximal $G(N,M)$ assignment $\{O_i\}$. Each output switch is assigned to $n_2 = r_2 n_1$ distinct input terminals. Let $S_i$, $i = 1, \ldots, r_2$, be the set of input switches having input terminals assigned to the output switch $OS_i$. For a maximal $G(N,M)$ assignment, each input switch is assigned to a maximum of $r_2 n_1$ output terminals, for any $t$ output switches, $OS_{i(1)}, \ldots, OS_{i(t)}, t = 1, \ldots, r_2$,

$$\left| \bigcup_{p=1}^{t} S_{i(p)} \right| \geq t$$

By Hall's theorem this implies that there exists an SDR for the set

$$\{S_i\} = \{S_1, \ldots, S_{r_2}\}.$$

Consider each of the input switches which are assigned to $r_2 n_1$ output terminals. Call this set of input switches

$$\{S_{i'}\} = \{IS_{i(1)}, \ldots, IS_{i(q)}\} \qquad 0 \leq q \leq r_2$$

Since each output switch is assigned to $n_2 = r_2 n_1$ input terminals, any $q'$ element subset of $\{S_{i'}\}$, where $q' \leq q$, is intersected by at least $q'$ of the $S_i$. By Hoffman and Kuhn's theorem there exists an SDR for $\{S_i\}$ which contains

$\{S_{i'}\}$. This SDR represents a subassignment of $\{O_i\}$ involving one output terminal on each output switch and one input terminal on $r_2$ of the $r_1$ input switches. In particular, $q$ of those $r_2$ input switches are input switches which, for the assignment $\{O_i\}$, are assigned to $r_2n_1$ output terminals. Such a subassignment can be realized by middle switch $MS_1$. The specific input terminals on the $r_2$ input switches which middle switch $MS_1$ connects to the $r_2$ output switches, together with one input terminal chosen from each of the remaining $r_1 - r_2$ input switches, form the set $\{M_1\}$.

The remaining unconnected subassignment of $\{O_i\}$ has each output switch assigned to $n_2 - 1$ input terminals and each input switch assigned to at most $r_2n_1 - 1$ output terminals.

Assume that this argument is repeated $j$ times. The remaining unconnected subassignment of $\{O_i\}$ would have each output switch assigned to $r_2n_1 - j$ input terminals and each input switch assigned to a maximum of $r_2n_1 - j$ output terminals. Let $S_i$, $i = 1, \ldots, r_2$, now be the set of input switches having input terminals assigned to output switch $OS_i$ in the remaining unconnected subassignment of $\{O_i\}$. Consider any $t$ output switches, $OS_{i(1)}, \ldots, OS_{i(t)}$, $t = 1, \ldots, r_2$. No input switch in this unconnected subassignment is assigned to more than $r_2n_1 - j$ output terminals,

$$\left| \bigcup_{p=1}^{t} S_{i(p)} \right| \geqslant t$$

By Hall's theorem this implies that there exists an SDR for the set $\{S_i\} = \{S_1, \ldots, S_{r_2}\}$. If $q$ of the input switches are assigned to exactly $n_1r_2 - j$ output terminals, any $q'$ element subset of this $q$ element subset of $\{I_j\}$

$$\{S_{i'}\} = \{IS_{i(1)}, \ldots, IS_{i(q)}\} \qquad 0 \leqslant q \leqslant r_2$$

is intersected by at least $q'$ of the $S_i$. This results because each output switch is assigned to $r_2n_1 - j$ input terminals. By Hoffman and Kuhn's theorem, there exists an SDR for $\{S_i\}$ which contains $\{S_{i'}\}$. This SDR represents a subassignment of $\{O_i\}$ involving one output terminal on every output switch and one input terminal on $r_2$ of the $r_1$ input switches. In particular, $q$ of those $r_2$ input switches are input switches for which the remaining unconnected subassignment of $\{O_i\}$ is assigned to $r_2n_1 - j$ output terminals. This subassignment can be realized by middle switch $MS_{j+1}$. The specific input terminals of the $r^2$ input switches which middle switch $MS_{j+1}$ connects to the $r_2$ output switches, together with one input terminal from each of the remaining $r_1 - r_2$ input switches, form the set $\{M_{j+1}\}$.

The remaining unconnected subassignment of $\{O_i\}$ has each output switch assigned to $r_2n_1 - j - 1$ input terminals and each input switch assigned to at most $r_2 n_1 - j - 1$ output terminals. If $j$ is set equal to $r_2 n_1 - 1$, then all $r_2 n_1$ output terminals on each output switch have been connected to their assigned input terminals with $r_2 n_1$ middle switches. If $n_2 = r_2 n_1$, then $m = n_2 = r_2 n_1$ middle switches are necessary and sufficient for the realization of any $G(N,M)$ assignment.

Suppose $n_2 > r_2 n_1$. Then there must necessarily be $n_2$ middle switches to realize any assignment in which some output switch is assigned to $n_2$ distinct input terminals. But because no input switch need be connected to more than $r_2 n_1$ output switches, the argument for sufficiency still holds with the exception that it is not necessary to find specific SDRs until $n_2 - r_2 n_1$ middle switches have been filled. If $n_2 > r_2 n_1$, then $n_2$ middle switches are necessary and sufficient for the realization of $G(N,M)$ assignments.

Suppose $n_2 < r_2 n_1$. Then any maximal $G(N,M)$ assignment is actually a subassignment of a maximal $G(N,M)$ assignment for the case where $n_2 = r_2 n_1$. Since in that case $r_2 n_1$ middle switches are sufficient for the realization of all maximal $G(N,M)$ assignments, then certainly $r_2 n_1$ middle switches are sufficient for all subassignments.

## Exercises

1. Design a rearrangeable three-stage 64 input-64 output circuit switch using both a crossbar and a TDM circuit switch as the elemental switch building block.

2. Design a strictly nonblocking 64 input-64 output circuit switch using both a crossbar and a TDM circuit switch as the elemental switch building block.

3. Compare the complexity of the switches developed in exercises 1 and 2.

4. Extend the concepts in chapter 4 to develop design guidelines for switches with more outputs than inputs and more inputs than outputs.

5. Consider a Lawrie omega network. Prove that if an array is stored using a $(d_1, d_2)$ skewing scheme, then (a) rows of the matrix are $d_2$-ordered; (b) columns of the matrix are $d_1$-ordered; (c) forward diagonals of the matrix are $d_1 + d_2$-ordered; and (d) backward diagonals of the matrix are $d_1 - d_2$-ordered.

## References

[ 1] S.R. Kimbleton and G.M. Schneider, "Computer Communications Networks: Approaches, Objectives, and Performance Considerations," *ACM Computing Surveys*, September 1975, pp. 129-173.

[ 2] Sperry Univac, *AN/USQ-67 Converter-Switching System, Signal Data*, PX 12233, June 1977, St. Paul, Minnesota.

[ 3] V.E. Benes, *Mathematical Theory of Connecting Networks and Telephone Traffic* (New York: Academic Press, 1965).

[ 4] W.H. Kautz, K.N. Levitt, and A. Waksman, "Cellular Interconnection Arrays," *IEEE Transactions on Computers*, C-17 (May 1968): 443-451.

[ 5] H.W. Gschwind, *Design of Digital Computers* (New York: Springer-Verlag, 1967).

[ 6] R.N. Canaday, "Two-Dimensional Iterative Logic," *AFIPS Conference Proceedings*, Fall Joint Computer Conference, 1965, vol. 27, pp. 343-353.

[ 7] R.E. Porter, "The RW400–A New Polymorphic Data System," *Datamation*, January-February 1960, pp. 4-14.

[ 8] G. Estrin et al., "Parallel Processing in a Restructurable Computer System," *IEEE Transactions on Electronic Computers* EC-12, no. 5 (December 1977): 747-755.

[ 9] D. Starr and J. Johnson, "Design of an Automatic Patching System," *Simulation*, June 1968, pp. 281-288.

[10] G. Hannauer, "Automatic Patching for Analog and Hybrid Computers," *Simulation*, May 1969, pp. 219-32.

[11] G. Hannauer, "Stored-Program Concept for Analog Computers," Final report NASA Contract NAS8-21228, George C. Marshall Space Flight Center, Huntsville Ala.

[12] M. Marcus, "Designs for Time Slot Interchangers," *NEC*, 1970, pp. 812-817.

[13] C. Clos, "A Study of Nonblocking Switching Networks," *Bell System Technical Journal* 32 (1953): 406-424.

[14] A. Duguid, "Structural Properties of Switching Networks," Brown University Progress Report BTL-7, 1959.

[15] D. Slepian, "Two Theorems on a Particular Crossbar Switching Network," Unpublished manuscript, 1952.

[16] P. Hall, "On Representatives of Subsets," *Journal of the London Mathematics Society* 10 (1935): 26-30.

[17] M. Paull, "Reswitching on Connection Networks," *Bell System Technical Journal* 41 (1962): 833-855.

[18] V.E. Benes, "On Rearrangeable Three-Stage Connection Networks," *Bell System Technical Journal* 41 (1962): 1481-1492.

[19] A. Waksman, "A Permutation Network," *Journal of the ACM* 9, (January 1968): 159-163.

[20] M. Paull, "Rearrangeability of Triangular Connection Networks," *Seventh Annual Allerton Conference of Circuit and System Theory, Proceedings*, 1969, pp. 489-496.

[21] J. Aggarwal, W. Mayeda, and C. Ramamoorthy, "On Multiple Transmission," *IEEE Transactions on Circuit Theory* CT017, no. 2 (May 1970 pp 245-248.

[22] M. Pinsker, "On the Complexity of a Concentrator," *Proceedings of the Seventh International Teletraffic Congress*, Stockholm, 1973, pp. 318/1-318/4

[23] M.C. Pease, "An Adaption of the Fast Fourier Transform for Parallel Processing," *Journal of the ACM* 15 (April 1968): 252-264.

[24] D.J. Kuck and A.H. Sameh, "Parallel Computation of Eigenvalues of Real Matrices," *Proceedings of the IFIP Congress*, 1971, p. TA-1-24.

[25] Duncan H. Lawrie, "Access and Alignment of Data in an Array Processor," *IEEE Transactions on Computers* C-24 (December 1975): 1145-1155.

[26] H.S. Stone, "Parallel Processing with the Perfect Shuffle," *IEEE Transactions on Computers* C20 (February 1971): 153-161.

[27] K.E. Batcher, "Flexible Parallel Processing and STARAN," *WESCON*, September, 1972, pp. 1/5.1-1/5.3.

[28] T.Y. Feng, "Data Manipulating Functions in Parallel Processors and Their Implementations," *IEEE Transactions on Computers*, March 1974. pp. 309-318.

[29] L.R. Goke and G.J. Lipovski, "Banyan Networks for Partitioning Multiprocessor Systems," *Proceedings of the First Annal Symposium on Computer Architecture*, December 1973, pp. 21-28.

[30] N. Pippenger, "The Complexity Theory of Switching Networks" (Sc.D. thesis, M.I.T., 1973).

[31] W. Peterson, *Error Correcting Codes* (Cambridge, Mass.: (M.I.T. Press, 1961).

[32] R. Fano, *Transmission of Information* (Cambridge, Mass.: M.I.T. Press, 1961).

[33] G. Margulis, "Explicit Construction of Concentrators," translated from *Problemy Peredachi Informatsil* 9, no. 4 (October-December 1973): 71-80, and published in *Problems in Information Transmission*, pp. 325-332, 1975.

[34] G. Masson, "On the Complexity of a Class of Concentration Switching Networks," *Proceedings of the Twelfth Annual Allerton Conference*, University of Illinois, 1974.

[35] G. Masson, "Binomial Switching Networks for Concentration and Distribution, *IEEE Transactions on Communication* C-25 (September 1977) pp. 873-883.

[36] N. Pippenger, "On the Complexity of Strictly Nonblocking Concentration Networks," *IEEE Transactions on Communication* C22 (November 1974): 1890-1892.

[37] C.E. Shannon, "Memory Requirements in a Telephone Exchange," *Bell System Technical Journal* 29 (1950): 343-349.

[38] W. Feller, *An Introduction to Probability Theory and Its Applications*, vol. 1, 3rd ed. (New York, John Wiley & Sons, Inc., 1968).

[39] A.E. Joel, Jr., "On Permutation Switching Networks," Bell System Technical Journal, 47 (1968): 813-822.

[40] D.C. Opferman and N.T. Tsao-Wu, "On a Class of Rearrangeable Switching Networks, Part I: Control Algorithms; Part II: Enumeration Studies and Fault Diagnosis," *Bell System Technical Journal*, 1971, pp. 1579-1618.

[41] N.T. Tsao-Wu and D.C. Opferman, "On Permutation Algorithms for Rearrangeable Switching Networks," *Proceedings of the IEEE 1969 International Conference on Communications*, pp. 10-29-10-34.

[42] G. Nakamura, "The Number of Reswitchings for a Cerain Three-Stage Connecting Network," *J. Inst. Elec. Commun. Engrs.*, Japan, 50, no. 8 (August 1967): 1419-1425.

[43] L.A. Bassalygo, I.I. Grushko, and V.I. Neyman, "The Number of Reswitchings for a 3-Stage Connecting Network," *Proceedings of the 6th International Teletraffic Congress*, 1970, pp. 245-1 to 245-9.

[44] L.A. Bassalygo and M.S. Pinsker, "On the Complexity of Optimal Non-blocking Switching Networks without Rearrangement," *Problems in Information Transmission*, 1973, pp. 84-87.

[45] D.G. Cantor, "On Non-blocking Switching Networks," *Networks* (1972): 367-377.

[46] D.G. Cantor, "On Construction of Nonblocking Switching Networks," Paper presented at the Symposium on Computer-Communications Networks and Teletraffic, Polytechnic Institute of Brooklyn, 1972.

[47] K.E. Batcher, "Sorting Networks and Their Applications," *AFIPS Conference 32* (1968), *Proceedings of the Spring Joint Computer Conference*, Atlantic City, N.J., 1968, pp. 307-314.

[48] M.J. Marcus, "New Approaches to the Analysis of Connecting and Sorting Networks" (Sc.D. thesis, M.I.T., 1972).

[49] D.C. VanVoorhis, "Large [g,d] Sorting Networks," Technical Report No. 18, Digital Systems Laboratory, Stanford Electronics Laboratories, Stanford University, Stanford, Calif., August 1971.

[50] R. Bose and R. Nelson, "A Sorting Problem," *Journal of the ACM* 9 (1962): 282-296.

[51] K.J. Thurber, "Circuit Switching Technology: A State-of-the-Art Survey," *COMPCON, IEEE Computer Society* Fall 1978.

[52] G. Masson, "Upper Bounds on Fanout in Connection Networks," *IEEE Transactions on Circuit Theory* CT-20 (1973): 222-230.

[53] G. Masson and B. Jordan, "Realization of a Class of Multiple Connection Assignments with Asymmetrical Three-Stage Connection Networks," *Proceedings of the Fifth Annual Princeton Conference on Information and Proceedings Systems Sciences*, 1971, pp. 316-320.

[54] G. Masson and B. Jordan, "Generalized Multi-stage Connection Networks," *Networks* 2 (1972): 191-209.

# 5 Bus Structures

## Introduction to Bus Control Techniques

One of the major issues involved with path-oriented systems is allocation of the path [1, 2, 3, 4]. With systems of dedicated links, the control of the link may be worked out in advance, and there is no dynamic control problem since there is no link contention problem. When the path is that of a memory, synchronization techniques such as semaphores and test-and-set instructions are available to provide for mutual exclusion or control of the memory location. However, if the path is a bus, an interesting control problem arises. This chapter addresses the problem of bus control and information-transfer techniques on the bus. Figure 5-1 indicates a hierarchical model of a bus-oriented communication system. The bus allocation techniques described here could be used in other areas of the computer system; for example, they could be useful in the design of channel priority logic. Further, the bus communication techniques would also be useful in I/O design, for example, fully interlocked request/ acknowledge interfaces to peripheral devices.

When a bus is shared by multiple devices, there must be some method whereby bus usage is assigned and a particular unit is allowed to transmit data over it. The major problem in this area is resolution of bus usage conflicts so that only one unit obtains the bus at a given time. The different control schemes can be roughly classified as being either centralized or decentralized. If the hardware used for passing bus control from one device to another is largely concentrated in one location, it is referred to as *centralized control*. The location of the hardware could be within one of the devices which is connected to the bus, or it could be a separate hardware unit. On the other hand, if the bus control logic is largely distributed throughout the different devices connected to the bus, it is called *decentralized control*.

The various bus control techniques are described here in terms of distinct control lines, but in most cases the equivalent functions can be performed with coded transfers on the bus data lines. The most basic tradeoff is allocation speed versus total number of bus lines.

## Arbitrator/Unit Control Model

Figure 5-2 illustrates a simple arbitrator/unit control model. This model consists of the arbitrator, a single unit, and a set of control lines. In this example,

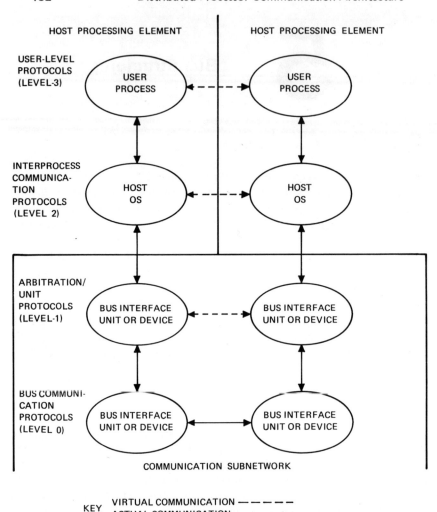

**Figure 5-1.** Bus Structure Hierarchical Communication System Model. Reprinted
with permission from K.J. Thurber, "Computer Communication Techniques," COMPSAC, IEEE Computer Society, 1978, pp. 589-594.

possible control interactions between an arbitrator and a single unit are considered
so that the functional issues become clear.

The basic concept of a bus is that there exists a set of shared lines over which
communication takes place. Some of the lines are used for control, and some are
used for information transfer. Essentially, the bus operates in a three-step cycle
as follows:

1.  Devices compete for allocation of the bus.

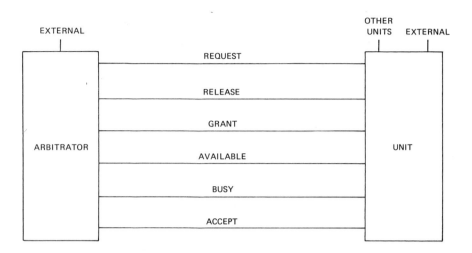

**Figure 5-2.** General Arbitrator/Unit System Model.


2.  The selected device is connected to the bus.
3.  Information is transferred on the bus from one device to another [1, 2].

The basic steps can be implemented in many ways. The following sections of this chapter detail the allocation process and information-transfer techniques. The connection issue is briefly discussed.

Connection is the technique via which the units are physically connected onto the bus lines. There are two basic techniques—connection at any point on the bus and connection only at the ends of the bus. Typically, connection only at the ends of the bus is via multiplexers, and the system may be viewed as an explicit multiplexing concept. Connection at any point on the bus requires that the arbitration function exist for the bus connections. This function actually acts as a control to multiplex the devices onto the bus. In a sense this type of system could be viewed as an implicitly multiplexed connection [1, 3].

Implicit multiplexing connection techniques are generally the fundamental design mode for bus structures. In this technique, connections may occur at any point on the bus. Typically, such connections are made using open-collector, tristate, or transformer techniques. Such techniques tend not to be used by common carriers. Explicit multiplexing techniques generally are used by common carriers. Such techniques allow connection only at the end(s) of the bus. Explicit techniques usually couple onto the bus by a multiplexer/demultiplexer subsystem. Some simple systems use selector chips for this function. The distinction between connection using explicit or implicit multiplexing techniques is important at an introductory level only to note that it exists.

**Arbitrator/Unit Design Issues**

A number of arbitration issues are symbolized by the interconnections shown on figure 5-2. In the arbitration process a request must be generated, at some future time the request will be honored (request granted), and eventually the unit releases the bus back to the controller. Further, information must be provided as to whether the bus is busy, available for assignment, and accepted for use. The details of this process are discussed later. The initial discussions concerning arbitration consider only control issues; thus no lines for information transfer are shown on the descriptive figures.

*Centralized or Decentralized Arbitrator*

The model shown in figure 5-2 pictures a centralized arbitrator. The arbitrator may be centralized, in which case the arbitration logic tends to be located at a single location, or it may be dispersed at a number of locations (known as decentralized).

*Complete or Incomplete Interconnection*

Figure 5-2 indicates six major interconnection lines between the arbitrator and unit. These lines are the bus-*request* line, bus-*release* line, bus-*grant* line, bus-*available* line, bus-*accept* line, and bus-*busy* line. Further, the unit may connect to other units or external devices (as may the arbitrator). In the model of figure 5-2, the arbitrator and unit are completely interconnected; that is, all the functions of request, release, granting, available, busy, and accept are explicitly provided. In some cases these lines may be functionally combined, time-shared, or encoded. The case where all functions are provided is described as complete interconnection. If one or more of the functions were implicit, the model would be considered incompletely connected. Whether a unit connects to other units is important in the context of decentralized arbitration and how the units connect and pass the control among themselves. External connections are important in the context of the impact of interrupts on the units and arbitration algorithm.

In addition to a system being complete or incomplete based on the control-line interconnection, the network itself may be completely interconnected (that is, the arbitrator is connected to all units identically) or not.

The detailed functioning of the control lines is discussed.

**Request.** There are two main request techniques:

1. *Formal.* In this case, the unit has a connection to the arbitrator, and the unit initiates a request which is transmitted to the arbitrator,

2. *No request.* In this case, the unit and arbitrator have prearranged for the bus usage conventions, and no request is made.

**Release**. Two major concepts for bus release exist:

1. *No notification.* In this case the unit simply releases the bus without notifying the arbitrator (this may be prearranged or may occur without any cognizance of the arbitrator).
2. *Arbitrator notification.* In this case the unit notifies the arbitrator explicitly that it no longer desires the bus (this may occur over a bus release line).

**Granting**. As with request and release concepts, bus granting has two major cases:

1. *Prearranged.* In this case the unit knows under what conditions it has control of the bus.
2. *Explicit notification.* In this case the arbitrator specifically notifies the unit that it has control of the bus (for example, over a bus granting line).

**Available**. There are two main availability signaling techniques:

1. *Passive.* In this case the unit waits for a bus-available signal from the arbitrator connection line.
2. *Prearranged.* In this case the unit knows that the bus is available because its use or conventions for its use have been prearranged.

**Accept**. There are three main bus acceptance techniques:

1. *Implicit acceptance.* In this case the bus acceptance may be prearranged.
2. *Explicit acceptance.* In this case the unit notifies the arbitrator that it is accepting the bus (most probably in response to a bus-granted signal).
3. *Arbitrary acceptance.* In this case the unit seizes the bus without notifying the arbitrator and without prearrangement (this technique may be subject to substantial transmission error).

**Busy**. There are four main bus-busy signaling techniques:

1. *Arbitrator assigned.* When an unit accepts a device, the arbitrator raises the bus-busy line.
2. *Unit accept.* When it takes control of the bus, the unit raises the bus-busy line.
3. *Arbitrator monitor.* When it detects bus traffic the arbitrator raises the bus-busy line.
4. *Random.* The devices do not care if the bus is in use and transmit whenever they want.

*Some Comments on the Design Issues*

The previous section discussed the types of functions that must be performed in a bus arbitration function. In an actual system, not all the functions may be present. For example, in some forms of "daisy-chaining," only a bus-available line is present. This signal is propagated, and all other information is implicit; that is, no request is issued, release and availability consist of propagating a bus-available signal to the next device, bus granting and accepting consist of accepting the bus by stopping the bus-available propagation, and bus busy is assumed unless the unit has control of the bus-available signal [5].

In other systems, the signals may be overlapped so that bus available causes units to compete for the next period of bus traffic [6]. Further, the amount of pipelining of signals depends on the complexity of the algorithm and the number of signal lines, as discussed later.

In the case of bus requests, formal requests may be viewed as mainly a dynamic technique (that is, the bus is designed to respond to actual system demands as expressed by bus allocation requests) [6]. On the other hand, the no-request technique tends to develop bus algorithms which are worked out in advance, and thus the bus allocation strategy tends to be static (does not respond to system demands) [7].

The combination of the release, grant, available, accept, and busy signals deals with bus timing. Through use of these signals, buses which provide arbitration at fixed intervals (synchronous arbitrators) or buses which automatically try to reallocate when not in use (asynchronous arbitrators) can be developed.

Previous studies of bus structures [1, 2, 3] have failed to note an important design consideration, the problem of data acceptance. Chen [2] did touch on similar issues in his consideration of bus deadlocks. Once bus control is gained by a sending device, the data must be transmitted. Yet, there is no guarantee that the intended receiving device is either available or operable. In the case of a single bus, the receiver may be busy computing. In a system with multiple buses, the receiver may be busy computing and/or busy with other data reception. A second important issue not typically dealt with is error acknowledgment (transmission error or transmission to a nonexistent device). The second issue is usually dealt with by requiring that devices acknowledge accurate transmission and that each transmission be encoded with check bits. Techniques to solve the first issue are discussed later.

In general, the designer cannot assume that the destination will always be available when the source has control of the bus. However, no systematic description of solutions to such problems can be given because they are implementation-dependent. Some typical design techniques include the following:

1.  *Buffering.* In this case all devices which can act as a destination are given either a single buffer (and a technique for message unscrambling) or a set of buffers (one for each source bus) to ensure that input data are accepted.

2. *Scheduling.* In this case a reservation is made for the destination, and the source is rescheduled for later bus allocation at a time mutually acceptable to the sender, receiver, and arbitrator. Alternatively, the arbitration algorithm may use destination reception information in the initial arbitration sequence.
3. *Control maintenance.* In this case the transmitter maintains control until the receiver is available (a concept which can easily create bus system deadlock problems).
4. *Retry.* In this case the transmitter simply aborts its request and at a later time attempts a retry of the transmittal.
5. *Time-out retry* (composition of solutions 3 and 4). Control is maintained for a specific period of time (solution 3). After the specified time has expired, a retry is scheduled (solution 4).
6. *Interrupt.* In this case, a set of interrupt lines is provided so that, depending on transmitter priority, the receiver can be interrupted. Depending on the transmitter's priority a retry solution may be required in conjunction with the interrupt concept.
7. *Data Accept.* In this case, the transmitter does not check to see if the receiver is available. It simply transmits, and if (at a later time) a message reception signal is received, no further action is required. If no message reception signal is received, then there was a busy receiver, a transmission error, or a nonexistent receiver, and appropriate system action must be initiated.

*Arbitrator Functional Issues*

The design of the arbitrator must take into consideration a number of issues in addition to augmenting the previously discussed design issues. For example, there is the issue of the arbitrator algorithm. Algorithms must consider such issues as unit priorities, whether units or external events may cause bus preemption, and, in the decentralized case, what unit is the current arbitrator. Further design issues include how units are addressed (virtual, name priority, real device names, or discretely by separate lines) and how information is passed on the lines (time-multiplexed, coded, or on separate lines).

*Cost Measures*

Any good design must be measured against a set of design tradeoffs. The major cost measures which should be considered in bus design include:

1. *Modularity*—the ease of adding another unit to the system
2. *Lines*—the number of lines necessary to support *n* units

3. *Hardware*—the number of gates necessary to implement the arbitration algorithm
4. *Allocation speed*—the amount of time required to reallocate the bus
5. *Overhead*—the ratio of allocation speed to transfer time
6. *Algorithm Flexibility*—the ability to change the algorithm to fit varying conditions such as system concept changes or a requirement for dynamic algorithm adaptability
7. *Fault tolerance*—the ability of the bus structure to adopt to varying levels of failures in the system

In the following paragraphs some specific bus control techniques are discussed. There are two major papers which previously discussed control techniques. Thurber et al. [1] use the simple classification of bus arbitration techniques given in figure 5-3. Chen [2] suggested the taxonomy shown in figure 5-4 and applied it to five sample bus implementations. This book selects the discussion of Thurber et al. and an extension of that concept for the following reasons:

1. The concepts used by Chen do not employ terminology common in industry.
2. Chen's "taxonomy" does not apply well to his selected algorithms (for example, with "buck passing," an algorithm selected by Chen, only three of Chen's four model dimensions apply).
3. The previous model of the arbitrator/unit interrelationships fits well with the examples used by Thurber et al. and illustrates common practical examples.

An extension has been made to the concepts considered by Thurber et al. to include a new concept—implicit control—which is not as common as techniques such as daisy-chaining but is being used in some systems currently under development. Some of the broadcast techniques can be modeled as decentralized implicit bus allocation [8, 9].

**Centralized Bus Control**

With centralized control, a single hardware unit is used to recognize and grant requests for the use of the bus. At least four different schemes have been proposed plus various modifications or combinations of these: daisy-chaining, polling, independent requests, and implicit requests.

Centralized daisy-chaining is illustrated in figure 5-5.

Each device can generate a request via the common bus-request line. Whenever the bus controller receives a request on the bus-request line, it returns a signal on the bus-available line. The bus-available line is daisy-chained through

CENTRALIZED
   DAISY CHAIN
   POLLING
   INDEPENDENT REQUESTS
DECENTRALIZED
   DAISY CHAIN
   POLLING
   INDEPENDENT REQUESTS

Figure 5-3. Bus Arbitration Mechanisms of Thurber et al.

ARBITER LOCATION
   DISTRIBUTED
   CENTRALIZED
      STATIC
      DYNAMIC
PRIORITY SORTING
   COMPARISON
   COUNTING
ADDRESSING
   PRIORITY
   UNIT
INFORMATION PASSING
   ENCODED
   DECODED

Figure 5-4. Bus Arbitration Taxonomy of Chen.

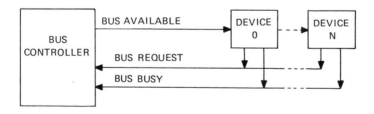

Figure 5-5. Centralized Daisy-Chaining. Reprinted with permission from K.J. Thurber, et al., "A Systematic Approach to the Design of Digital Bussing Structures," Proceedings of the FJCC, Montvale, N.J.: AFIPS Press.

each device. If a device receives the bus-available signal and does not want control of the bus, it passes the bus-available signal onto the next device. If a device receives the bus-available signal and is requesting control of the bus, then the bus-available signal is not passed onto the next device. The requesting device places a signal on the bus-busy line, drops its bus request, and begins its data transmission. The bus-busy line inhibits the bus-available signal while the transmission takes place. When the device drops the bus-busy signal, the bus-available signal is reenabled. If a bus request still exists on the bus-request line, the allocation procedure repeats.

The bus-busy line can be eliminated, but this essentially converts the bus control technique to a decentralized daisy chain. This technique is discussed in the second on decentralized bus control.

The obvious advantage of such a daisy-chaining scheme is its simplicity—very few control lines are required, and their number is independent of the number of devices. Hence, additional devices can be added by simply connecting them to the bus.

A disadvantage of the daisy-chaining scheme is its susceptibility to failure. If a failure occurs in the bus-available circuitry or a device, it could either prevent succeeding devices from ever getting control of the bus or allow more than one device to transmit over the bus at the same time. However, the logic involved is quite simple and could easily be made redundant to increase its reliability. A power failure in a single device or the necessity to take a device offline can also be problems with the daisy-chain method of control.

Another disadvantage of the daisy-chaining scheme is the fixed priority structure which results. The devices which are "closer" to the bus controller always receive control of the bus in preference to those which are "farther away." If the closer devices had a high demand for the bus, the farther devices could be locked out.

Since the bus-available signal must sequentially ripple through the devices, this bus-assignment mechanism can also be quite slow.

Finally, it should be noted that with daisy-chaining, cable lengths are a function of system layout; and so adding, deleting, or moving devices is physically awkward.

Figure 5-6 illustrates a centralized polling system. As in the centralized daisy-chaining method, each device on the bus can place a signal on the bus-request line. When the bus controller receives a request, it begins polling the devices to determine who is making the request. The polling is done by counting on the polling lines. When the count corresponds to a requesting device, that device raises the bus-busy line. The controller then stops the polling until the device has completed its transmission and removed the busy signal. If there is another bus request, the count may restart from zero or may continue from where it stopped.

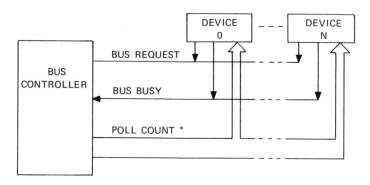

**Figure 5-6.** Centralized Polling: Poll Count. Reprinted with permission, from K.J. Thurber, et al., "A Systematic Approach to the Design of Digital Bussing Structures," Proceedings of the FJCC, Montvale, N.J.: AFIPS Press.

Restarting from zero each time establishes the same sort of device priority as proximity does in daisy-chaining, while continuing from the stopping point is a round robin approach which gives equal opportunity to all devices. The priorities need not be fixed because the polling sequence is easily altered.

The bus-request line can be eliminated by allowing the polling counter to continuously cycle except while it is stopped by a device using the bus. This alternative impacts the restart (that is, priority) philosophy and the average bus assignment time.

Polling does not suffer from the reliability or physical placement problems of daisy-chaining, but the number of devices in figure 5-6 is limited by the number of polling lines. Attempting to poll bit-serially involves synchronous communication techniques (as described later in this chapter) and the attendant complications of such a technique.

Figure 5-7 shows that centralized polling may be made independent of the number of devices by placing a counter in each device. Then the bus controller is reduced to distributing clock pulses which are counted by all devices. When the count reaches the code of a device wanting the bus, the device raises the busy, line which inhibits the clock. When the device completes its transmission, it removes the busy signal and the counting continues. The devices can be serviced either in a round robin manner or on a priority basis. If the counting always continues cyclically, when the busy signal is removed, the allocation is round robin; and if the counters are all reset when the busy signal is removed, the devices are prioritized by their codes. It is also possible to make the priorities adaptable by altering the codes assigned to the devices. The clock skew problems

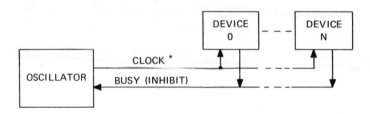

**Figure 5-7.** Centralizing Polling: Clock. Reprinted with permission from K.J. Thurber, et al., "A Schematic Approach to the Design of Digital Bussing Structures," Proceedings of the FJCC, Montvale, N.J.: AFIPS Press.

tend to limit this technique to small, slow systems; it is also exceptionally susceptible to noise and clock failure.

Polling and daisy-chaining can be combined into schemes where addresses or priorities are propagated between devices instead of a bus-available signal. This adds some priority flexibility to daisy-chaining at the expense of more lines and logic.

The third method of centralized bus control, independent requests, is shown in figure 5-8. In this case each device has a separate pair of bus-request and bus-granted lines, which it uses for communicating with the bus controller. When a device requires use of the bus, it sends the bus request to the controller. The controller selects the next device to receive service and sends a bus-granted line to it. The selected device lowers its request and raises bus-assigned line, indicating to all other devices that the bus is busy. After the transmission is complete, the device lowers the bus-assigned line and the bus controller removes bus-granted line and selects the next requesting device.

The overhead time required for allocating the bus can be shorter than for daisy-chaining or polling since all bus requests are presented simultaneously to the bus controller. In addition, complete flexibility is available for selecting the next device for service. The controller can use prespecified or adaptive priorities, a round-robin scheme, or both. It is also possible to disable requests from a particular device which, for instance, is known or suspected to have failed.

The major disadvantage of independent requests is the number of lines and connectors required for control. Of course, the complexity of the allocation algorithm is reflected in the amount of bus-controller hardware.

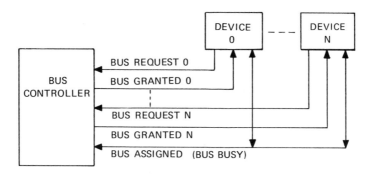

**Figure 5-8.** Centralized Independent Requests. Reprinted with permission from K.J. Thurber, et al., "A Schematic Approach to the Design of Digital Bussing Structures," Proceedings of the FJCC, Montvale, N.J.: AFIPS Press.

The fourth technique for centralized bus control, implicit request, is illustrated in figure 5-9. With this concept, the bus controller has been designed to allocate the bus to the set of devices in some algorithmic fashion. The devices do not contend with one another dynamically to obtain time to utilize the bus. A priori the bus time has been allocated. Using a specified algorithm (which could be implemented with a stored program), the bus controller raises and lowers the bus-granted lines. During the time that device $i$ sees its bus-granted line raised, it may transmit information onto the bus. When a device's bus-granted line is not raised, the device is inhibited from using the bus.

The centralized implicit bus-allocation technique is much like that of centralized independent requests except that the devices do not request bus allocation. All allocation of the bus must be worked out a priori (although this does not preclude algorithmic allocation). There is a simple control allocation in this case. The bus controller simply ensures that only one bus-granted line is in the raised condition at any given instant.

Further, the implicit technique requires fewer lines than the independent-request case, but as with independent requests, the number of lines is directly proportional to the number of devices. The bus-granted line is not constrained to be a single line. It could be a set of lines used to pass some type of information to the device which describes the allocation parameters of the bus when the bus is granted to a device.

The design of an implicit bus control algorithm could be quite difficult. There is no constraint on the allocation algorithm (whether a stored program, hardwired, and so forth), but the algorithm must be aware of the physical

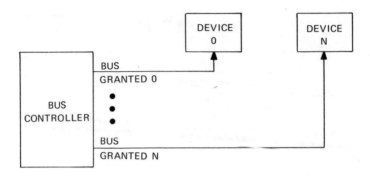

**Figure 5-9.** Centralized Implicit Arbitration.

spacing, transfer characteristics, speed, failure characteristics, and overhead of all devices and the resultant subsystem connected on the bus. If the system or a device fails, the algorithm may have to be completely reorganized and redeveloped. Thus centralized implicit allocation is not conducive for a system design which may change during development. All failure modes in the system must be prespecified and incorporated into the allocation to achieve fail-safe operation. The implicit-allocation concept can be very flexible once the system is designed because of the capability of the algorithms that can be provided. It holds the hope of being able to allocate bus bandwidth so that maximum advantage is taken of device characteristics, system configuration, and other bus parameters. There is no overhead paid by the device to generate and process a request, thus making allocation very fast. A major drawback of this concept is that the entire subsystem controlled by this bus controller must be brought up in a known, synchronized set of states to ensure proper action. This set of states may be established from the bus controller, however. The allocation algorithms must also include consideration of system timing delays and topology since the device does not return control of the bus to the controller. One major advantage of the implicit-control concept is that computation can proceed with results being stored in a buffer which is transmitted in total when the bus is allocated to the buffered device. However, if no information is to be transferred when the bus is allocated or if the device falls out of synchronization, bus bandwidth or system integrity may be lost, respectively.

If allocation of the bus by the bus controller is performed utilizing an implicit-request technique and the allocation also dictates a specific bus information transfer, then this variation of implicit bus control is referred to as a *command/response allocation technique*. The set of bus-grant lines is sometimes used to describe the transaction parameters, type of information transferred, recipients, error controls imposed, and so on. Using this addition to implicit bus control, a common practice is to time-multiplex the bus-grant signals over the same set of lines (parallel communication architecture) or line (serial communication architecture) as the data information. The command/ response allocation technique is mainly used when not only bus allocation but also information transactions are directly controlled by the bus controller.

A modification of the centralized inplicit-request concept is to delete the bus-grant lines and allow devices to transmit at arbitrary times. This concept leads to control concepts such as the random access techniques discussed in chapter 3.

**Decentralized Bus Control**

In a decentrally controlled system, the control logic is (primarily) distributed throughout the devices on the bus. As with the centralized case, there are at least four distinct schemes, plus combinations and modifications of daisy-chaining, polling, independent requests, and implicit request.

A decentralized daisy chain can be constructed from a centralized one by omitting the bus-busy line and connecting the common bus-request line to the "first" bus-available line, as shown in figure 5-10. A device requests service by raising its bus-request line if the incoming bus-available line is low. When a bus-available signal is received, a device which is not requesting the bus passes the signal on. The first device which is requesting service does not propagate the bus-available line and keeps its bus-request line until it is finished with the bus. Lowering the bus-request line lowers bus-available line if no successive devices also have bus-request signals up, in which case the "first" device wanting the bus gets it. On the other hand, if some device "beyond" this one has a bus-request line; control propagates down to it. Thus, allocation is always on a round robin basis.

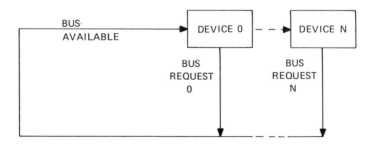

**Figure 5-10.** Decentralized Daisy Chain; Bus Request. Reprinted with permission from K.J. Thurber, et al., "A Schematic Approach to the Design of Digital Bussing Structures," Proceedings of the FJCC, Montvale, N.J.: AFIPS Press.

A potential problem exists in that if a device in the interior of the chain releases the bus and no other device is requesting it, the fall of bus-request control is propagating back toward the "first" device while the bus-available signal propagates "forward." If devices on both sides of the last user now raise bus-request signals, the one to the "right" obtains the bus momentarily until its bus-available line drops when the "left" device gets control. This dilemma can be avoided by postponing the bus assignment until such races have settled out, either asynchronously with one-shots in each device or with a synchronizing signal from else where in the system.

A topologically simpler decentralized daisy chain is illustrated in figure 5-11. Here, it is not possible to unambiguously specify the status of the bus by using a static level on the bus-available line. However, it is possible to determine the bus status from transitions on the bus-available line. Whenever the bus-available line coming into a device changes state and that device needs to use the bus, it does not pass a signal transition onto the next device; if the device does not need the bus, it then changes the bus-available signal to the next device. When the bus is idle, the bus-available signal oscillates around the daisy chain. The first device to request the bus and receive a bus-available signal change terminates the oscillation and takes control of the bus. When the device is finished with the bus, it causes a transition in bus-available line to the next device.

Dependence on signal edges rather than levels renders this approach somewhat more susceptible to noise than the previous one. This problem can be minimized by passing control with a request/acknowledge type of mechanism such as described later for communication, although this slows bus allocation. Both of these decentralized daisy chains have the same single-point failure mode and physical layout liabilities as the centralized version. Specific systems may prefer either the (centralized) priority or the (decentralized) round robin algorithm, but they are equally inflexible (albeit simple).

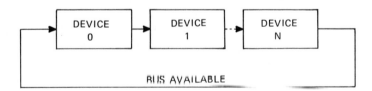

**Figure 5-11**. Decentralized Daisy Chain: Circular. Reprinted with permission from K.J. Thurber, et al., "A Schematic Approach to the Design of Digital Bussing Structures," Proceedings of the FJCC, Montvale, N.J.: AFIPS Press.

Decentralized polling can be performed as shown in figure 5-12. When a device is willing to relinquish control of the bus, it puts a code (address or priority) on the polling lines and raises the bus-available signal. If the code matches that of another device which desires the bus, that device responds with a bus-accept signal. The former device drops the polling and bus-available lines, and the latter device lowers the bus-accept line and begins using the bus. If the polling device does not receive a bus-accent signal (a bus-refused line could be added to distinguish between devices which do not desire the bus and those which are failed), it changes the code according to some allocation algorithm (round robin or priority) and tries again. This approach requires that exactly one device be granted bus control when the system is initiated. Since every device must have the same allocation hardware as a centralized polling bus controller, the decentralized version utilizes substantially more hardware. This busy enhanced reliability in that failure of a single device does not necessarily affect operation of the bus.

Figure 5-13 illustrates the decentralized version of independent requests. Any device desiring the bus raises its bus-request line, which corresponds to its priority. When the current user releases the bus by dropping bus-assigned line, all requesting devices examine all active bus requests. The device which recognizes itself as the highest-priority requester obtains control of the bus by raising the bus-assigned line. This causes all other requesting devices to lower their bus requests (and to store the priority of the successful device if a round robin algorithm is to be accommodated).

The priority logic in each device is simpler than that in the centralized counterpart, but the number of lines and connectors is higher. If the priorities are fixed rather than dynamic, not all request lines go to all devices, so the

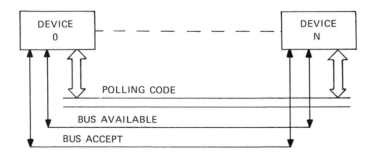

**Figure 5-12.** Decentralized Polling. Reprinted with permission from K.J. Thurber, et al., "A Schematic Approach to the Design of Digital Bussing Structures," Proceedings of the FJCC, Montvale, N.J.: AFIPS Press.

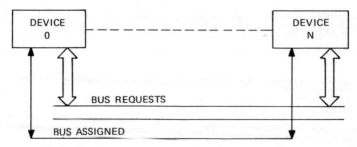

**Figure 5-13**. Decentralized Independent Requests. Reprinted with permission from K.J. Thurber, et al., "A Schematic Approach to the Design of Digital Bussing Structures," Proceedings of the FJCC, Montvale, N.J.: AFIPS Press.

decentralized case uses fewer lines in systems with up to about ten devices. Again, the decentralized method is somewhat more reliable than the centralized one.

The clock-skew problems limit this process to small, dense systems, and it is exceptionally susceptible to noise and clock failure.

There are a number of possible subcases of the decentralized implicit control concept. These are illustrated in figures 5-14 to 5-16. In figure 5-14 each device is computing the allocation algorithm, synchronously with every other device. When the device recognizes that the algorithm allows it to use the bus, the device takes control of the bus. When the algorithm passes control to another device, the device in control must relinquish control of the bus. An obvious disadvantage to this control scheme is that if the devices are physically disjoint or fall out of synchronization, there is no way to retain system integrity. Further, the system must assume that there are no malicious users who would throw the system out of synchronization.

A more realistic decentralized implicit control technique is shown in figure 5-15. In this case a set of lines connects the devices, and it is assumed that each device is capable of computing the allocation algorithm. All devices compute the allocation algorithm synchronously and place the result of the computation onto the allocation lines. The set of all allocation computation answers is voted. All devices monitor the allocation lines; and when a device recognizes its code, it takes control of the bus. This technique allows the system some level of fault tolerance.

A preferred and more useful form of decentralized implicit control is shown in figure 5-16. In this case, each device can compute the allocation algorithm. Further, each device has a set of input and output lines connecting it to all devices from which it may receive or to which it may pass control of the bus. This bus control technique may be operated as previously discussed. For fault-tolerant operation, all devices compute the algorithm; and before

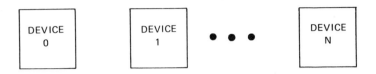

**Figure 5-14.** Decentralized Implicit Arbitration—Synchronous Access.

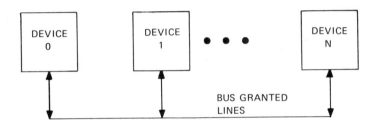

**Figure 5-15.** Decentralized Implicit Arbitration—Monitor.

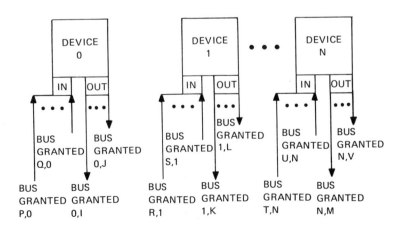

**Figure 5-16.** Decentralized Implicit Arbitration—Discrete Munitor.

a device may take control of the bus, a specified number of input lines must be raised. Alternatively, control may be passed sequentially with the allocation algorithm being executed only when the device in control of the bus is deciding on the next device to receive control of the bus. One notable advantage of the decentralized control technique shown in figure 5-16 is that the network does not have to be fully connected; that is, a device does not have to have input and output connectors to every other device. The speed of allocation can be quite fast since the algorithm computation can be overlapped with bus usage. Additionally, some physical interconnection problems can be eased by allowing reallocation to occur when the first input pulse denoting allocation is received from another device. A safer technique is to wait to take control of the bus when the bus-allocation pulse has been received from the device known to currently have control of the bus or from all devices which can input a bus-granted signal.

Each of the three implicit control techniques described can be used in the command/response mode as described in the section on centralized implicit bus control techniques.

Further, broadcast techniques [8, 9] could use a configuration similar to figure 5-14. However, instead of synchronously computing the allocation algorithm, the general broadcast concept is that any device that desires to transmit proceeds; if multiple devices are trying to transmit and these transmissions "collide," upon detection of the collision the devices compute a new time to retry their transmission. This new transmission-time computation is designed to resolve the transmission collisions. Broadcast techniques are summarized in the section discussing random-access (Aloha) algorithms in chapter 3. Further, comments on broadcast implementations are contained in the conclusion of this chapter.

**Tradeoffs**

A number of design issues were mentioned with respect to the previously described bus control techniques. This section discusses some of the most important issues that the designer should consider in the selection of a bus control technique. The main issues discussed are modularity, logical complexity, number of lines, flexibility, allocation speed, fault tolerance, contention, and deadlock problems.

*Modularity* is defined to be the incremental cost of adding a device to the system. If the cost is near zero, the system is quite modular; if the cost is proportional to $n$ (for a system with $n$ devices), then the system is not modular. For example, case 3 (figure 5-16) of decentralized implicit control is not modular since it may require the addition of $2n$ lines. Decentralized daisy-chaining is, however, physically quite modular. Most of the bus control techniques work equally well with systems of homogeneous or nonhomogeneous devices. Some of the decentralized control techniques may require that the bus control portion of the devices be identical to ensure proper system action (decentralized implicit control, figure 5-14) whereas other techniques (decentralized polling) may be able to utilize nonhomogeneous bus controllers. There are tradeoffs which force the designer to choose a less modular system. A typical tradeoff would involve the modularity versus speed tradeoff of decentralized daisy-chaining compared to centralized independent requests. At some point the designer has to face the tradeoff between speed and modularity.

Chen [2] addressed this tradeoff problem by using multiple bus controllers, which led to the deadlock problem discussed later. Other tradeoff issues with respect to modularity that the designer must address include the constraints placed on the bus controller for physical locality. Some of the very modular decentralized control techniques suffer from severe constraints, allowing the choice of use only with physically compact systems (for example, decentralized independent requests). The topology of the network itself may have some impact on the control choice. If the system is ring-structured, then a daisy chain may be a very effective control choice. However, if the network contains a central communications processor, the most logical choice may be centralized independent requests. A final practical design issue that must be addressed (but is beyond the scope of this book) is the detailed hardware components available to implement the controller and its cabling.

A major consideration in the design process is the number of allowable lines. Some application environments (say, aircraft avionics or networks which are physically separated by long distances) cannot afford the weight or cost of a large number of cables and must choose a single-line technique like decentralized daisy-chaining. The previously described techniques provide a large variation in the number of control lines, thus allowing the designer great flexibility in choice of the final design.

To achieve both speed and modularity, the designer may have to utilize multiple bus controllers operating in parallel on the same set of devices. This can be a very effective technique; but as was pointed out by Chen [2], the bus design can have the classical resource-contention problems of deadlock. A solution to the probme is to place some synchronization logic between the bus controllers to solve contention problems. However, such designers should be avoided unless it is chosen for redundancy or fault-tolerance purposes. Fault-tolerant bus designs should select a control technique (other than replication) that makes it easy to check other bus controllers and remove a device without losing the bus control system. Techniques like decentralized independent requests are much more fault-tolerant than daisy-chain techniques.

The last main issue that should be considered is the tradeoff between flexibility, speed, and complexity. Allocation techniques which are fast and flexible (decentralized implicit) may be very difficult to understand, analyze, and simulate. Yet for an effective design, much analysis may be required. Slow allocation schemes such as daisy-chaining are easy to model. Unless the system requirements dictate a complex technique, the designer should utilize the more simplistic control techniques.

*Bus Communication*

When a communication path on a bus has been established between devices which in some way transfer data, the problem of coordinating or synchronizing the information exchange(s) must be addressed. In the following sections we consider various approaches and techniques to accomplish this.

For the purpose of explanation, the framework on which our discussions are based is the most simplistic one consisting of a device pair—a single information-sending device transmitting to a single information-receiving device. This is illustrated in figure 5-17. Note that in figure 5-17 the bus lines are divided into two sets—coordination bus lines and information or data bus lines. The former are said to carry coordination signals while the latter carry information or data signals. It should be kept in mind that we separate these signals primarily for pedagogical reasons, since coordination and information signals can be implemented on the same bus lines by embedding the necessary coordination signals within the data. In fact, in bit-serial transmission schemes the data and coordination signals must be carried on a single line. Nonetheless, the coordination aspects of the communication between the devices would still have to be (at least) considered separately from the data-transmission aspects. Hence, our framework suffers no loss in generality. We are also assuming at this point that these two devices have already obtained control of and been connected to the bus.

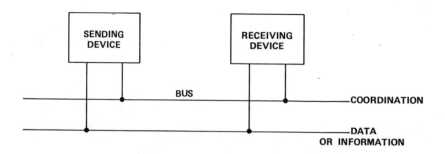

Figure 5-17. Sender/Receiver Model.

## Information

Communication between two devices is primarily for the purpose of transferring information, and therefore bus communication could certainly be characterized (and, indeed, often is characterized) by the type of information transferred. In this chapter, however, the type of information involved is not our dominant concern. Instead, our concern is with the strategy that governs the coordination by means of which the data transfer is accomplished. This strategy is given many names in the literature—data communication synchronization procedures, bus synchronization procedures, bus or line protocols, bus communication, bus or line disciplines. We refer to our strategies somewhat less specifically as simply bus communication techniques. Details on and examples of contemporary line protocols and bus structures are given in chapters 6 and 7.

It should be kept in mind that the nature or type of information or data that can be transferred is quite broad. It could be, for example, source address, destination address, communication class, or action class.

The source address is often implicit, and the destination address may be also (for example, in the case of a dedicated bus). Communication class refers to the type of information to be transferred—data, command, status, interrup, and so on. This, too, might be partially or wholly implicit or might be merged with the action class, which determines the function to be performed, such as input, output, and so forth. After this initial coordination or message format has been set up and agreed on, the actual data communication can proceed.

## Information Transfer

Five basic information-transfer approaches can be considered for a bus: single-word[1] transfers only, fixed-length block transfers only, variable-length block transfers only, single-word or fixed-length block transfers, and single-word or variable-length block transfers. It should be noted that here the term *word* is used functionally to denote the basic information unit on the bus; bus width factors are covered later. Further, the last case, single-word or variable-length block transfers, may be viewed as a special case of variable-length block transfers (as may single-word or fixed-length block transfers).

The information transfer is directly involved with three other major aspects of the system—the access characteristics of the devices using the bus, the control mechanism by which the bus is allocated (if it is nondedicated), and the bus communication techniques. Of course, if the bus connects functional units of a computer such as processors and memories, the information transfer may severely impact programming, memory allocation and utilization, and so on.

The choice of allowing only single words to be transferred has a number of important system ramifications. First, it precludes any effective use of purely block-oriented devices, such as disks or drums. These devices have a high latency, and their principal value lies in amortizing this time across many words in a block. To a lesser extent, this concern also applies to other types of devices. There can be substantial initial overhead in obtaining access to a device—bus acquisition, bus propagation, busy-device delay, priority resolution, address mapping, intrinsic device-access time, and so on. Prorating these against a block of words would reduce the effective access time.

The second factor in a single-word-only system is the bus control method. Since a nondedicated bus must be reassigned to another device for each word, the allocation algorithm may have to be very fast to meet the bus throughput specifications. Even if bus assignment occurs in parallel with data transfer, this could restrict the sophistication of the algorithm, the bus bandwidth, or both. Judiciously selected parameters (speed, priorities, and so on) conceivably could enable a bus controller to handle blocks from a slow device on a word-by-word basis.

A single-word-only bus requires that the communication scheme operate at the word rate, whereas with block transfers it might be possible for devices to effect higher throughput by interchanging communication signals only at the beginning and end of each block.

Bus bandwidth may be increased at the expense of flexibility by transferring only fixed length blocks of information. Problems arise when the bus block size does not match that of a block-oriented device on the bus. If the bus blocks are smaller, some improvement is achieved over the single-word-only bus. If the bus blocks are too large, however, extraneous information is transferred, which wastes bus bandwidth and buffer space and unnecessarily ties up both devices. However, there are applications such as look-aside memories where locality of procedure and data references make effective use of a purely fixed-length block transfer.

Since the bus is assigned for entire blocks, the control can be slower and thus simpler. Likewise, the communication validity check can be restricted to blocks because this is the smallest unit that could be retired in case of an error. The data-ready aspect of communication would have to remain on a word basis unless a self-clocked modulation scheme is used.

The use of dynamically variable-length blocks is significantly more flexible than the two previous approaches, because the block size can be matched to the physical or logical requirements of the devices involved in the transfer. This capability makes more efficient use of bus bandwidth and device time in transferring blocks. On the other hand, the overhead involved in initiating a block transfer would also be expanded for single-word transfers (blocks of length 1). Thus, a compromise between bandwidth and flexibility may have to be arranged, based on the throughput requirements and expected average block size. An example of such a compromise would be a system in which the sizes of the data blocks depended on the source devices. This avoids explicitly block-length specification, reducing the overhead and improving throughput.

The facility for one-word blocks requires that the control scheme be able to reallocate the bus rapidly enough to minimize wasted bandwidth. Date-error response may also be required at the word rate.

In a system where there are high-priority devices with low data requirements, this might be a reasonable alternative. The single-word option reduces the number of cases where the oversized block would waste bandwidth, buffer space, and device availability, but it still suffers from poor device and bus utilization efficiency when more than one word but less than one block is needed.

The expected mix of block and single-word transfers would be a primary influence on the selection of control and communication mechanisms to achieve a proper balance of cost and performance.

As might be expected, the capability for both single words and variable-length blocks is the most flexible, efficient, and expensive data-transfer philosophy. Single words can be handled without the overhead involved in initializing a block transfer. Data blocks can be sized to suit the devices and applications, which optimizes bus usage. The necessity for reassigning the bus as often as every word time imposes a speed constraint on the control method which must be evaluated in light of the expected bus-traffic statistics. If data-validity response is desired below a message level, the choice of a communication scheme will be affected.

*Signal Form*

By the *form* of a signal, we mean the physical nature of the signal—pulse, level, or transition. These forms are sometimes referred to as *signal modes*. There are, of course, advantages and disadvantages to each type. Signal in the form of a current or voltage pulse, for example, may be more susceptible to being masked by noise than signals in the form of a current or voltage level. However, a signal in the form of a level requires greater energy or power to maintain as well as more time on the bus line(s). Transition signals may be complex to sense. A summary of the relative features of these three forms is given in table 5-1.

Although the form of a signal primarily refers to its physical nature, the form also has implications regarding the bus communication technique as well. This is a result of the potential coupling or tightening of device communication signals resulting from the use of level and transition forms of signals as opposed to the pulse form. If bus communication is implemented entirely in the form of pulse signals, then regardless of the response signals used, there is the possibility that a pulse might, at times, be transmitted which was or either insufficient amplitude or duration for recognition at its destination; or noise might contaminate the bus and be reacted to by a device as though the noise were actually a communication signal. Each type of error would put a device or device pair into an uncertain or incorrect state. The proper use of response signals would,

**Table 5-1**
**Summary of Signal-Form Characteristics**

|  | ADVANTAGES | DISADVANTAGES |
|---|---|---|
| PULSE | — SPEED | — NOISE SUSCEPTIBILITY<br><br>— MISSED SIGNALS<br>    • AMPLITUDE<br>    • WIDTH |
| LEVEL | — CAN BE INTERLOCKED (AVOIDS DISADVANTAGES OF PULSE SYSTEMS)<br><br>— LOW NOISE SUSCEPTIBILITY<br><br>— EASILY ADAPTED TO DEVICES WITH WIDELY VARYING SPEED CHARACTERISTICS | — SLOWER THAN PULSE TECHNIQUES<br><br>— USES SIGNIFICANT POWER |
| TRANSITION | — CAN BE INTERLOCKED<br><br>— LOW NOISE SUSCEPTIBILITY<br><br>— USEFUL WITH VARYING SPEED DEVICES<br><br>— UNNECESSARY TRANSITIONS NECESSARY TO BUILD PULSES OR LEVELS CAN BE ELIMINATED<br><br>— FASTER THAN LEVEL TECHNIQUES | — MAY HAVE TO BE ABLE TO MAINTAIN TWO LEVELS<br><br>— TRANSITIONS MAY BE DIFFICULT TO SENSE |

of course, prevent the devices from proceeding with faulty operation; but note that, in addition, some type of roll-back or recovery procedure would have to be enacted in order to diagnose the situation. Such procedures, of course, imply additional costs in a system in terms of time and hardware.

An alternative is the use of communication signals in the form of levels. In effect, each signal has associated with it an "on-level" and an "off-level." Usually "on" and "off" denote the power-dissipation aspects of the signal.

If a signal in the form of a level is sent from one device to another, the on-level can continue to be held by the sending device until a response is received by that device from the device to which the signal was sent. Clearly, this opens up many coordination possibilities. Maintaining the on-level until notification of its reception is referred to as the *interlocking* of that signal. This is obviously more than simply using responses because of the time and power costs of such a technique.

Note that the response signal in this discussion could itself be in the form of either a pulse or a level. If it is in the form of a pulse, of course, we risk the possibility of its being missed. If it is in the form of a level, then it, too, can be interlocked. But note further that it can be interlocked to not only another signal but also the off-level or the transition from on to off of the signal which it interlocked. In other words, we can produce simply a closed form of interlocking which significantly tightens the coordination of the devices.

Transitions are the last major form of signal technique. In this form, transitions between levels (signal phases, signal frequency, and so on) are the meaningful information. The system must be able to detect the transitions and interpret them as meaningful information. (Further, in some systems, if time also has a value, no transition after a specific time interval can convey meaningful information—see chapter 6.) Like level systems, transition systems can be interlocked and thus can be used with variable-speed devices. Further, the transitions necessary to build a pulse or a proper polarity level can be eliminated in transition-oriented system.

Bus communication techniques can be compared on the basis of power, complexity, noise susceptibility, and so on but most importantly on time. Estimates of the amount of time involved can be made on the basis of some time-increment assumptions regarding the durations of certain fundamental operations which would be involved in all techniques:

$\Delta_p$ = propagation time of a signal from one device to another

$\Delta_1$ = time length of the signal (Certainly, the length of a signal in level form is greater than the length of a signal in pulse form.)

$\Delta_r$ = response time of a device to a signal

It is also important to consider skewing increment. When two signals are sent (to the same destination) in parallel, they can arrive at their destination at slightly different times. We must then take into account this time difference since we cannot expect the destination device to begin responding to the signals until the entire signal set has been received. Often, however, it is possible to ignore this skew because it actually implies two different values for $\Delta_p$, and it usually is quite small relative to $\Delta_p$, $\Delta_1$, and $\Delta_r$. When this skew time does become nonnegligible, $\Delta_p$ can simply be increased to describe the worst case. This is commonly known as *clock skew*.

*Synchronous versus Asynchronous Categorization*

Different researchers have different concepts as to what, by definition, constitutes synchronous versus asynchronous communication. Part of this nomenclature problem depends on the designer's model of the phenomena being studied. In the context of synchronism versus asynchronism in bus systems, we consider only the views given in works dealing solely with bus structures. Three important but slightly disagreeing approaches are discussed by Thurber et al. [1], Chen [2], and Jensen, Thurber, and Schneider [3]. In Thurber et al. synchronous is viewed as requiring a clock, asynchronous is viewed as nonclocked, and "self-clocking" is viewed as asynchronous. In Chen, synchronous is viewed as being associated with some pulse techniques; asynchronous is viewed as being associated with pulse, level, or transition techniques which utilize acknowledgment techniques. Self-clocking techniques are viewed as "synchronous." In Jensen, Thurber, and Schneider synchronous techniques are viewed as any system in which there exist timing agreements between devices.

Carried to its logical extent, this latter concept means that all communication is "synchronous." The debate is resolved as follows in this book. Synchronous techniques involve timing agreements between devices, but we do not consider interlocking as a timing agreement. Asynchronous techniques are techniques which operate without a clock. Self-clocking systems are discussed as a separate category since logically they could be viewed as a locally clocked system or interlocking at the device level and thus could be either synchronous or asynchronous. Chen gives the generic protocol types shown in figures 5-18 and 5-19. Thurber et al. use a more limited set, as shown in figure 5-20. Thurber et al. introduced the concept of "semi-synchronous." Later Jensen, Thurber, and Schneider pointed out that semisynchronous could also (and maybe more correctly) be interpreted as a combination of a bus arbitration algorithm and an asynchronous communication technique. However, the arbitration technique was used as a pseudo-clock as in self-clocking techniques and therefore could be classified as either synchronous or asynchronous per the previous discussion.

```
                    PULSE  MODE
                  *PRIMITIVE USED
                    ACKNOWLEDGMENT
                      SEPARATE
                      COMBINED
                    NO  ACKNOWLEDGMENT
                  *PRIMITIVE  NOT USED
```

**Figure 5-18.** Asynchronous Path Pulse-Mode Taxonomy.

```
*LEVEL MODE
 #PRIMITIVE USED
   NO ACKNOWLEDGMENT
   ACKNOWLEDGMENT
     NOT INTERLOCKED
       SEPARATE ACKNOWLEDGMENT
       COMBINED ACKNOWLEDGMENT
     INTERLOCKED
       SEPARATE ACKNOWLEDGMENT
         ACKNOWLEDGMENT NOT INTERLOCKED
         ACKNOWLEDGMENT INTERLOCKED
       COMBINED ACKNOWLEDGMENT
         ACKNOWLEDGMENT NOT INTERLOCKED
         ACKNOWLEDGMENT INTERLOCKED
```

**Figure 5-19.** Asynchronous Path Level and Pulse-Mode Taxonomy.

```
SYNCHRONOUS
ASYNCHRONOUS
  ONE-WAY COMMAND
    SOURCE-CONTROLLED
    DESTINATION-CONTROLLED
  REQUEST/ACKNOWLEDGE
    NON-INTERLOCKED
    HALF-INTERLOCKED
    FULLY INTERLOCKED
SEMISYNCHRONOUS
  ONE-WAY COMMAND
  REQUEST/ACKNOWLEDGE
    NON-INTERLOCKED
    HALF-INTERLOCKED
    FULLY INTERLOCKED
```

**Figure 5-20.** Path Communication Taxonomy.

Thus the reason why Thurber et al. coined the term *semisynchronous*. For the following discussion Thurber's synchronous and asynchronous discussions are used because Chen's approach, although more exhaustive, is overly complex for most designers. Self-clocking schemes are discussed in a special section. For a discussion of semisynchronous techniques, see Thurber et al. [1].

*Basic Asynchronous Communication*

Asynchronous bus communication techniques fall into two general categories— one-way command and request-acknowledge. In the following, a number of figures are used to illustrate the various asynchronous bus communication techniques which are commonly used. These figures utilize some primitive coordination signals, namely, data ready, data request, and data accept/bus available. More is said about these primitives (and other possible primitives) later in this chapter. However, for the remainder of this section, the reader should associate with these signals the rational interpretation which their names suggest.

*One-way command* refers to the fact that the data-transfer mechanism is completely controlled by only one of the two devices communicating—once the transfer is initiated, there is no interaction (except, perhaps, for an error signal). A one-way command (OWC) interface may be controlled by either the source or the destination device.

With a source-controlled OWC interface, the transmitting device places data on the bus and signals data ready to the receiving device, as seen in figure 5-21. Timing of data ready is highly dependent on implementation details, such as exactly how it is used by the destination device. If data ready itself directly strobes in the data, then it must be delayed long enough for the data to have propagated down the bus and settled at the receiving end before data ready arrives. Instead of "pipelining" data and data ready, it is safer to allow the data to reach the destination before generating data ready; but this makes the transfer rate a function of the physical distance between devices. A better approach is to make data ready as wide as the data and let the receiving device internally delay before loading.

The principal advantages of the source-controlled OWC interface are simplicity and speed. The major disadvantages are that there is no validity verification from the destination, it is difficult and inefficient to communicate between devices of different speed, and noise pulses on the data-ready line might be mistaken for valid signals. The noise problem can be minimized by proper timing, but usually at the expense of transfer rate.

The validity-check problem can be avoided with a destination-controlled OWC interface, such as shown in figure 5-22. The receiving device raises data request, which causes the source to place data on the bus. The destination now has the problem of deciding when to look at the data lines, which is related to the physical distance involved. If an error is detected in the word, the receiving device sends a data-error signal instead of another data request, so the validity-check time may limit the transfer rate. The speed is also adversely affected by higher initial overhead, and by twice the number of bus propagation delays as used by the source-controlled interface.

The request/acknowledge method of asynchronous communication can be separated into three cases—noninterlocked, half interlocked, and fully interlocked.

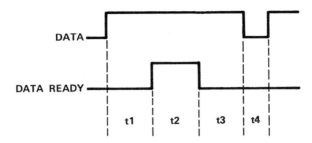

**Figure 5-21.** Asynchronous, Source-Controlled, One-Way-Command Communication. Reprinted with permission from K.J. Thurber, et al., "A Schematic Approach to the Design of Digital Bussing Structures," Proceedings of the FJCC, Montvale, N.J.: AIFPS Press.

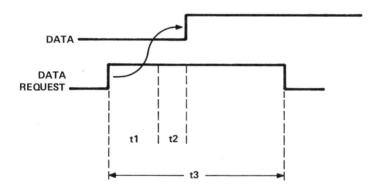

**Figure 5-22.** Asynchronous, Destination-Controlled, One-way-Command Communication. Reprinted with permission from K.J. Thurber, et al., "A Schematic Approach to the Design of Digital Bussing Structures," Proceedings of the FJCC, Montvale, N.J.: AFIPS Press.

Figure 5-23 illustrates the noninterlocked method. The source puts data on the bus and raises data ready; the destination stores the data and responds with data accept, which causes data ready to fall and new data to be placed on the lines. If an error is found in the data, the receiving device raises data error instead of data accept. This signal interchange not only provides error control but also permits operation between devices of any speeds. The price is primarily speed, although some added logic is also required. As with the one-way command interface, the exact timing is a function of the implementation. There are

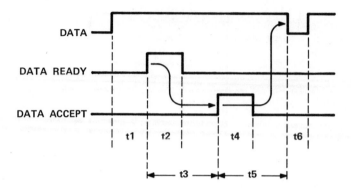

DATA

DATA READY

DATA ACCEPT

t1    t2         t4         t6

|◄— t3 —►|◄— t5 —►|

**Figure 5-23.** Asynchronous, Noninterlocked, Request/Acknowledge Communi-
cation. Reprinted with permission from K.J. Thurber, et al., "A
Schematic Approach to the Design of Digital Bussing Structures,"
Proceedings of the FJCC, Montvale, N.J.: AFIPS Press.

now two lines susceptible to noise and twice as many bus delays to consider.
Improper ratios of bus propagation time and communication-signal pulse widths
could allow another data ready to come and go while data accept is still high
in response to a previous one, which would hang up the entire bus.

This can be avoided by making data ready remain up until data accept (or
data error) is received by the source, as seen in figure 5-24. In this half-interlocked interface, if data ready comes up while data accept is still high, only the
transfer is delayed. Furthermore, the variable-width data ready tends to protect
it from noise. There is no speed penalty and very little hardware cost associated
with these improvements over the noninterlocked case.

One more potential timing error is possible if data accept extends over the
source buffer reload period and masks the leading edge of the next data ready.
Figure 5-25 shows how this is avoided with a fully interlocked interface where
a new data ready does not occur until the trailing edge of the old data accept
(or data error). Also, both communication signals are now comparatively noise-
immune. The device logic is again slightly more complex, but the major
disadvantage is that the bus delays have doubled over the half-interlocked case,
nearly halving the upper limit of the transfer rate.

*Basic Synchronous Communication*

In synchronous communication techniques, bus timing is generated via either
a global clock or with a combination of global and local clocks. In the global
case each pulse pair determines a "time slot" during which information may

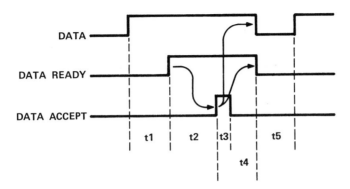

**Figure 5-24.** Asynchronous, Half-Interlocked, Request/Acknowledge Communication. Reprinted with permission from K.J. Thurber, et al., "A Schematic Approach to the Design of Digital Bussing Structures," Proceedings of the FJCC, Montvale, N.J.: AFIPS Press.

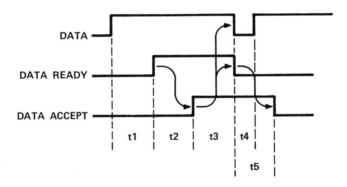

**Figure 5-25.** Asynchronous, Fully Interlocked, Request/Acknowledge Communication. Reprinted with permission from K.J. Thurber, et al. "A Schematic Approach to the Design of Digital Bussing Structures," Proceedings of the FJCC, Montvale, N.J.: AFIPS Press.

be transmitted. Global and local systems use the global clock to generate a frame. Local clocks then use the frame to generate subframe boundaries which are analogous to time slots. Such techniques are usually associated with long-distance communication. Since many of the tradeoffs associated with synchronous systems can best be discussed in terms of line-sharing or multiplexing techniques used in conjunction with the "time slots," that approach is used for the following discussion. Further, we assume that time slots have fixed duration; however, it is conceivable to generate variable-length time slots.

The bus timing can be generated globally or both globally and locally. A globally timed bus contains a central oscillator which broadcasts clock signals to all units on the bus. Depending on the logical structure and physical layout of the bus, clock skew may be a serious problem. This can be somewhat alleviated by distributing a globally generated frame signal which synchronizes a local clock in each device. The local clocks drive counters which are decoded to identify the time slot assigned to each device. A sync pulse occurs every time the count cycle (that is, frame) restarts. The device clocks must be within the initial frequency and temperature-coefficient tolerances determined by the bus timing characteristics. Skew can still exist if a separate frame sync line is used, but it can be avoided by putting frame sync in the data. The sync signal then must be separable from the data, generally through amplitude, phase, or coding characteristics. If the identifying characteristic is amplitude, the line drivers and receivers are much more complex analog circuits than those for simple binary data. If phase is used, the sync signal must be longer than a time slot, which costs bus bandwidth and again adds an analog dimension to the drivers and receivers. If the sync signal is coded as a special binary sequence, it could be confused with normal data, and can require complex decoders. All the global and global/local synchronization techniques are susceptible to noise errors.

There are two basic approaches to synchronous buses—the time slots may be assigned to devices on either a dedicated basis or a nondedicated basis. A mix of both dedicated and undedicated slots can also be used. If time slots are dedicated, they are permanently allocated to a device regardless of how frequently or infrequently that device uses them. Each device on the bus is allowed to communicate on a rotational (time-division multiplex) basis. The only way that any priority can be established is by assigning more than one slot to a device (sometimes called supercommutation). More than one device may be assigned to a single time slot by submultiplexing (subcommutating) slower or mutually exclusive devices.

Generally, not all devices will wish to transmit at once; system requirements may not even require or permit it. If any expansion facilities for additional devices are provided, many of the devices may not even be implemented on any given system. These two factors tend to waste bus bandwidth, and lowering the bandwidth to an expected "average" load may risk unacceptable conflicts and delays in peak traffic periods.

Another difficulty that reduces throughput on a dedicated-time-slot bus is that frequently not all devices are at the same speed. This means that if a device operates slower than the time-slot rate, it cannot run at its full speed. The time-slot rate could be selected to match the rate of the slowest device on the bus, but this slows down all faster devices. Alternatively, the time-slot rate can be made as fast as the fastest device on the bus, and buffers can be incorporated into the slower devices. Depending on the device-rate mismatches and the length of data blocks, these buffers could grow quite large. In addition, the buffers must be capable of simultaneous input and output (or one read and one write in a time-slot period), or else the whole transfer is delayed until the buffer is filled. Another approach is to run the bus faster than the slowest device and assign multiple time slots to that device, which complicates the control and wastes bus bandwidth if that device is not always transferring data. Special logic must also be included if burst or block transfers are to be permitted, since a device normally does not get adjacent time slots.

For reliability, it is generally desirable that the receiving device verify and acknowledge correct arrival of the data. This is most effectively done on a word basis unless the physical nature of the transmitting device precludes retry on anything other than a complete block or message. If a synchronous time slot is wide enough to allow a replay for every word, then data transmission will be slower than with an asynchronous bus because the time slots would have to be defined by the slowest device on the bus. One solution is to establish a system convention that verification is by default, and if any error does occur, a signal is returned to the source device $N$ time slots later (pipelined response). The destination has time to do the validity test without slowing the transfer rate; however, the source must retain all words which have been transmitted but not verified.

Nondedicated time slots are provided to devices only as needed, which improves bus utilization efficiency at the cost of slot-allocation hardware. Block transfers and priority-assignment schemes are possible if the bus-assignment mechanism is fast enough. The device-speed and error-checking limitations of the dedicated case are also shared by nondedicated systems.

*Self-Clocking Techniques*

Previously we discussed whether such techniques (self-clocking) were synchronous. In this section briefly describe some of these techniques and their potential implementation. Consider the following module: (1) a sending device $D_S$, (2) a receiving device $D_R$, and (3) a set of information lines. Assume that there are three time states: (1) $T_B$, time before transmission; (2) $T_S$ time of "synchronization"; (3) $T_D$, time of data transfer.

Assume that $D_S$ wishes to transmit to $D_R$. Further, ignore the problems of getting $D_S$ and $D_R$ connected to the bus and concentrate on the actual transmission of information. A typical self-clocked system operates as follows. During $T_B$, $D_S$ and $D_R$ are connected to the bus; during $T_S$, $D_S$ begins the "information" transfer and $D_R$ derives the appropriate synchronization information from the "transmitted" information; after $D_R$ has synchronized itself to the $D_S$-transmitted data stream, it then, during $T_D$, interprets the information stream as data. Thus, $D_S$ sends a two-part message—timing information followed by data. $D_R$ may use the timing information to synchronize a local clock, or it may operate asynchronously. If it operates asynchronously (without a clock), at specified intervals the timing data may have to be resent. Logically, self-clocking techniques may be viewed as clocks generated by $D_S$ any interpreted by $D_R$. Typically, the timing information may be transmitted by using a special bit sequence (see the special ASCII character SYN in chapter 6); bit stuffing (see the discussion of SDLC in chapter 6); a special phase, frequency, or amplitude; or any other characteristics that the designer can isolate. The semisynchronous transmission technique suggested by Thurber uses the bus-available line as the logical clock. The $D_r$ monitors the lines looking for the synchronizing information; and when it sees the appropriate information, it synchronizes itself to the information sequence and then begins to receive the data. One advantage of such a concept occurs with a transition system. Once the devices become synchronized, only bit changes need be sent (0 and 1 and 1 to 0) because no transmission during a "time slot" indicates no change in data value.

Logically, carrying the clock with the data is equivalent to a central clock.

## Characterization of Techniques

Given a complex bus communication technique, there is a description problem which exists in attempting to specify its nature. One way to specify such techniques to form a set consisting of the signals used in the bus communication technique wherein the entries in the set partially characterize the technique. In addition, the bus communication techniques can be characterized by a state diagram or an extended version of the previously given timing diagrams which shoe arbitration, connection, and so on in addition to communication details. The transitions between states for a bus communication technique can be shown in a state diagram. If state techniques are used, then classical minimization and modifying techniques for state diagrams can be utilized such that the bus communication techniques can be composed and analyzed, and in a more abstract and hopefully efficient fashion. The same techniques could be applied to protocols and so on. To set up a presentation of characterization of bus communication techniques by such means, the coordination signals transferred between devices must first be further described beyond the signal descriptions used in the earlier consideration of bais communication techniques.

In general, the set of coordination signals used for a communication technique can usually be grouped according to their information content as (1) state signals, (2) action signals, and (3) response signals. As we have seen, a physical coordination signal on a line of the bus can, at times, fall into more than one group. In particular, we discuss in the following cases where state signals or action signals also serve as response signals. However, before such joint classification can be appreciated, we must further discuss each of the groupings.

Generally two types of state signals are used for coordination in bus communication techniques. The first type consists of signals sent by (what will be when the data transfer is in progress) the data-sending device to (what will be when the data transfer is in progress) the data-receiving device. These state signals notify the data-receiving device that the data-sending device is in a state in which a data transfer can take place. The second type consists of signals sent by (what will be when the data transfer is in progress) the data-receiving device to (what will be when the data transfer is in progress) the data-sending device. These state signals notify the data-sending device that the data-receiving device is in a state in which a data transfer can take place. In the following, we refer to the former as a sending-device-ready (SDR) signal and to the later as receiving-device-ready (RDR) signals.

Note that both these signals indicate a state of preparedness of one of the devices relative to an impending information transmission. Moreover, these state signals can also be implemented to indicate degrees of preparedness in the sense that such a signal can indicate either that the device is in a completely prepared state for commencement of information transmission or a degree of progress toward such a state. We therefore refer to the former as zero-order state signals and the latter as higher-order state signals (that is, first-order state signals. second-order state signals, and so on). We denote such signals $SDR_0$, $SDR_1$, $SDR_2$, ... and $RDR_0$, $RDR_1$, $RDR_2$, ..., respectively. It shall be kept in mind here that the term *degree* is used in a somewhat abstract sense. It implies that the progression of the data-sending or data-receiving device toward a state in which the transmission of data is necessary can be measured or quantified in some way. The extent to which this is true depends, of course, on the application. Intuitively, it is clear that knowledge of such progress is theoretically useful for reliability and efficiency considerations.

A partial characterization of a bus communication technique would thus be an association of the technique with the set consisting of an $i$-tuple ($SDR_0$, $SDR_1$, ..., $SDR_i$) and a $j$-tuple ($RDR_0$, $RDR_1$, ..., $RDR_j$) corresponding to the state signals implemented in the technique: $S = [(SDR_0, SDR_1, ..., SDR_i), (RDR_0, RDR_1, ..., RDR_j)]$.

In most bus communication techniques, there are primarily two types of action signals used for coordination—signals sent by the data-sending device to the data-receiving device notifying the data-receiving device that data have been placed on the data bus lines, and signals send by the data-receiving device to the data-sending device notifying the data-sending device that the data bus lines have been read. In the following we refer to the former as data-sent (DS) signals and to the latter as data-accepted (DA) signals. Note that both these signals indicate an action that has taken place.

Another partial characterization of a bus communication technique would then be an association of the schema with the set $A$, where $A$ is the subset of the two-element action class set, $[DS,DA]$, which are implemented in the schema: $AC[DS,DA]$. Clearly, $A$ is not necessarily a proper or nonempty subset of $[DS,DA]$.

In a bus communication technique, response signals are acknowledgments to state, action, or other response signals. They can be used to indicate simply that a previously sent signal was, indeed, received; or, on a somewhat higher level, they can be used to indicate that not only was previously sent signal received, but also some condition was met or operation was accomplished in response to it. They are, in effect, a means of tightening the coordination between the sending and receiving devices.

A response signal can be implemented separately or by combining the response with a state or action signal. The former requires an additional coordination bus line and additional hardware; the latter requires that a particular signal have multiple implications. We denote a signal and a response by an ordered pair, the first entry of the pair being the signal designation and the second entry being the response-signal designation. When the response signal is separate, the second entry in the ordered response pair is denoted by $K$ (signal designation); otherwise, the standard signal designation is used for the second entry. For example, suppose we have a separate response signal to SDR; then this would be denoted as (SDR,$K$(SDR)). Suppose, instead, we have the RDR as the response to SDR; this would be denoted as (SDR,RDR). Finally, suppose we have a separate response to the $K$(SDR); this would be denoted as ($K$(SDR), $K$($K$(SDR))).

The response signal originates at a device as an acknowledgment of reception with, perhaps, some indication of a condition to a coordination signal transmitted by the other device of the sender-receiver pair.

Another partial characterization of a bus communication technique would then be an association of the technique with a set of ordered pairs $K$, where, as described, each ordered pair represents a signal (state, action, or response) and its response. The absence of an ordered pair in $K$ having a particular signal as its first entry indicates that the signal has no generated response in the associated bus communication technique.

A final characterization of a bus communication technique would then be the association of the technique with a set of interlocked pairs denoted as $I$. For each pair contained in $I$, the first entry of the pair is the signal designation and the second entry is the response with which it is interlocked. Because the response with which a signal can be interlocked might be a particular aspect of a signal, we use brackets [ ... ] following the signal designation to add the necessary information which will make the interlocking schema clear. For example, suppose that DR was interlocked with the on-level of $DA$; furthermore, suppose that $DA$ was interlocked with the off-level of $DR$. Then we would have that $(DR,DA\,[=on\,]) \in I$, and $(DA,DR\,[=off\,]) \in I$. As an alternative, suppose that the $DA$ was instead interlocked with the on-to-off transition of DR. Then $(DR,DA\,[on \rightarrow off\,]) \in I$.

Thus, a bus communication technique can be characterized by the four-tuple $[S,A,K,I]$. Chapter 2 in Chen's thesis [2] deals with the problems and schemes for bus synchronization. Chen defines a terminology that allows simple arithmetic computations to be done to determine such things as "reliability" of a synchronization protocol, minimum period of each protocol, and "cost" to implement a protocol.

The terminology he uses is in the form of a vector whose elements are binary values representing the use (1) or disuse (0) of a particular protocol signal. The vector **P** contains four elements, and they are $P[1] = 1$ *SR* (sender ready), $P[2] = 1$ *RR* (receiver ready), $P[3] = 1$ *DR* (data ready), and $P[4] = 1$ *DA* (data accept). For example, $P[1] = 1$ means that *SR* is used in the protocol; or if $P[1] = 0$, then *SR* is not used in the protocol. In a similar way Chen defines vectors **K**[.] , each of which contains four elements corresponding to the four possible protocol signals used. The **K**[.] vector contains a 1 for an element if the protocol signal used has a separate acknowledge and 0 if it does not. The **C**[.] vector contains a 1 for an element if the protocol signal used has a combined acknowledge/synchronization. In addition to these vectors two other possible specifications can be made. They are *i* meaning that that particular protocol signal is interlocked with its acknowledge, and *a*, meaning that that particular protocol signal is fully interlocked with its acknowledge.

Chen also defines certain time quantities that are used in his computations for the minimum period for the execution of a protocol. He defines them as follows: $T_p$, propagation time; $T_t$, transition time; $T_s$, skewing time; and $T_r$, recording time. By using these times in combination with the vectors containing the information of what protocol signals are used, Chen formulates equations giving the minimum period for a particular case of protocol signals.

Chen classifies three modes of synchronization primitives—pulse, level, and transition. With each mode, considerations are made in terms of the time quantities defined, and the minimum period equations are reformulated for each operation mode of synchronization. When Chen deals with the use of acknowledgments, he considers two problems—missing a synchronization signal and overlapping (or runover) synchronization signals. Both problems are talked about, and he proposes a simple test for the occurrence of each problem and a possible way of correcting the problem in terms of interlocking the signals.

However, in addition to the four-tuples suggested by Chen, we could also use state diagrams to describe bus communication techniques, say, IEEE bus standard [10] and Sunshine's gateway concepts [11].

### Summary and Conclusion

A number of example systems utilize various forms of the previously discussed bus control and communication techniques. The majority of systems tend to use either a centralized independent request [12] or a decentralized daisy-chain [5] technique. Some systems have adopted polling techniques [13]. Tandem Computer Corporation is building a fault-tolerant system around its DYNABUS (registered trademark), but because of patent considerations details are unavailable at this time [14]. Other important busses and their arbitrator techniques include independent requests and daisy-chaining, DEC Unibus [15]; independent requests and daisy-chaining, INFIBUS [16]. A bus design using a priority algorithm is given in Pirtle [17]. Random-access techniques could be viewed as a form of implicit requests [8, 9].

Bus communication techniques have been considered broadly in the literature. Most authors, however, consider the subject in a somewhat secondary manner or in discussions concerning input-output systems. Reference 18 discusses the information lines necessary to communicate in a system. References 19, 20, and 21 cover synchronous systems. References 22 and 23 are good presentations of the synchronous clock-skew problem. Reference 24 deals with the design of a frame and slotted system. Reference 25 describes the design of modems. Reference 26 discusses bit stuffing for synchronization. The synchronous system in reference 27 uses a combination of global and local timing. Reference 28 deals with a synchronous system with nondedicated time slots. Reference 29 is about transmission error checking and serial-by-byte transmission. References 30, 31, and 32 cover buffering and block size from a statistical point of view in simple bus structures such as loops. Reference 33 studies the choice of block sizes. Reference 34 considers the buffering problem.

Reference 2 includes a unique and detailed examination of deadlock prevention and detection and recovery algorithms from the standpoint of hardware interconnection mechanisms.

Implicit versus explicit multiplexing was discussed earlier in this book and in reference 3.

Lamport [35] gives an elegant description of the problems associated with synchronizing a distributed system.

Before concluding this chapter, some comments on the importance of four papers are in order. There are two classic papers in the bus structure field—Thurber et al. [1] and Chen [2]. Two new papers, Levy [36] and Luczak [37], also deserve considerable attention. The paper by Thurber et al. is a classic in this field. Its importance is due to its complete architectural coverage of the subject which provides a timeless design guide. Chen's article is important because of its coverage of deadlocks and its notational development. Chen also provides an extensive discussion of asynchronous communication possibility; however, the concept, while elegant, leaves too many choices to be practically useful. Chen's arbitration discussion does not meet the standards of excellence of his other developed material. Levy presents the most important implementation-oriented description of bus structures done to date. For a designer wishing a machine-oriented discussion of bus structure design issues with extensive discussion of each issue keyed to successful buses used in DEC computers, Levy is a "must."

Luczak provides a significant discussion of random-access bus structure concepts in the overall context of channel access algorithms categorized into selective, random access, and reservation. The random-access development is quite good; however, it does mix implementation and architecture issues. The discussion on selective-access techniques is remarkably close to that of Thurber et al., and the reservation techniques described can be implemented as special cases of "selective" architectures. The extensions (implicit control) to the Thurber et al. arbitration concepts given in this book encompass all of Luczak's categories. The details of random-access implementation techniques given in Luczak are extremely important.

This chapter discussed the main generic types of centralized and decentralized control techniques—daisy-chaining, polling, independent requests, and implicit. The major tradeoffs and comparison between each of the techniques were discussed along with the major tradeoffs to be considered in selecting a control technique. The most important thing to be learned from studying these generic control techniques is the ability to visualize the different system performances that may be obtainable from the designer's choice.

Further, the chapter discussed the main forms of synchronous, asynchronous, and self-clocking communications. The major tradeoffs and implementation problems were discussed for each of the considered techniques. Techniques for characterizing and describing the complete design were discussed as well as contemporary representation techniques to specify the design.

## Note

1. For the purposes of discussion a *word* is defined as the basic unit of information regardless of the number of contained bits, and a *block* consists of contiguous words.

## Exercises

1. Construct a tradeoff table which tabulates arbitration speed, number of lines, possible algorithms, and so on, for the bus arbitration schemes discussed in this chapter.

2. Design a centralized independent-request bus arbitrator for an eight-device system which can be used in a redundant system with two identical bus arbitrators that connect to all eight devices. *Note*: Ensure that deadlocks cannot occur in the redundant configuration. Use state diagrams to describe the design.

3. Design a decentralized daisy-chain arbitration scheme which passes control by using a coded transfer.

4. Construct a tradeoff table which tabulates speed, data-error possibilities, number of control signals, and so on for the asynchronous and synchronous communication schemes discussed in this chapter.

5. Design a fully interlocked request/acknowledge transmission interface. Use state tables to describe the design.

6. Design a bit-serial 32-MHz synchronous time-slotted transmission interface which time-multiplexes/demultiplexes sixteen 2-MHz bit-serial synchronous sources onto a single line.

## References

[ 1] K.J. Thurber et al., "A Systematic Approach to the Design of Digitial Bussing Structures," *Proceedings of the FJCC* Montvale, N.J.: AFIPS Press, portions reprinted with permission.

[ 2] R.C. Chen, *Bus Communication Systems* Montvale, N.J.: AFIPS Press, Dissertation, Carnegie-Mellon 1974).

[ 3] E.D. Jensen, K.J. Thurber, and G.M. Schneider, "A Review of Systematic Methods in Distributed Processor Interconnection," *Proceedings of the International Communications Conference*, 1976.

[ 4] G.A. Anderson and E.D. Jensen, "Computer Interconnection Structures: Taxonomy, Characteristics, and Examples," *ACM Computing Surveys*, December 1975.

[ 5] R.L. Alonso et al., "A Multiprocessor Structure," *Proceedings of the IEEE*, September 1967.

[ 6] K.J. Thurber et al., "Master Executive Control for AADC," Navy Contract N62269-72-C-0051, National Technical Information Service, June 1972.

[ 7] G.A. Anderson, "Interconnecting a Distributed Processor System for Avionics," First Annual Symposium on Computer Architecture, IEEE Computer Society, December 1973.

[ 8] R.M. Metcalfe and D.R. Boggs, "Ethernet: Distributed Packet Switching for Local Computer Networks," *CACM*, July 1976.

[ 9] N. Abramson, "The Aloha System," *Computer-Communication Networks* (Englewood Cliffs, N.J.: Prentice-Hall 1973).

[10] IEEE Standard 488-1975; D.E. Knoblock, D.C. Loughry, and C.A. Vissers, "Insight into Interfacing," *IEEE Spectrum*, May 1975.

[11] C.A. Sunshine, "Interprocess Communication Protocols for Computer Networks" (Ph.D. thesis, Stanford University, 1976).

[12] S.J. Andelman, "Real-Time I/O Techniques to Reduce System Costs," *Computer Design*, May 1966.

[13] P.E. Payne, "A Method of Data Transmission Requiring Maximum Turnaround Time," *Computer Design*, November 1968.

[14] J.A. Katzman, "System Architecture for Non-Stop Computing," *COMPCON West*, 1977.

[15] Digital Equipment Corporation, *PDO-11 Peripherals Handbook*, Maynard, Mass.: 1975.

[16] Lockheed, *Sue Computer Handbook*, Los Angeles, Calif. 1972.

[17] M. Pirtle, "Intercommunication of Processors and Memory," *FJCC*, 1967.

[18] R. Rinder, "The Input/Output Architecture of Minicomputers," *Datamation*, May 1970, pp. 119-124.

[19] N. Clark and A.C. Gannet, "Computer-to-Computer Communication at 2.5 Megabit/sec," *Proceedings of IFIP Congress*, North-Holland Publishing Company, September 1962, pp. 347-353.

[20] Collins Radio Corporation, *C-System Overview*, Dallas, Texas, October 1, 1969.

[21] J.S. Mayo, "An Approach to Digital System Network," *IEEE Transactions on Communication Technology*, April 1967, pp. 307-310.

[22] G.P. Hyatt, "Digital Data Transmission," *Computer Design* 6, no. 11, (November 1967): 26-30.

[23] J.W. Schwartz, "Synchronization in Communication Satellite Systems," *NEC*, 1967, pp. 526-527.

[24] C.D. Smith, "Optimization of Design Parameters for Serial TDM," *Computer Design*, January 1972, pp. 51-54.

[25] J.R. Davey, "Modems," *Proceedings of the IEEE* 60 (November 1972): 1284-1292.

[26] M.W. Willard and L.J. Horkan, "Maintaining Bit Integrity in Time Division Transmission," *NAECON*, 1971, pp. 240-247.

[27] R.H. Hardin, "Self Sequencing Data Bus Technique for Space Shuttle," *Proceedings Space Shuttle Integrated Electronic Conference* 2 (1971): 111-139.

[28] M.P. Ristenbatt and D.R. Rothschild, "Asynchronous Time Multiplexing," *IEEE Transactions on Communication Technology*, June 1968, pp. 349-357.

[29] A. Avizienis, "Design of Fault-Tolerant Computers," *Proceedings FJCC*, AFIPS Press, 1967, pp. 733-743.

[30] G.N. Cedarquist, "An Input/Output System for Multiprogrammed Computer," Report No. 223, Department of Computer Science, University of Illinois, Urbana, Ill. April 1967.

[31] W.W. Chu, "A Study of Asynchronous Time Division Multiplexing for Time Sharing Computer Systems," *Proceedings FJCC*, AFIPS Press, 1969, pp. 669-678.

[32] W.W. Chu, "Demultiplexing Considerations for Statistical Multiplexers," *IEEE Transactions on Computers*, June 1972, pp. 603-609.

[33] D.H. Gibson, "Considerations in Block-Oriented Systems Design," *Proceedings SJCC*, AFIPS Press, 1967, pp. 75-80.

[34] A.L. Leiner, "Buffering between Input/Output and the Computer" *Proceedings FJCC*, 1962, pp. 22-31.

[35] L. Lamport, "Time, Clocks, and Ordering of Events in a Distributed System," *CACM*, July 1978, pp. 558-565.

[36]  J.V. Levy, "Buses, The Skeleton of Computer Structures," *Computer Engineering: A DEC View of Hardware Systems Design*, eds. G.G. Bell et al. (Maynard, Mass: Digital Press, 1978).

[37]  E.C. Luczak, "Global Bus Computer Communication Techniques," *Proceedings of the 1978 Computer Networking Symposium*, pp. 58-67.

# 6

# Transmission Techniques and Data-Link Controls

## Introduction

In chapter 5, digital bus communication techniques were discussed. In this chapter, more general communication design issues are considered [1 to 8]. The reason for this chapter is that it is common to have to interface to devices other than processors, for example, a remote dial-up, a modem, a satellite, and so on. Thus, it is necessary to have an understanding of different types of transmission and data-link techniques.

A number of different techniques can be used to encode data onto lines. This chapter describes a large number of these techniques. The major design issues covered are:

1. Transmission direction and overlap
2. Transmission-rate measurements
3. Modulation techniques
4. Multiplexing
5. Modems
6. Character assembly
7. Message assembly
8. Code standards
9. Data-link control (DLC) protocols

The techniques described in this chapter are representative of the design issues encountered at the data-link control level (level 0) discussed in chapter 3. In a sense this chapter could be considered as part of chapter 3, since in chapter 3 we primarily discussed level 1 considerations. Further, the detailed techniques discussed in this chapter could be the basis of the actual transmission implementation of a circuit switch (chapter 4). In chapter 4, we dealt only with the global switch design and control problem; thus the level 0 design issues for the circuit switch could be implemented using the techniques developed here or via techniques discussed under the communication topics in chapter 5 on bus structure techniques.

## Transmission Direction and Overlap

Three major techniques are commonly applied to signal transmission: (1) simplex, (2) half-duplex, and (3) full duplex. Each of these techniques incorporates different direction and overlap concepts.

In a simplex system, signals may travel only from point $A$ to point $B$. Further, since there is only one signal in the system, there is no opportunity for simultaneous overlap.

A half-duplex system allows for signals to travel in both directions, that is, from point $A$ to point $B$ and from point $B$ to point $A$. However, only one signal may be present at any given time. Thus, it is not legal for both point $A$ and point $B$ to simultaneously overlap transmission.

Full-duplex systems, on the other hand, allow for transmission from point $A$ to point $B$ and from point $B$ to point $A$ simultaneously. Thus, transmission may be simultaneous; however, at least two wires are necessary.

The concepts of simplex, half-duplex, and full-duplex transmission do not imply any inherent speed, length, or constancy of transmission issues. They simply denote direction and signal-overlap capabilities. The different techniques previously discussed are summarized in table 6-1.

**Transmission-Rate Measurements**

The speed at which messages are exchanged in a system may vary considerably. Thus systems must have a means of measuring and calculating this exchange rate. In digital equipment, the rate may be expressed in bits per second, where a bit consists of the normal digital quantity, a bit which is in either the 0 or 1 state. However, since equipment in a distributed processor may also connect to analog or telephone devices, bit rates are not a totally satisfactory measurement technique. Another measure of transmission rate is the baud rate. A *baud* consists of a change in signal state which represents a defined signal intelligence. Thus the baud rate is the rate of signal modulation. Further, the baud rate may

**Table 6-1**
**Summary of Transmission Techniques**

| TYPE OF OPERATION | MESSAGE FLOW | SIGNAL OVERLAP |
|---|---|---|
| SIMPLEX | A TO B | NOT ALLOWED |
| HALF DUPLEX | A TO B AND B TO A | NOT ALLOWED |
| FULL DUPLEX | A TO B AND B TO A | ALLOWED |

not equal the bit rate. If a system were defined, for example, where a particular phase shift represented a particular bit pair (dibit), then the baud rate would be half the bit rate. If, however, the system were defined such that a signal change represented a bit (for example, a positive pulse represented a 1 and a negative pulse a 0), then the bit rate and baud rate would be equal.

## Modulation Techniques

Many techniques can be used to modulate a signal. A large number of these are discussed, along with their tradeoffs:

1. Amplitude modulation (AM)
2. Frequency modulation (FM)
3. Phase modulation (PHM)
4. Pulse modulation (PUM)

These transmission techniques differ in their noise susceptability, rate of effective transmission, reliability characteristics, economic constraints, standardization and current usage, effectiveness versus distance characteristics, and ability to interface to currently deployed equipments.

### Amplitude Modulation

Amplitude modulation (AM) techniques vary the amplitude of a carrier wave. This, in effect, superimposes an envelope on the carrier wave of a lower frequency. This envelope then contains the modulated information. The amount of modulation may vary. In some cases the maximum modulation may be limited to 50 percent of the carrier level; in another case the modulation may be 100 percent; in a third case, the carrier may actually be stopped and started (figure 6-1). AM systems tend to be sensitive to noise (which is usually present in a digital system) and therefore tend to be useful in systems where (1) signal amplitude is not subject to rapid level fluctuations, (2) low noise levels can be expected, and (3) there exist inherent frequency-interference conditions. If those conditions cannot be met, then an FM concept would probably be a better choice.

### Frequency Modulation

Frequency modulation (FM) techniques tend to be useful in environments where (1) considerable signal-level variations are expected, (2) noise is expected, and (3) inherent frequency stability exists. The concept of FM is to keep the signal

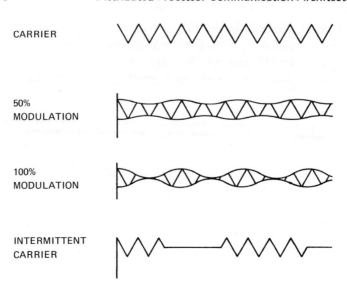

**Figure 6-1.** Amplitude Modulation.

amplitude constant but vary the frequency about some carrier frequency. Some common terms need to be defined for FM:

1. *Baseband* is the carrier frequency.
2. *Sideband* is the modulated baseband signal.
3. *Space bandwidth* is the frequency spectrum which separates multiple baseband signals.

Figure 6-2 indicates an FM transmission scheme known as FSK (frequency-shift keying). In this scheme the presence of the baseband frequency indicates a no-data condition, the presence of the upper sideband represents a binary 1, and the presence of the lower sideband represents a binary 0. Clearly, only one sideband can be present at any given time. In FM systems, several base-bands may be present simultaneously. Thus, there is a tradeoff to be made among channel spacing (space bandwidth) and distortion, available frequency spectrum, and filter characteristics. In general, the transmitters' spaceband requirements are much less stringent than the receivers' spaceband requirements, thus causing the receiver to require better filter hardware. This occurs because transmitters must avoid only encroaching on other basebands, while receivers must not only select the proper baseband but also suppress unwanted interference resulting from other signals. Generally, frequency stability is a problem in FM systems, and frequency oscillators must be accurate to within at least one part in at least $10^6$. Typically, the larger the difference between sidebands, the less sensitive the receiver must be.

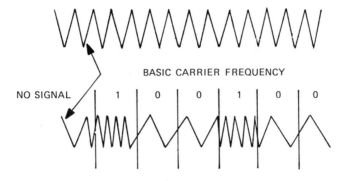

BASIC CARRIER FREQUENCY

NO SIGNAL

| 1 | 0 | 0 | 1 | 0 | 0 |

FREQUENCY IS SHIFTED BETWEEN A
HIGHER AND LOWER FREQUENCY
TO TRANSMIT 1's AND 0's.

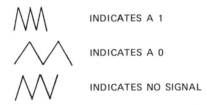

INDICATES A 1

INDICATES A 0

INDICATES NO SIGNAL

**Figure 6-2.** Frequency Modulation.

*Phase Modulation*

Phase modulation (PHM) techniques operate on the phase characteristic of the carrier wave (usually a sine wave). Each change in phase indicates a transmission. In such systems, the change in phase is keyed (referenced) to the current signal phase and is not keyed to a fixed or zero-phase position. The signal may be viewed as being contained in a phase change which is the absolute value of the amount that the phase is increased. Because phase-change detectors can detect only large changes in phase, digital data are the major type of information transmitted using PHM techniques. It is possible to utilize a combination of phase modulation and amplitude modulation to simultaneously transmit two channels of information on a single carrier. An example of a phase-modulation system with 90° denoting a 1 and 180° denoting a 0 transmitting 1011 is illustrated in figure 6-3.

*Pulse Modulation*

The last major type of modulation is pulse modulation. Pulse modulations may be either encoded or not encoded. If the pulse modulation is encoded,

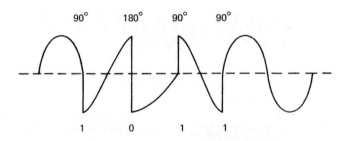

**Figure 6-3**. Phase Modulation.

its "value" is interpreted into more than two values; that is, it is interpreted into a multibit value which consists of a digital representation of the data value. For example, 8-bit bytes could be transmitted utilizing pulse techniques if the receivers could discriminate between 256 different pulse combinations. Pulses may be differentiated via three major techniques—(1) amplitude, (2) width, and (3) time—since a pulse has three main characteristics—height, width, and spacing. The three pulse-modulation techniques (see table 6-2 and figure 6-4 to 6-6) are:

1. Pulse-amplitude modulation (PAM)
2. Pulse-width modulation (PWM)
3. Pulse-position modulation (PPM)

In PAM, the spacing and width of the pulse are constant. The modulation occurs when the pulse's amplitude is varied. This varying amplitude can then be interpreted either as a sine wave envelope or as encoded pulses to obtain the digital data stream. Similarly, in PWM and PPM, the width and position are varied with the amplitude/position and amplitude/width being held constant, respectively. Note, that the digital pulse techniques discussed in chapter 5 could be considered as additional cases of pulse-transmission techniques.

*Implemented Techniques*

In practice, the most common techniques used for data transmission are frequency-shift keying (FSK) and phase-shift keying (PSK). Both techniques are discussed in more detail.

Typically, in FSK systems either two frequencies (representing 0 and 1) or three frequencies (representing 0, 1, and no signal) are used. Obviously, FSK does not use all the capabilities of FM techniques. The main problem with FSK is *jitter*, that is, fluctuation in the waveform caused by waveform

**Table 6-2**
**Summary of Pulse-Modulation Techniques**

| TECHNIQUE | CONSTANT | VARIABLE |
|-----------|----------|----------|
| PAM | WIDTH/POSITION | AMPLITUDE |
| PWM | AMPLITUDE/POSITION | WIDTH |
| PPM | AMPLITUDE/WIDTH | POSITION |

CONSTANT PULSE WIDTH AND FREQUENCY CARRIER
(COULD ALSO USE BOTH POLARITY PULSES IF DESIRED)

**Figure 6-4**. Pulse-Amplitude Modulation.

CONSTANT SPACING

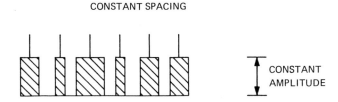

CONSTANT
AMPLITUDE

**Figure 6-5**. Pulse-Width Modulation.

discontinuity when the frequency is shifted. This problem can be solved by restricting frequency shifts to occur only when the waveform crosses zero. This technique is known as *FSK-synchronous*. (Synchronous in this case has a different meaning from that defined in chapter 5.) Nonsynchronous FSK does not restrict the frequency shift to occur at the zero crossing (half-cycle points) and thus can handle a larger message volume; however, nonsynchronous techniques

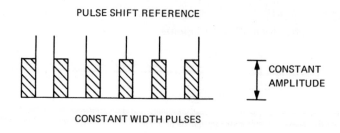

Figure 6-6. Pulse-Position Modulation.

incur jitter, and thus a tradeoff must be made between jitter (and its impact on reliability) and message volume. Jitter in FM systems is analogous to noise in an AM system.

In certain systems, the carrier may be filtered out at the transmitter. In this case, the carrier must be reintroduced at the receiver. This process is known as *carrier regeneration* and allows the designer to optimize the design for line distance, distortion and so forth. The major problem with this technique is that the oscillators at the receiver and transmitter may not be the same, thus introducing errors and distortion. Carrier regeneration is beyond the scope of this discussion and is mentioned only for completeness.

Phase-shift keying (PSK) is used to transmit binary data in an analogous fashion as FSK; however, only two phase shifts are typically used. The Bell System has introduced a very clever and important concept which they have used in some modems. It is known as *dibit PSK*. In this case they let a phase shift represent a bit pair; that is, 00, 01, 10, and 11 are represented by four distinct phase shifts. In this system, then, the bit rate is twice the baud rate. Further, to allow for maximum practical use of channel bandwidth, two channels are defined. Channel 1 uses phase shifts of $\theta$, $\theta + 90°$, $\theta + 180°$, and $\theta + 270°$. Channel 2 is offset 45° from channel 1; that is, it uses phase shifts of $\theta + 45°$, $\theta + 135°$, $\theta + 225°$, and $\theta + 315°$. The system then sends two channels of information by alternating between channel 1 and channel 2 transmissions. Thus, the channels are kept track of by knowing that they are operating in an alternating fashion using different phase shifts.

### Multiplexing

Previously, the concept of alternating data from two channels onto a single channel was mentioned. Multiplexing a channel or line is the technique used to alternate signals on a line. There are two forms of multiplexing—time-division multiplexing (TDM) and frequency-division multiplexing (FDM).

Time multiplexing divides the transmitted signal into discrete time slots. Typically, several lines supply inputs to the TDM system. The system then samples the inputs and composes a single output message for transmission. If every channel is sampled sequentially $(1, 2, \ldots, n, 1, 2, \ldots, n, 1, 2, \ldots)$ in round robin fashion and the data on each channel are sent, then no identifier is necessary with the data. If, however, not every channel is sent every time it has a slot available to it, then an identifier must be provided so that the multiplexer at the other end can unscramble the received data. Which type of TDM is designed depends on the complexity allowed for the multiplexer and a trade-off between the bandwidth needed for the identifier and the bandwidth wasted by transmitting unnecessary information.

FDM techniques also use a single line to transmit multiple channels. Typically, each channel is assigned its own separate baseband frequency. Then several channels may be simultaneously transmitted on a single line. The baseband and sideband frequencies must be chosen so they do not overlap into the assigned frequencies of other channels.

## Modems

Modems are the device which typically is used to connect a digital device to a phone line or other analog channel. Typically, a modem performs four functions:

1. It converts the digital stream to an "analog" data stream and controls the transmission.
2. It converts the "analog" data stream to a digital data stream.
3. It controls data flow through the modem.
4. It provides error recovery and test signals.

A typical FSK modem is block-diagrammed in figure 6-7.

## Character Assembly and Messages

So far we have discussed bit transmission. The system must make sense out of bit streams. This is accomplished by extracting characters out of bit streams and extracting messages out of characters.

There are three main types of characters: (1) fixed-pattern control characters, (2) variable-pattern control characters, and (3) variable-pattern data characters. Control characters are used to signal such things as start of message, synchronization functions, error control, and so on. These characters can be extracted from the bit stream by hardware or software techniques. After the devices have been initiated and synchronized, data are transmitted. Data

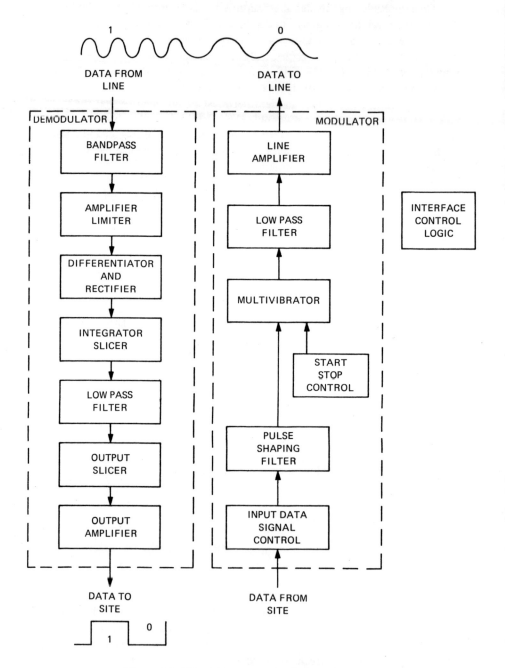

**Figure 6-7.** Block Diagram of a Typical Modem.

characters have bit patterns that correspond to symbols, numbers, alphabetic characters, and so forth. Figure 6-8 shows a simple message format. Messages may be of fixed length and format, or the format or length may be variable. Sometimes complete messages may have to be exchanged in a "request/acknowledge" format when equipment is first turned on to set up the appropriate system connections (bootstrapping). These special messages may have special formats and characters.

## Codes

A number of standard codes are in use today. These codes assign bit patterns to specific characters. Some of the more important codes are ASCII (more properly known as USASCII—United States of America Standard Code for Information Interchange), Excess-3 (XS-3) code, and EBCDIC (Extended Binary-Code Decimal Interchange Code). Figures 6-9, 6-10, and 6-11 illustrate the alphabetic, numeric, and miscellaneous ASCII code conventions, respectively.

ASCII is an 8-bit code, but functionally it is really a 7-bit code since only 7 of the 8 bits are available for a fixed bit pattern. The unassigned eighth bit is usually used for parity (error control).

In some cases it may be necessary to process at a rate which exceeds that available in a bit-serial link. There is nothing that would preclude the transmission of a code in characters, that is, on a set of parallel data paths with one

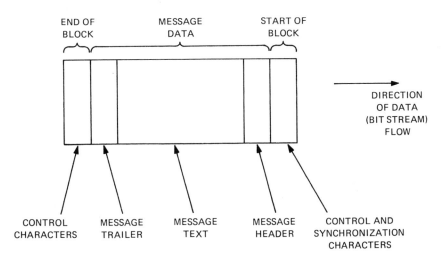

**Figure 6-8.** Typical Message Format.

| NUMERICAL ORDER OF ALPHABET | BINARY DIGIT VALUE | | | | | CODE PULSE (1's) BIT POSITIONS | |
|---|---|---|---|---|---|---|---|
| | $(2^4)$ 16 | $(2^3)$ 8 | $(2^2)$ 4 | $(2^1)$ 2 | $(2^0)$ 1 | | |
| A – 1 — 0 | 0 | 0 | 0 | 1 — 1 | | & 7 |
| B – 2 — 0 | 0 | 0 | 1 | 0 — 2 | | & 7 |
| C – 3 — 0 | 0 | 0 | 1 | 1 — 1, 2 | | & 7 |
| D – 4 — 0 | 0 | 1 | 0 | 0 — 3 | | & 7 |
| E – 5 — 0 | 0 | 1 | 0 | 1 — 1, 3 | | & 7 |
| F – 6 — 0 | 0 | 1 | 1 | 0 — 2, 3 | | & 7 |
| G – 7 — 0 | 0 | 1 | 1 | 1 — 1, 2, 3 | | & 7 |
| H – 8 — 0 | 1 | 0 | 0 | 0 — 4 | | & 7 |
| I – 9 — 0 | 1 | 0 | 0 | 1 — 1, 4 | | & 7 |
| J – 10 — 0 | 1 | 0 | 1 | 0 — 2, 4 | | & 7 |
| K – 11 — 0 | 1 | 0 | 1 | 1 — 1, 2, 4 | | & 7 |
| L – 12 — 0 | 1 | 1 | 0 | 0 — 3, 4 | | & 7 |
| M – 13 — 0 | 1 | 1 | 0 | 1 — 1, 3, 4 | | & 7 |
| N – 14 — 0 | 1 | 1 | 1 | 0 — 2, 3, 4 | | & 7 |
| O – 15 — 0 | 1 | 1 | 1 | 1 — 1, 2, 3, 4 | | & 7 |
| P – 16 — 1 | 0 | 0 | 0 | 0 — 5 | | & 7 |
| Q – 17 — 1 | 0 | 0 | 0 | 1 — 1, 5 | | & 7 |
| R – 18 — 1 | 0 | 0 | 1 | 0 — 2, 5 | | & 7 |
| S – 19 — 1 | 0 | 0 | 1 | 1 — 1, 2, 5 | | & 7 |
| T – 20 — 1 | 0 | 1 | 0 | 0 — 3, 5 | | & 7 |
| U – 21 — 1 | 0 | 1 | 0 | 1 — 1, 3, 5 | | & 7 |
| V – 22 — 1 | 0 | 1 | 1 | 0 — 2, 3, 5 | | & 7 |
| W – 23 — 1 | 0 | 1 | 1 | 1 — 1, 2, 3, 5 | | & 7 |
| X – 24 — 1 | 1 | 0 | 0 | 0 — 4, 5 | | & 7 |
| Y – 25 — 1 | 1 | 0 | 0 | 1 — 1, 4, 5 | | & 7 |
| Z – 26 — 1 | 1 | 0 | 1 | 0 — 2, 4, 5 | | & 7 |

**Figure 6-9.** ASCII Alphabetic Code.

wire for each bit in the code. In such a case, significant hardware or time may be able to be saved by not having to assemble bits into characters.

### Line Protocols

The most fundamental protocol in distributed computing is the line protocol [9, 10]. This is the data-link protocol which provides for the transmission of information between digital devices. Line protocols are necessary to ensure orderly transfer of error-free digital data. Because of the potential of error

| DECIMAL NUMBER | BINARY DIGIT VALUE | | | | CODE PULSE (1's) BIT POSITIONS | |
|---|---|---|---|---|---|---|
| | $(2^3)$ | $(2^2)$ | $(2^1)$ | $(2^0)$ | | |
| | 8 | 4 | 2 | 1 | | |
| 0 —— | 0 | 0 | 0 | 0 —— | | 5 & 6 |
| 1 —— | 0 | 0 | 0 | 1 —— | 1, | 5 & 6 |
| 2 —— | 0 | 0 | 1 | 0 —— | 2, | 5 & 6 |
| 3 —— | 0 | 0 | 1 | 1 —— | 1, 2, | 5 & 6 |
| 4 —— | 0 | 1 | 0 | 0 —— | 3, | 5 & 6 |
| 5 —— | 0 | 1 | 0 | 1 —— | 1, 3, | 5 & 6 |
| 6 —— | 0 | 1 | 1 | 0 —— | 2, 3, | 5 & 6 |
| 7 —— | 0 | 1 | 1 | 1 —— | 1, 2, 3 | 5 & 6 |
| 8 —— | 1 | 0 | 0 | 0 —— | 4, | 5 & 6 |
| 9 —— | 1 | 0 | 0 | 1 —— | 1, 4, | 5 & 6 |

NOTE

The eighth bit is used for either odd or even parity checking and is not part of the fixed bit pattern. Depending upon the hardware design, the system may use either odd or even parity. Even parity is used for asynchronous transmission, and odd parity is used for synchronous transmission.

**Figure 6-10**. ASCII Numeric Code.

occurrences, the information cannot be simply transmitted between source and destination. Instead, techniques must be provided to send messages in an orderly correct sequence to an active, ready device which can advise of reception errors. Specific control characters and control sequences which provide this capability are termed *line protocols*.

## Protocol Functions and Tradeoffs

The major design issues with a line protocol must consider the following functions [9, 10] : data exchange, error control, information encoding, line utilization, synchronization, communication data transparency, and bootstrapping. Within each function, important design issues need to be considered. These are summarized here.

*Data exchange* is generally accomplished by three considerations—message format, message control sequences, and message reception handshaking procedures. A typical message format includes a message header, information field, and error check field, in that order. The header specifies such information as

| b4 | b3 | b2 | b1 | COL → ROW ↓ | 0 | 1 | 2 | 3 | 4 | 5 | 6 | 7 |
|----|----|----|----|----|----|----|----|----|----|----|----|----|
| | | | | | 0 | 0 | 0 | 0 | 1 | 1 | 1 | 1 |
| | | | | | 0 | 0 | 1 | 1 | 0 | 0 | 1 | 1 |
| | | | | | 0 | 1 | 0 | 1 | 0 | 1 | 0 | 1 |
| 0 | 0 | 0 | 0 | 0 | NUL | DLE | SP | 0 | @ | P | ` | p |
| 0 | 0 | 0 | 1 | 1 | SOH | DC1 | | 1 | A | Q | a | q |
| 0 | 0 | 1 | 0 | 2 | STX | DC2 | " | 2 | B | R | b | r |
| 0 | 0 | 1 | 1 | 3 | ETC | DC3 | # | 3 | C | S | c | s |
| 0 | 1 | 0 | 0 | 4 | EOT | DC4 | $ | 4 | D | T | d | t |
| 0 | 1 | 0 | 1 | 5 | ENQ | NAK | % | 5 | E | U | e | u |
| 0 | 1 | 1 | 0 | 6 | ACK | SYN | & | 6 | F | V | f | v |
| 0 | 1 | 1 | 1 | 7 | BEL | ETB | ' | 7 | G | W | g | w |
| 1 | 0 | 0 | 0 | 8 | BS | CAN | ( | 8 | H | X | h | x |
| 1 | 0 | 0 | 1 | 9 | HT | EM | ) | 9 | I | Y | i | y |
| 1 | 0 | 1 | 0 | 10 | LF | SUB | * | : | J | Z | j | z |
| 1 | 0 | 1 | 1 | 11 | VT | ESC | + | ; | K | [ | k | { |
| 1 | 1 | 0 | 0 | 12 | FF | FS | , | < | L | \ | l | ¦ |
| 1 | 1 | 0 | 1 | 13 | CR | GS | - | = | M | ] | m | } |
| 1 | 1 | 1 | 0 | 14 | SO | RS | . | > | N | ^ | n | ~ |
| 1 | 1 | 1 | 1 | 15 | SI | US | / | ? | O | _ | o | DEL |

NOTE: $b_R$ = Parity Bit (either odd or even parity, depending upon hardware design).

LEGEND FOR USASCII CODE:

| | | | |
|----|----|----|----|
| NUL | NULL/IDLE | DC1 | DEVICE CONTROL |
| SOH | START OF HEADER | DC2 | DEVICE CONTROL |
| STX | START OF TEXT | DC3 | DEVICE CONTROL |
| ETX | END OF TEXT | DC4 | DEVICE CONTROL (STOP) |
| EOT | END OF TRANSMISSION | NAK | NEGATIVE ACKNOWLEDGE |
| ENQ | ENQUIRE | SYN | SYNCHRONOUS IDLE |
| ACK | ACKNOWLEDGE | ETB | END OF TRANSMISSION BLOCK |
| BEL | AUDIBLE SIGNAL | CAN | CANCEL |
| BS | BACKSPACE | EM | END OF MEDIUM |
| HT | HORIZONTAL TABULATION | SUB | SUBSTITUTE |
| LF | LINE FEED | ESC | ESCAPE |
| VT | VERTICAL TABULATION | FS | FILE SEPARATOR |
| FF | FORMAT EFFECTOR | GS | GROUP SEPARATOR |
| CR | CARRIAGE RETURN | RS | RECORD SEPARATOR |
| SO | SHIFT OUT | US | UNIT SEPARATOR |
| SI | SHIFT IN | SP | SPACE |
| DLE | DATA LINK ESCAPE | DEL | DELETE/IDLE |

Figure 6-11. ASCII Miscellaneous Codes.

synchronization, start of header, start of text, addressing (source and/or destination), control flags, sequencing information (for submessage assembly), and so on. The information field is the message content. The error control field specifies the details of the error control and/or recovery concepts to be used with the information if a transmission has occurred. The control information determines details of the transmission.

Upon "receipt" of a message, the destination typically responds with a message received (acknowledgment—ACK) or message not accepted (not acknowledgment—NAK). How messages are checked or errors detected (error control) depends on specific implementations; however, the general procedure is as follows. During each transmission the source generates an error control block (set of check bits) which are transmitted as the error-check field in the message. The check bits are generated from the information content of the message. As the message is received, the destination generates a set of check bits, and it compares the source- and destination-generated bits to ensure that they are the same (no error). Depending on the result of this error-no error determination, a specific handshaking procedure occurs between the source and destination to complete the message acceptance and transmission. Typical *error control* procedures may include vertical redundancy (character checking) or longitudinal or cyclic redundancy (message-block checking) techniques. Further, errors may include protocol sequence errors. Handshaking techniques differ based on items such as synchronous or asynchronous transmission and point-to-point or multipoint transmission implementations.

As described earlier in this chapter, a number of different information *encodings* of characters are possible. However, data-link controls such as Synchronous data-link control (SDLC) are bit-oriented, and the encoding is transparent to the protocol.

A number of detailed *line utilization* design issues include:

1. Simplex, half-duplex, or full-duplex communication
2. Serial or character transmission
3. Point-to-point or multipoint line device concepts
4. The overhead/acknowledgment tradeoffs (acknowledgment messages as separate entities: acknowledgment information in another block; one acknowledgment for multiple blocks; and so on)
5. Synchronous or asynchronous transmission
6. Pipelining
7. Message overhead
8. Error recovery procedures

If the protocol uses synchronous transmission, the message control stream must include a *synchronization* pattern to enable the destination to frame the reception properly. It is desirable for this synchronizing sequence to be unique (to prevent false synchronization), but in some codes (ASCII) all bit patterns have been assigned. This may necessitate extensive synchronization sequences to ensure correct system operation.

*Communication data transparency* is the ability to send any bit pattern as data. It is desirable for the line facilities to use the same protocol whether they are parallel or serial, synchronous or asynchronous. A certain amount of transparency may be achieved by setting a data count (see later discussion on DDCMP), bit stuffing (see later discussion on SDLC), or by character stuffing (see discussion on BISYNC).

*Bootstrapping* is the technique via which a device may start an inoperative system at the end of a line.

### Common Protocols

Currently there are three major protocols—IBM's binary synchronous communication (BISYNC), IBM's synchronous data-link control (SDLC) used with the system network architecture (SNA), and DEC's digital data communication message protocol (DDCMP). These are summarized in table 6-3 and discussed later. SDLC is discussed in detail in the following sections [11 to 21].

*DDCMP*

The message format of DDCMP [10] is shown in figure 6-2. The only control character is the first character (SOH, which is shown, indicates data; ENQ specifies control; SLE specifies bootstrap). The header contains the count (of 8-bit bytes), control flags, response field for positive acknowledgment of received messages, message sequence number, and multipoint destination address. CRC-1 (CRC-2) is a cyclic redundancy check for the header (information). The information may be up to 16,383 bytes transmitted in 8-bit bytes with no specific information coding specified.

Transmissions may be full duplex, half duplex, serial or parallel, point-to-point, and/or multipoint. The count field allows for data transparencies. Techniques to share error acknowledgments (255 messages per ACK) and cut down on synchronization overhead (delete the 8-bit SYN characters if there is no gap) are available. Other important features of DDCMP are summarized in table 6-3.

*BISYNC*

BISYNC [11] is shown in figure 6-3. In a BISYNC protocol the header is optional. If provided, it starts with SOH (start of header) and ends with STX (start of text). The header is user-defined. Addressing for multipoint and/or polling is implemented using a special control message. Text is variable in length

**Table 6-3**
**Protocol Characteristics**

|  | DDCMP | BISYNC | SDLC |
|---|---|---|---|
| TRANSFER CONTROL | SEE FIGURE 10.1 | SEE FIGURE 10.2 | SEE FIGURE 10.3 |
| ERROR CONTROL |  |  |  |
| RETRANSMIT | YES | YES | YES |
| ERROR RECOVERY | CYCLIC | CYCLIC (EBCDIC) | CYCLIC |
| ERROR DETECTION |  | VERTICAL 6-BIT TRANSCODE & LONGITUDINAL (ASCII) |  |
| INFORMATION ENCODING | NONE | ASCII OR EBCDIC 6-BIT TRANSCODE | BIT ORIENTED |
| LINE UTILIZATION |  |  |  |
| FULL DUPLEX | YES | NO | YES |
| HALF DUPLEX | YES | YES | YES |
| SERIAL | YES | YES | YES |
| PARALLEL | YES | NO | NO |
| POINT-TO-POINT | YES | YES | YES |
| MULTIPOINT | YES | YES | YES |
| SYNCHRONIZATION |  |  |  |
| SYNCHRONOUS | YES | YES | YES |
| ASYNCHRONOUS | YES | NO | NO |
| DATA TRANSPARENCY |  |  |  |
| COUNT | YES | – | – |
| CHARACTER STUFFING | – | YES | – |
| BIT STUFFING | – | – | YES |
| BOOTSTRAPPING | YES | NO | NO |

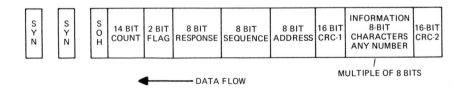

| S Y N | S Y N | S O H | 14 BIT COUNT | 2 BIT FLAG | 8 BIT RESPONSE | 8 BIT SEQUENCE | 8 BIT ADDRESS | 16 BIT CRC-1 | INFORMATION 8-BIT CHARACTERS ANY NUMBER | 16-BIT CRC-2 |

MULTIPLE OF 8 BITS

◀———— DATA FLOW

**Figure 6-12.** DDCMP Message Format.

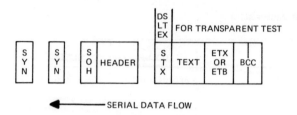

**Figure 6-13.** BISYNC Message Format.

and uses character stuffing for transparency. Transparent mode is defined by DLE STX in the text field instead of STX. Further control characters are preceded by a DLE bit pattern to differentiate them from transparent data. The DLE DLE sequence recognizes the second DLE as control function data. Transmission is half duplex, serial in parallel by byte, point-to-point, or multipoint and synchronous. At least two synchronizing characters (SYN) must precede the message. Bootstrapping is not included in the line protocol. Coding can be ASCII, EBCDIC, or 6-bit transcode. Error checking is dependent on code type—ASCII uses vertical redundancy on each character and longitudinal on a message, EBCDIC and 6-bit transcode use cyclic redundancy.

*SDLC*

SDLC [12 to 21] is a link control. Currently it appears that SDLC will be the main (eventually only) link control supported by IBM. Thus it is very important in the context of distributed system design.

The frame of the SDLC is shown in figure 6-14. SDLC is a bit synchronous protocol. The only specified fields consist of two flags (F), an address (A), a control field (C), a frame check (FCS), and an arbitrary-length information field. Note that the information field (I) may contain additional control information (say, source/destination address, poll control, and so on). The length and form of the I field are strictly under design control. The SDLC protocol is not concerned with I-field details. Each field is discussed.

The flag field (F) appears at the beginning of the frame and at the end of the frame. The flag consists of the specific 8-bit sequence: 01111110. Flags delimit the SDLC frame. Any arbitrary number of flags can be sent between frames. F denotes frame start. The device notes that a frame has started when it detects a flag followed by an 8-bit nonflag sequence. Upon detection of the next flag, the receiver knows that the frame is complete, the 16 bits prior to the flag are the FSC, and the bit (previous seventeenth bit) received prior to FSC bits was the last information bit. The flag is discussed in more detail later.

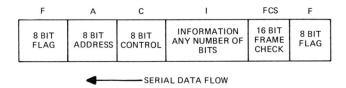

| F | A | C | I | FCS | F |
|---|---|---|---|---|---|
| 8 BIT FLAG | 8 BIT ADDRESS | 8 BIT CONTROL | INFORMATION ANY NUMBER OF BITS | 16 BIT FRAME CHECK | 8 BIT FLAG |

◄──────── SERIAL DATA FLOW

**Figure 6-14.** SDLC Message Format.

The address field follows the first flag. Define a *secondary station* as a remote station and a *primary station* as a controlling station. The address specifies the following:

1. If the frame is going from a primary station to a secondary station, A specifies the secondary station(s) intended to receive the frame.
2. If being sent by a secondary station, A specifies the transmitter.

The control field (8 bits following A field) conveys information about frame number, responses, and so forth. There are three basic formats—information transfer, supervisor, and nonsequenced (see figure 6-15). On figure 6-15, $N_S$ is the frame number being sent, $N_R$ is the frame number last received, $P/F$ specifies the poll/final frame bit, $C_1$ specifies specific transmission functions, and $C_2$ can specify a number of command/response functions. The receiver can infer the frame being sent for up to eight frames. Acknowledgments can be sent without acknowledgment. After seven frames are sent without an acknowledgment, the transmitter will stop and wait for acknowledgment. If an error is detected, a particular frame can be specified (by sending the proper $N_R$ value) so only the bad frame and the frames transmitted thereafter must be retransmitted (selective restart property). Frames with supervisory or nonsequenced information in them do not change the $N_S$ or $N_R$ values. The supervisory format is used to poll a secondary station. The nonsequenced format is used to initialize, disconnect, and check status of stations.

The FCS field contains the check bits generated by the error control polynomial. To be compatible with IBM equipment, the correct polynomial must be used. The polynomial has been changed from that used with BSC.

SDLC transmissions may be full or half duplex, and point-to-point and multipoint systems are supported. Since SDLC is synchronous and bit-oriented, a technique must be available to ensure that the flag (01111110) is a unique sequence. This is accomplished using "bit stuffing." If six (or more) 1's are received, a flag could become a nonunique sequence. Thus, after every five consecutive 1's, a 0 is automatically inserted (unless the character is the flag).

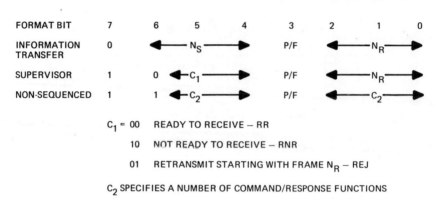

$$C_1 = 00 \quad \text{READY TO RECEIVE} - RR$$
$$10 \quad \text{NOT READY TO RECEIVE} - RNR$$
$$01 \quad \text{RETRANSMIT STARTING WITH FRAME } N_R - REJ$$

$$C_2 \text{ SPECIFIES A NUMBER OF COMMAND/RESPONSE FUNCTIONS}$$

**Figure 6-15.** SDLC Control Field Formats.

Whenever the receiver detects five 1's followed by a 0, the 0 is removed (ignored). The flag can be unique using this process since a flag is the only way six consecutive 1's can be transmitted. Data transparency overhead is a function dependent on the transmitted data.

Bit stuffing will probably make near-asynchronous operation possible. Consider the situation where received-data timing is not available to the station. Non-return-to-zero-inverted (NRZI) coding is used, but stuffing provides a "timing signal" after every five consecutive 1's. Since NRZI switches state every time a 0 is transmitted, the maximum time period between transitions would be 5-bit times, and thus the devices should have enough information to keep their sample timings properly "synchronized" even if the device is basically asynchronous because clocking can be set up. It should be fairly easy to keep the devices synchronized as a result of the bit stuffing and NRZI code transmission. The devices can be initially synchronized from the flag field.

SDLC seems to be very efficient, particularly in full-duplex operation. Timing analysis and comparison to BISYNC are found in references 5 to 9. Because of IBM's dominance of the world markets, SDLC (or SDLC-compatible) protocols will probably become the communication protocol standard. The ANSI standard (AADCP) and the ISO standard (HDLC) are very similar to SDLC.

In some SDLC-compatible protocols, the address field is expanded to 16 bits, as is the control field. Further, bootstrapping functions, for example, can be implemented using a subcontrol field contained in the I field of the SDLC frame. Thus, even though SDLC appears quite rudimentary (it is only oriented to control physical links between primary and secondary stations), it does allow information necessary to perform complex functions to be conveyed. Importantly, the structure, size, and content of I are solely dependent on the equipment and not on SDLC.

## Summary

This chapter discussed general techniques available to implement data-transmission schemes and line protocols. In contrast to the techniques mentioned in chapter 5 for buses, a wide variety of techniques are available for general data transmission. These techniques would be most useful in a general switching environment and could be used to develop the communication-link protocols and link transmission schemes necessary to implement the level 0 protocols for either a packet (message) switch or a circuit switch and then implement the actual circuit designs. Various techniques and tradeoffs for signal modulation, multiplexing, modem design, message formatting, typical code sets, and data-link control procedures were discussed with the emphasis on conceptual understanding and developing a knowledge of relative advantages and disadvantages. This chapter could be viewed as an extension of chapters 3 and 4 in terms of the level 0 design issues.

## Exercises

1. Develop a tradeoff chart which compares the modulation techniques discussed in this chapter.

2. Develop a tradeoff chart which compares the multiplexing techniques discussed in this chapter.

3. Using the basic SDLC concept, design equipment that can interface to both BISYNC and SDLC protocols. Further, design equipment which can process SDLC but can emulate the BISYNC protocol. (*Hint*: Let the BISYNC basic frame be one of the possible information fields that can be transmitted in an SLDC frame).

4. Design a line-protocol interpretation strategy that provides for use of (or compatibility with) BISYNC, SDLC, and DDCMP.

## References

[ 1] J.R. Davey, "Modems," *Proceedings of the Institute of Electrical and Electronics Engineers* 60 (November 1972): 1284-1292.

[ 2] L.C. Hobbs, "Terminals," *Proceedings of the IEEE* 60 (November 1972), pp. 1273-1284.

[ 3] D.R. Doll, "Multiplexing and Concentration," *Proceedings of the IEEE* 60 (November 1962): 1313-1321.

[ 4] C.R. Cahn, "Combined Digital Phase and Amplitude Modulation Communication Systems," *Institute of Radio Engineers Transactions on Communication Systems*, September 1960, pp. 150-155.

[ 5] W.R. Bennett and J.R. Davey, *Data Transmission* (New York: McGraw-Hill, 1965).

[ 6] R.W. Lucky et al., *Principles of Data Communication* (New York: McGraw-Hill, 1968).

[ 7] E.D. Sunde, "Theoretical Fundamental of Pulse Transmission: Part I," *Bell System Technical Journal*, May 1954, pp. 721-788.

[ 8] E.D. Sunde, "Theoretical Fundamentals of Pulse Transmission: Part II," *Bell System Technical Journal*, July 1954, pp. 987-1010.

[ 9] S.R. Kimbleton and G.M. Schneider, "Computer Communication Networks: Approaches, Objectives, and Performance Considerations," *Association for Computing Machinery Computing Surveys*, September 1975, pp. 129-173.

[10] E.F. Stelmach, *Introduction to Minicomputer Networks* (Maynard, Mass.: Digital Press, 1974).

[11] IBM, *Binary Synchronous Communication: General Information Manual*, IBM SRL GA 27-3004.

[12] "Communications Clinic: Synchronous Data Link Control; Part 1— General Concepts and Structure," *Modern Data*, February 1975, pp. 25-26.

[13] "Communications Clinic: Synchronous Data Link Control; Part 2— The Control Field," *Modern Data*, March 1975, pp. 32-33.

[14] "Communications Clinic: Synchronous Data Link Control; Part 3— Supervisory and Non-Sequenced Control Field Formats," *Modern Data*, April 1975, pp. 46-47.

[15] "Communications Clinic: Synchronous Data Link Control; Part 4— Throughput Calculations," *Modern Data*, June 1975, pp. 24-25.

[16] "Communications Clinic: Synchronous Data Link Control; Part 5— Response Time Performance," *Modern Data*, September 1975, pp. 30-33.

[17] J.P. Gray, "Line Control Procedures," *Proceedings of the IEEE*, November 1972, pp. 1301-1312.

[18] R.A. Donnan and J.R. Kersey, "Synchronous Data Link Control: A Perspective," *IBM Systems Journal*, April 1974, pp. 140-162.

[19] IBM, *Synchronous Data Link Control: General Information Manual*, March 1974, IBM SRL GA 27-3093.

[20] J.R. Kersey, "Synchronous Data Link Control: SDLC," *Data Communications*, May/June 1974, pp. 49-60.

[21] S.K. Kar, "Advanced Report on Synchronous Data Link Control (SDLC)," *Telecom Computer Technology Report*, May 1974.

# 7

# Example Systems and Concepts

## Introduction

This chapter contains summary descriptions of major bus and communication system concepts for distributed processing and network systems including:

1. IBM's system network architecture [1 to 6]
2. MU5 exchange network [7]
3. Honeywell's experimental distributed processor [8, 9, 10]
4. Barrel switch design concepts [11]
5. Collins C-System [12]
6. DEC UNIBUS [13]
7. IEEE bus standard [14]
8. A Waksman permutation switch [15, 16, 17]

## System Network Architecture

System network architecture (SNA) is IBM's architecture for data communication systems [1 to 6]. It consists of a set of formats and protocols designed to allow a series of machines and programs to be interconnected to provide a distributed-system architecture (see figure 7-1). One of the possible data-link controls for SNA is the previously described SDLC.

SNA may be viewed as a set of interacting system components. The highest level of component is the *node*, usually a single equipment controlled by a particular program level. SNA nodes are as follows:

1. *Host node*—the equivalent of a central processor [central processing unit (CPU)] along with its operating system and access method; oversees the network and contains user applications.
2. *Communication controller node*—manages the line control and network data routing. Routing data to another communication controller is called performing an *intermediate* function; routing data to a cluster controller node or terminal node is called performing a *boundary* function.
3. *Cluster controller node*—provides for connection (attachment) of I/O devices.
4. *Terminal node*—provides for connection of I/O devices; differs from a cluster controller node by capability and capability rather than by function.

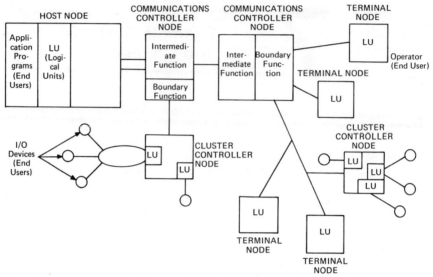

**Figure 7-1.** An SNA Data Communication System Showing Major Components.

End users are at the "ends" of the network. End users may be operators, programs, or I/O devices. End users access the network via logical units (LUs). Each LU has a unique network name, and an LU is really an access port to the network. The LUs may be either hardware or software.

Below (within) each SNA node a set of layers is provided. SNA defines requests and responses to be used by each layer and protocols to be used between layers. The layers are as follows:

1. *Application layer*—the origin and destination of all network messages; represents the end user.
2. *Function management layer*—presents message data between applications; takes into account and resolves device dependencies. An end user gains access to another end user by using the network name of the appropriate LUs in the function management layer of the other end user; this coupling of the representative LUs is called a *session*. After a session is initiated, the end users can exchange data.
3. *Transmission subsystem layer*—responsible for message routing, path selection, and flow control of messages.

Because most network nodes are programmable, SNA claims the advantage of being able to distribute the computing (processing) function, thus allowing for CPU off-loading. Further claimed advantages resulting from the ability to place the processing capability at the node where it can be used most effectively are improved response time, lower line costs, higher system availability, less duplication of effort, a basis for system growth, and insulation of the end user from data communication details.

Typically, standard IBM equipment is used in SNA networks:

1. *CPUs*—any IBM System/370 with the relocate feature.
2. *Operating-system software*—DS/VS and DOS/VS.
3. *Communication software access methods*—Virtual telecommunications access method (VTAM) alone; VTAM in conjunction with telecommunications access method (TAM); customer information control system (CICS), information management systems (IMC), and/or remote job entry (RJE) provide the link to the communication network. Extended telecommunications modules (EXTM) can provide the access method with CICS/VS and DOS/VS systems.
4. *Communication control units*—3704 and 3705 communication controllers with the network control program (NCP); use of the partitioned emulation programming (PEP) extension in the 3704 and 3705 allows communication channels to operate in either emulation mode or network control mode, thus allowing operation of both SNA and pre-SNA networks simultaneously. This feature is used to bridge applications as the user converts to SNA network systems.
5. *Channels*—point-to-point or multipoint channels.
6. *Terminals*—IBM 3270 (remotely via IBM 3704/3705; locally via System/370 I/O channel); information display system, IBM 3600 finance communication system, IBM 3650 retail store system, IBM 3660 supermarket system, IBM 3767 communication terminal, IBM 3700 data communication system, IBM 3790 communication system (remotely via IBM 3704/3705; locally via System/370 I/O channel), and IBM System/32.

Details of SNA operation are summarized here.

End users "communicate" via sessions. Resources known as network addressable units (NAUs) are managed by the communication system, all elements in nodes which support communication from end user to end user. SNA defines the structures, protocols, and so on of a communication system. The NAU provides an end-user port to the communication system. Information flows between NAUs in the communication system. Each NAU has a network address (used by the communication system) and a network name (used by the end user to identify the NAU). To communicate, end users must establish a pairing between their respective NAUs, known as a session. This is accomplished by an end user invoking a protocol to initiate a session. The session is then established between the named NAU of the requesting end user. Paths are established during a session to connect the NAUs, and a function management service, presentation service, is bound to the NAUs to support the session. This is pictured in figure 7-2. Multiple sessions may also be supported.

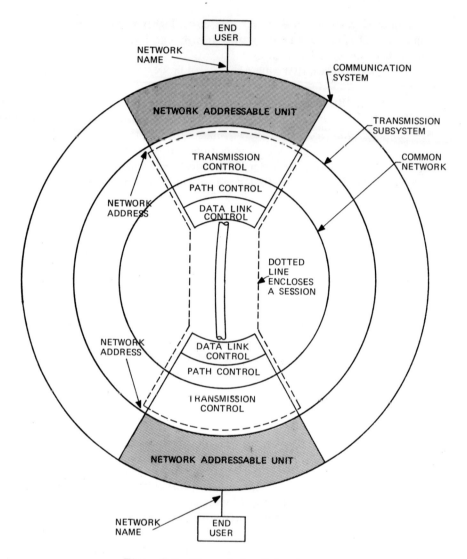

**Figure 7-2.** Transmission Subsystem.

The transmission subsystem has two major elements (figure 7-2) the common network which provides for path control and data-link control, and the transmission subsystem which provides for transmission control. Data-link control manages the links between network nodes; path control provides for data routing over the paths established between network addresses; transmission control controls sessions and data flow into and out of the common network.

SNA defines three types of NAUs:

1. System services control point (SSCP)–services provided for management functions and performed by command processors; for example, network services processor is responsible for network bootstrapping, session establishment, and so on.
2. Physical unit (PU)–each mode known to exist by SSCP has a PU; SSCP uses SSCP/PU sessions for bootstrapping, configuration control, and so on.
3. Logical unit (LU)–the user port used to access SSCP services (say, session establishment) or to communicate with other users.

Sessions allowed between NAU consist of (1) LU to LU, (2) LU to SSCP, and (3) PU to SSCP.

The function management (FM) services provided within the different NAU types are:

1. *Presentation services* (PS)–FM services provided within an LU to support LU-to-LU sessions.
2. *Logical-unit services* (LUS)–FM services provided within an LU to support LU-to-SSCP sessions.
3. *Physical-unit services* (PUS)–FM services provided within a PU to support PU-to-SSCP sessions.
4. *Network services* (NS)–FM services provided within an SSCP to provide network configuration management and support for SSCP-to-PU and SSCP-to-LU sessions.

The transmission control element provides for direct access to the transmission subsystem. The access is used by function management within an NAU when requests or responses are sent on the common network to counterpart FM services. The main elements of transmission control are:

1. *Connection point* (CP) *manager*–provides a mechanism for session control, network control, and NAU to communicate with their counterparts via the common network via a response unit (RU); uses control information to build a response header (RH); constructs the basic information unit (BIU) for transmission by constructing an RH-RU combination.
2. *Session control* (SC)–used to obtain resources necessary for a session and establish the session.
3. *Network control* (NC)–provides a means for CP managers and path control to communicate through the common network using sessions that were established for NAU/NAU communication.

The path control (PC) elements manage the shared data links and route the BIUs. PC must be aware of the NAU locations and connection paths. Depending on the BIU site, it may be broken up for transmission as a series of segments. Whether segments or BIU are transmitted depends on BIU size and buffer size at the destination node. Path control adds a transmission header (TH) to the BIU (or BIU segment) to form a path information unit (PIU). If necessary, path control may block several PIUs together into a basic transmission unit. This is commonly done when several PIUs are destined for transmission over a link common to several paths.

The actual data-link control used can be SDLC or System/370 data channels. A header and trailer are added to the basic transmission unit to form a basic link unit (BLU). The BLU is transmitted over the actual data link.

Data reception is the opposite of data transmission. An actual data transmission is summarized in figures 7-3 and 7-4. An example of a presentation class design using IMS, CICS, and VTAM is given in figure 7-5, illustrating the relationships between the user and the various software subsystems.

Network names are associated with each physical unit, link, and logical unit in the system. Network names are transformed, via SSCP, into a network address. Network addresses comprise 16 bits and consist of two parts—subarea and element within the subarea. These two fields of the 16-bit quantity must be selected at system generation time, but until then they are completely variable. Certain nodes are responsible for a specific subarea. An example view of the subarea concept is given in figure 7-6.

SDLC is discussed in another chapter. More details on SNA may be found in references 1 to 6.

## MU5 Exchange Network

A very innovative "bus structure," the MU5 exchange network [7], is described in this section (figure 7-7). The exchange consists of the hardware between $A_E$ and $B_E$ of the diagram. Figure 7-7 ignores the control and priority resolution circuits necessary to run the exchange and shows only the data paths. The Lavington et al. article [7] details the switch design; here we summarize only the design.

The key to the switch concept is that data transfers differ significantly in concept from the view normally seen in a bus. The exchange does not use concepts normally associated with shared buses, crossbar switches, or multiported memories. Rather, it can be viewed as a multiplexer ($A_E$ to $A_D$), a high-speed data link ($A_D$ to $B_D$), and a demultiplexer ($B_D$ to $B_E$)

The two key concepts are as follows. (1) The hardware to drive a very high-speed short data link (12 centimeters) has been provided along with the necessary priority and control circuits. (2) Data transfers are broken into two distinct parts—a transfer request providing the required address and a data-available request. The short link provides for high-speed and centralized hardware. Further, the hardware can be simply controlled.

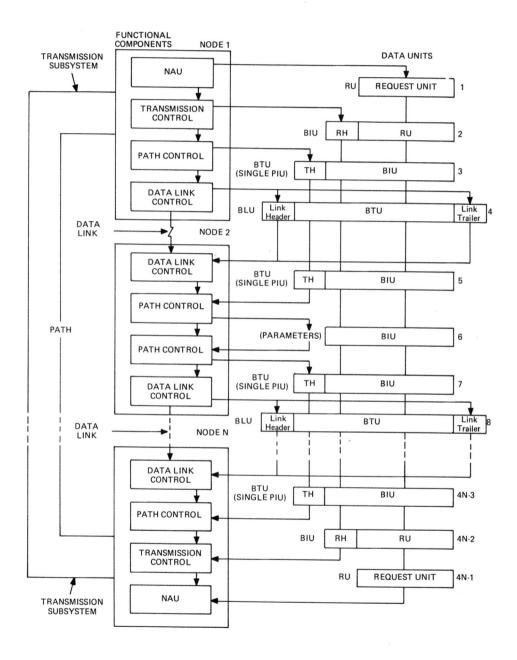

**Figure 7-3.** Transmission Subsystem Control Data Flow through $N$ Nodes.

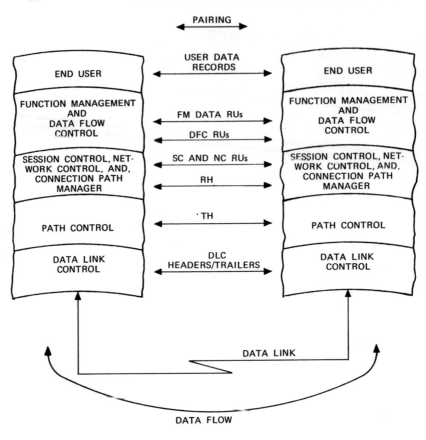

**Figure 7–4.** SNA Internal Communication Data-Flow Correspondences between End Users.

The effect of the data-transfer division is much more subtle. Consider a bus with device $A$ requesting information from device $B$. The data transfer is basically source-controlled (device $A$), and the transfer speed depends on the slowest device. In the exchange the transfer request is source-controlled (device $A$); however, the data-available request is controlled by the "destination," or device $B$. The impact of this is that device $A$ kicks off the transfer. At some later time, device $B$ responds. In the meantime, every device $B$ must remember where the transfer requests originated; and when the data are available, the exchange must schedule (via priority and control logic) the appropriate use of the data link. Clearly, each transfer involves two competitions for the exchange, and setting up such a system for complex device interactions could be very difficult.

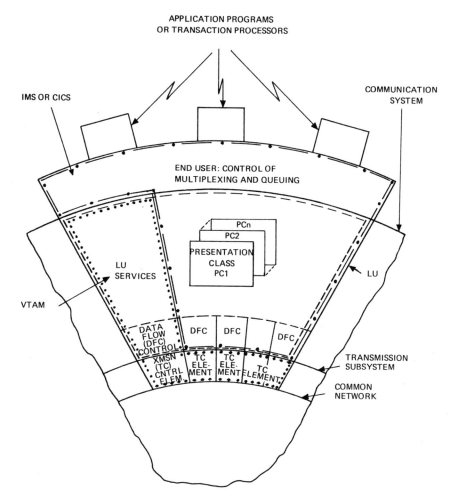

**Figure 7-5.** Example of Presentation Levels (Host Node).

The MU5 system contains some significant system concepts designed to take advantage of the exchange properties, but these issues are beyond the scope of this discussion.

## Honeywell Experimental Distributed Processor

The experimental distributed processor (XDP) [8, 9, 10] was built for a feasibility demonstration of distributed processing for Small Ships Command and

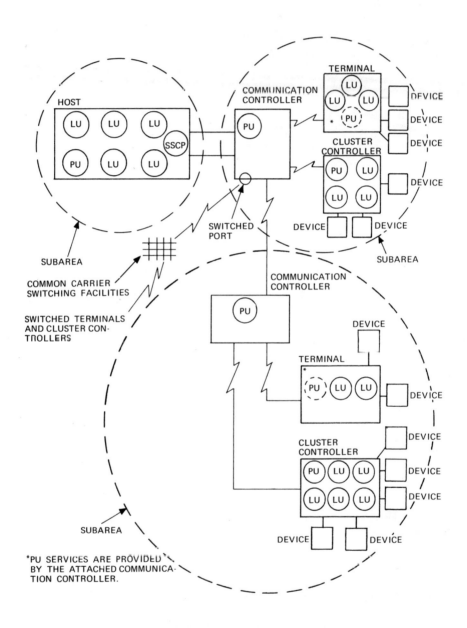

**Figure 7-6.** Potential Physical Configuration of Subareas.

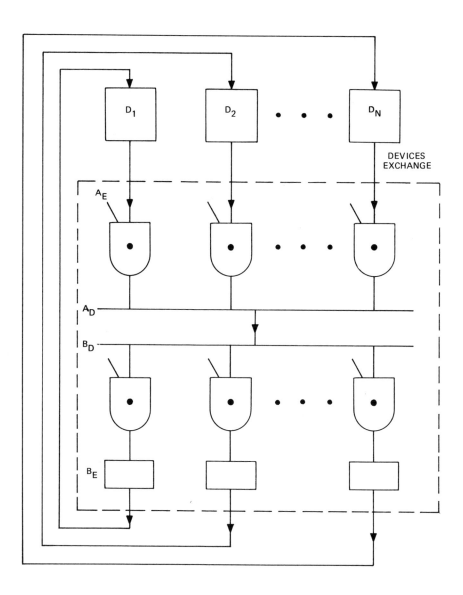

**Figure 7-7.** MU5 Exchange Network.

Control (SSCC) under contract to the Naval Electronics Laboratory Center (NELC). The objective of the contract was to develop and demonstrate a laboratory distributed-processor system oriented toward the requirements of SSCC data processing. A two-processor system was delivered in May 1976; however, the design was completed for sixty-four processors.

Honeywell performed requirements studies [8, 9, 10] for the SSCC problem. The system description can be found in reference 8. The XDP concept based on the requirements analysis is to provide the capability to configure systems in a wide range of system sizes for many SSCC applications using the same system design.

XDP is a "direct shared-bus" system consisting of PEs, which are connected via a bus interface unit (BIU) to a bit serial global bus (see figure 7-8). It is a direct bus concept because all transmissions go directly from source to

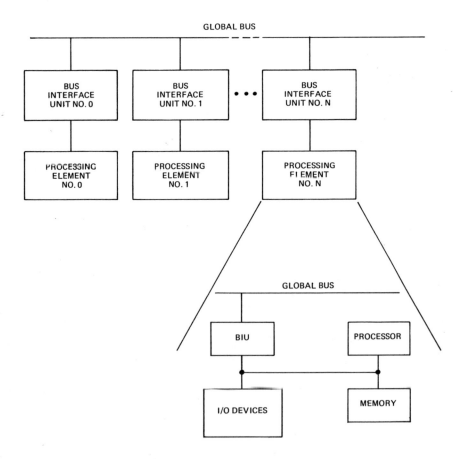

**Figure 7-8.** XDP System Configuration.

destination PE. It is a shared-bus concept since all PEs take turns on the same bus. I/O devices are connected to one or more PEs.

Software for XDP is a collection of processes running on PEs, where a process is defined to be the smallest computational unit of concurrency.

A BIU is a programmable device which performs the interconnection tasks associated with interprocess communication (IPC) in XDP. The IPC protocol is managed by the BIU (to minimize overhead in the PE software) and is enforced by the BIU (to maintain IPC uniformity for all processes).

The PEs were computer automation LSI-2 minicomputers. PEs connect to bus interface units in two ways—programmed I/O (PIO) and direct memory access (DMA). The BIU design is marginally dependent on the particular PE selected. The XDP system was designed to allow up to sixty-four PEs to be connected on a bus with a maximum length of 2000 feet. The initial system has two PEs on an 1100-foot bus. The bus is a double-shielded twisted pair cable with a raw data rate of 1.25 million bits per second.

Each process in the system has a unique logical name. The names in the XDP system identify destinations as opposed to sources. The message recipient identifies messages sent to it by recognizing its own name. Using destination names, a process can transmit a message without knowing in what PE the destination process resides. Each XDP BIU can recognize up to eight destination names. Messages are sent by the hardware. The process need only format the message and request its transmission. Messages are sent and received through circular queues. Each PE has (in its memory) an output queue (OQ) and up to eight input queues (IQ). Queue size and location parameters are software-specified.

Each BIU (figure 7-9) has three functions—global bus synchronization and allocation, message output from memory to the bus, and message input from the bus to memory.

The microprogrammed input controller (IC) has overall control of BIU functions. It monitors all bus traffic, determines when the BIU has control of the bus and relinquishes bus control if it has no message to send or causes the output controller to send a message from the OQ, handles input messages from the bus to the IQ, generates PE interrupts for exceptional conditions, and maintains system-status operation lists. Bus transmissions are prefixed with a bus synchronization signal: a specific modulation violation, followed by two data bits. The synchronization signal and the two bits are referred to as a *sync*. The two bits indicate one of four sync types—start of transaction (SOT), end of transaction (EOT), acknowledge (ACK), and negative acknowledge (NAK). The XDP global bus allocation mechanism is decentralized and asynchronous; that is, each BIU decides independently whether it controls the bus during the next opportunity "time slot." The time slots are not fixed in length but vary with the traffic.

The output controller (OC) handles the transmission of messages from the OQ to the global bus. The PIO interface provides the capability to control and

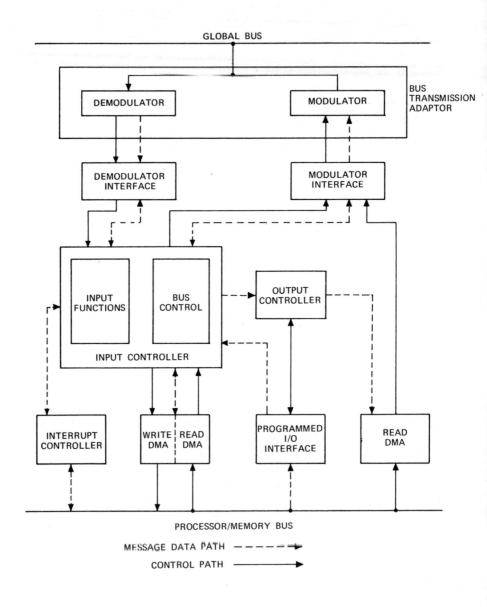

**Figure 7–9.** Block Diagram of a Bus Interface Unit (BIU).

monitor the BIU. The modulator interface (MI) accepts bus-sync transmit requests from the IC and 16-bit message data words from the OC. The modulator and demodulator comprise the bus transmission adapter (BTA). The modulator sends bus-sync signals and message bits using Manchester coding. The demodulator recognizes sync signals on the bus and converts data from Manchester coding to nonreturn-to-zero (NRZ) form. The demodulator interface (DI) receives serial data and bus sync from the BTA. The DMA controller coordinates all DMA requests in the BIU. The interrupt controller (ITC) causes interrupts to appear in the PE.

Since the system is a laboratory system, it includes significant facilities for hardware diagnosis and hardware monitoring.

The bus allocation mechanism works as follows (see figure 7-10): each BIU has a 256-bit time-slot vector and a time-slot pointer register. The time-slot vector is used to determine when a BIU can transmit; the 256 bits correspond to a maximum of 256 variable-length time slots. Time slots are assigned to the BIUs based on their system transmission-rate requirements. A given BIU has a 1 in its time-slot vector for each time slot in which it controls the bus and 0's in all other vector bits. Reallocation of the bus occurs in each BIU when it receives the bus synchronization signal (end of transaction, or EOT). When an EOT is received, each BIU increments its time-slot pointer register, which indicates which time-slot bit should be tested to determine control of the bus for the next time slot. When a BIU gets a time slot, it can either relinquish control or send one message.

When a start of transaction (SOT) is detected, all BIUs begin inputting the message currently on the bus. The first message word is the destination name. Each BIU compares the name against its list of resident process names. The BIU which matches the name will store the message (but not the name) in the appropriate input queue. The format of a message in the OQ is shown in figure 7-11.

When the OC transmits the message from the OQ on the GB, it adds some information (see figure 7-12).

The input queue message is the same as the output queue message format except that there is no destination name word.

## Barrel-Switch Network Design

The operation of data shifting in a digital computer is one of most fundamental and important operations [11]. It is also a special case of a data-routing network and is thus interesting as an example. One of the primary means of accomplishing this shifting operation in a processor is a parallel shift register. At low and moderate speeds this is a simple and acceptable method. In high-speed applications, however, this concept becomes unacceptable because of its time delay in shifting the data. One faster alternative is the barrel switch. The basic barrel-switch concept is a combinational network consisting of a matrix of logic

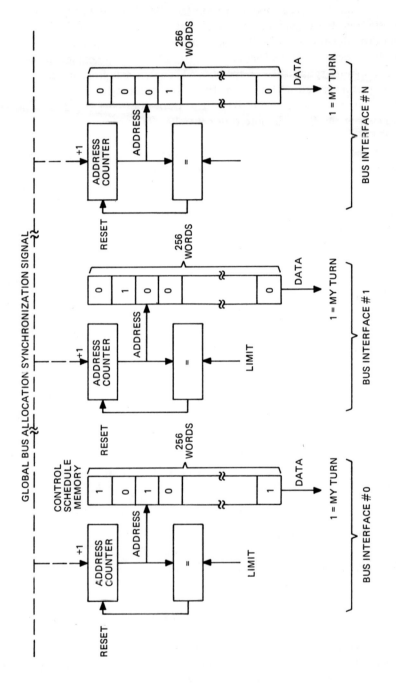

**Figure 7-10.** Time-Slot Vectors.

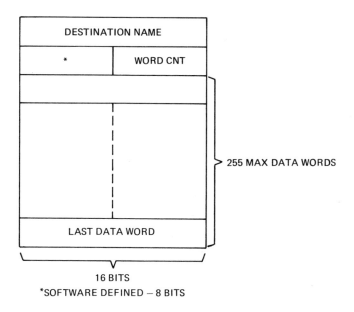

**Figure 7-11.** Output Queue Message.

blocks, each acting as an $n$-line to one-line multiplexer. The arrangement is shown in figure 7-13 for a two-line to one-line multiplexer. We use a two-line multiplexer to illustrate the barrel shifter design philosophy and tradeoffs.

A 4-bit switch capable of one shift to the right is shown (figure 7-13). It becomes a simple matter to rearrange this switch to provide a shift of two or four places to the right by connecting units of one, two, and four shifts in series. Cascading such devices makes it possible to shift the input data any number of positions from 0 to 7 to the right (figure 7-14).

It may be noted here that the three control lines may be thought of as a 3-bit binary number representing the number of positions shifted.

We have thus designed a simple switch capable of shifting up to seven places to the right in an end-off manner. The total delay involved three levels of logic. The next function necessary for a reasonable barrel switch is a capability for an end-around shift (controlled by an end-around/end-off (EAO line). This implementation is illustrated in figure 7-15. In a similar manner two "and" gates are used to couple the last two inputs of the two-shift level to its first two inputs and likewise four gates for the four-shift level. All EAO lines are tied

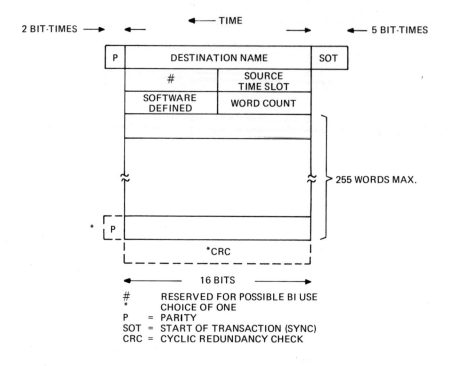

Figure 7–12. Global Bus Message Format.

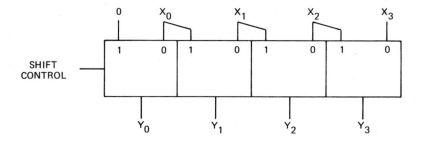

Figure 7–13 Basic 4-Bit Shift Network.

together, and the resulting circuit is capable of zero to seven right shift in either end-around or end-off.

We might like to make a left end-around shift possible. This is easily done by noticing that right end-around and left end-around shifts are radix complements.

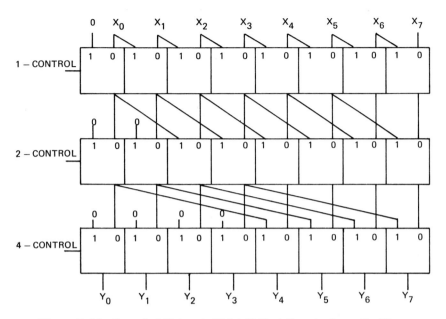

**Figure 7–14.** Cascaded Network Right-Shifted Zero to Seven Positions.

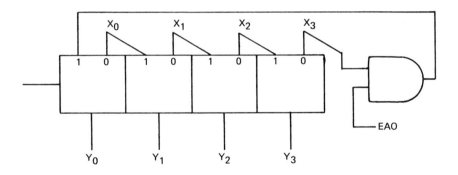

**Figure 7–15.** Barrel-Switch End-around Shift.

That is, a right shift of $n$ places is the same as a left shift of $m - n$ places, where $m$ is the bit capacity of the switch. Thus an additional network could be added in the shift-amount control lines to change the shift amount depending on a shift right/shift left control line (table 7-1). It can be seen that the left-shift outputs are equal to $\bar{R} + 1$ where $R$ is the right-shift output (figure 7-16).

**Table 7–1**
**Shift-Distance Control**

| INPUT | OUTPUT | |
|---|---|---|
| | $L/\bar{R} = 0$ | $L/\bar{R} = 1$ |
| 000 | 000 | 000 |
| 001 | 001 | 111 |
| 010 | 010 | 110 |
| 011 | 011 | 101 |
| 100 | 100 | 100 |
| 101 | 101 | 011 |
| 110 | 110 | 010 |
| 111 | 111 | 001 |

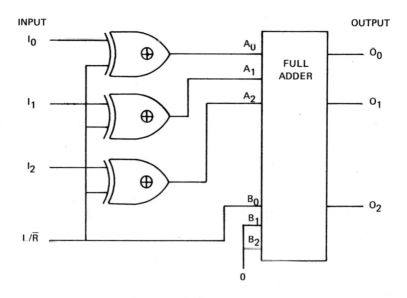

**Figure 7–16.** Shift Control Logic.

Another major function is the left end-off shift. This could be accomplished by using the left end-around function and inhibiting to zero the proper number of bits on the right end (figure 7-17).

These "cancellation units" are connected as shown in figure 7-18.

The resulting operation is as follows. The bit will be inhibited if either input two or three is high. Thus by connecting two to output four of the previous block, a single left-shift cancel (LSC) line may be held high to cancel a series of bits. Each LSC line therefore corresponds to a given number of bit cancellations from one to seven. Since the number of bits canceled is the same as the left-shift amount, a demultiplexer may be used to drive the LSC lines. The inputs to the demultiplexer are connected directly to the shift amount inputs. In order to prevent unwanted cancellations, the strobe input of the demultiplexer is controlled by the $L/\overline{R}$ and EAO lines (figure 7-19). Thus

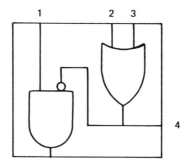

**Figure 7-17.** Cancellation Unit.

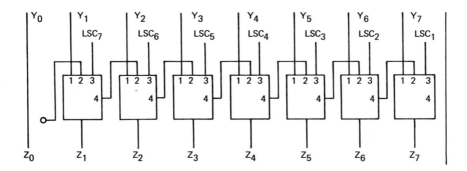

**Figure 7-18.** Resultant Network.

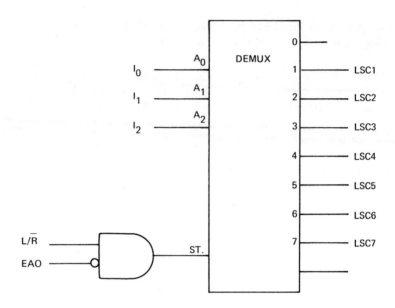

**Figure 7-19.** Demultiplexer Control.

bit cancellations can occur only when the network is set up for left end-off shifts.

We now have the design fundamentals for a high-speed network capable of four shift functions. Becuase of its modular construction, the barrel switch may be extended to handle any number of bits and any shift amount by simply adding more logic cells. For instance a 16-bit switch would require an additional level of shift cells (to produce an 8-bit shift) and the appropriate end-around and cancellation cells. Further, additional shift modes could be devised using this or similar implementation schemes.

This section mentioned two major shifter concepts—the parallel shift register approach and a multilevel combinational shift matrix. Off-the-shelf integrated circuits are available which perform many of these same functions using single-level combinational designs with wired-on or tristate bus techniques, for example, Motorola 10808 and AMD AM25510. Further, many shift modes are possible (table 7-2).

Additional variations of shifters possible include use for floating-point normalization and sign-magnitude machine arithmetic shifters.

In the future one can expect to see shifter-oriented chips with thirty to fifty built-in shift modes: however, as with the shift register solution to the data-shifting problem, whether to utilize such chips or build a special barrel shifter will depend on cost/performance tradeoffs.

**Table 7–2**
**Possible Shift Modes**

| TYPE OF SHIFT MODE | DIRECTION | FILL | COMMENTS |
|---|---|---|---|
| LOGICAL | RIGHT & LEFT | ZERO/ONE FILL | |
| ARITHMETIC | | SIGN FILL | 1's OR 2's COMP |
| CIRCULAR | | LSB-MDB OR MSB-LSB | ROTATE |
| CIRCULAR | | SS-MSB OR SS-LSB | MULTIPRECISION |
| DOUBLE PRECISION LOGICAL | | ZERO/ONE | |
| DP ARITHMETIC | | SIGN FILL | 1's OR 2's COMP |
| DP CIRCULAR | | LSB-MSB OR MSB-LSB | ROTATE |
| DP CIRCULAR | | SS-MSB OR SS-LSB | MULTIPRECISION |

## C-System

The Collins C-system presents an interesting bus design for high-speed communications [12]. The basic system is shown in figure 7–20, the processor organization is shown in figure 7–21, and the programmable channel termination group (PCTG) is shown in figure 7–22.

The basic concept is quite simple. The processors interconnect to each other via a high-speed data exchange [time-division exchange (TDX)]. Each processor also connects to a TDM (time-division multiplex) loop for communication to its peripherals and local and/or remote PCTG facilities. PCTG facilities are used to communicate with data collection facilities.

The TDX system is a synchronous coaxial loop which operates at 32 million bits per second. Using a bit-interlaced time-division multiplexing scheme, up to sixteen channels operating at 2 million bits per second are derived. If required, channels of 4 or 8 million bits per second could be derived by combining several individual channels of 2 million bits per second. Facilities are also provided to subdivide channels into slow-speed channels with rates from 7.8 to 250 kilobits per second. The system disks, tape units, host interface units, and so on are assigned dedicated TDX communication channels. Special communication capabilities and requirements such as processor-to-processor communication

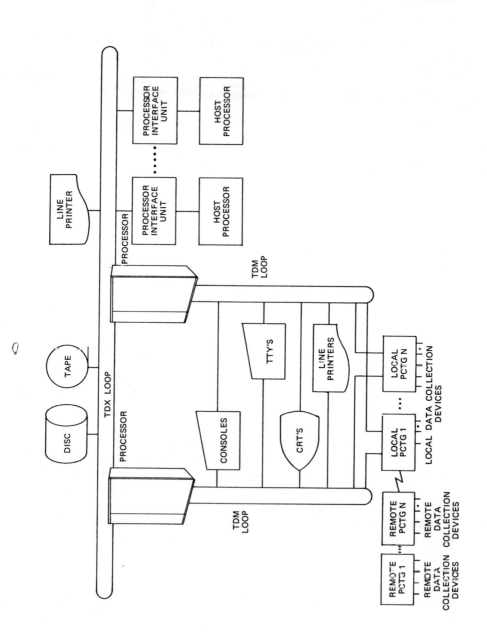

**Figure 7-20.** Typical C-System Data Communication System

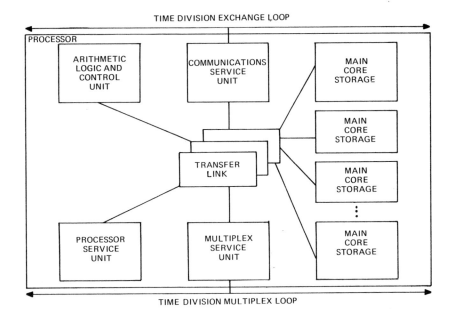

**Figure 7-21.** Processor Organization.

are also assigned specific channels or subchannels of the TDX. The TDX facilities along with the processor organization provide for segmenting the C-system into a set of hosts and a communication subnetwork. The basic processor is shown in figure 7-22, and it provides a capability to transfer data between the TDX and TDM links.

The TDM links are serial data links of 1.2288 million bits per second. The TDM is word-interlaced and provides for up to 256 channels at 4.8 kilobits per second. A device may be assigned one, eight, sixteen, or thirty-two basic channels and thus has effectively access to 4.8-, 38.4-, 76.8-, or 153.6-kilobit channels. Channels are dedicated to devices, and devices communicate to the processor via the multiplex service unit (MSU).

The PCTG provides user communication lines, line management and TDM communication (figure 7-22). It is basically a minicomputer operating in a packet-switched mode. Each PCTG can handle sixty-four lines.

## UNIBUS

Figure 7-23 illustrates the UNIBUS basic block diagram [13]. Table 7-3 is a summary of UNIBUS interface lines. Figure 7-24 illustrates the typical interface

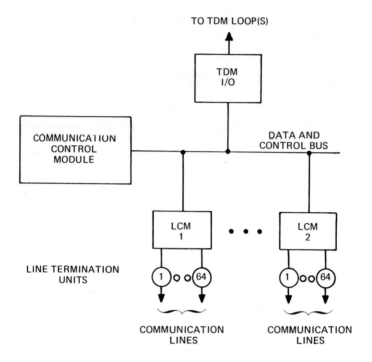

**Figure 7–22.** PCTG Organization.

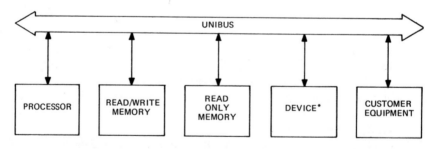

*FOR EXAMPLE, TELETYPE, DISK, PAPER TAPE, ETC.

**Figure 7–23.** Simplified Block Diagram of a PDP-11 System.

between a processor, memory, and device. The operation of the UNIBUS is discussed here.

The UNIBUS is a set of common signal wires designed to provide for connection and interfacing of equipment to PDP-11 systems. All devices on the

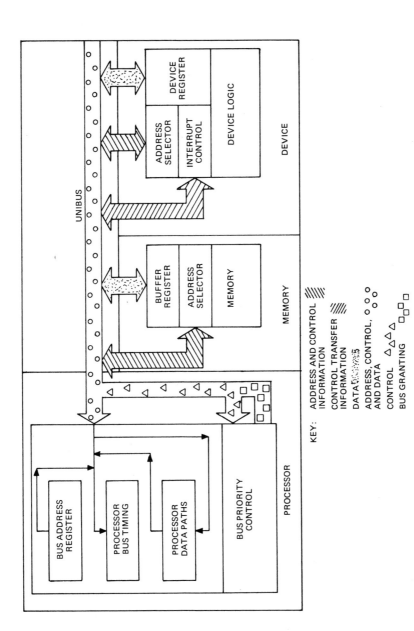

**Figure 7-24.** Block Diagram of the PDP-11 Interface.

**Table 7–3**
**Summary of UNIBUS Signals**

| NAME OF SIGNAL | MNEMONIC | SOURCE OF SIGNAL | DESTINATION OF SIGNAL | TIMING | FUNCTION OF SIGNAL | NO. OF LINES | COMMENTS |
|---|---|---|---|---|---|---|---|
| DATA TRANSFER SIGNALS (FOR TRANSFER OF DATA TO OR FROM MASTER) | | | | | | | |
| ADDRESS | A | MASTER | ALL | MSYN | SELECTS SLAVE DEVICE | 18 | |
| DATA | D | MASTER | SLAVE | MSYN (DATO, DATOB) | | 16 | |
|  |  | SLAVE | MASTER | SSYN (DATI, DATIP) | | | |
| CONTROL | C | MASTER | SLAVE | MSYN | SELECTS TRANSFER OPERATION | 2 | |
| MASTER SYNC | MSYN | MASTER | SLAVE | BEGINNING OF TRANSFER | INITIATES OPERATION AND GATES A,C AND D SIGNALS | 1 | |
| SLAVE SYNC | SSYN | SLAVE | MASTER | DATA ACCEPTED (DATO, DATOB) DATA AVAILABLE (DATI, DATIP) | RESPONSE TO MSYN | 1 | |
| PARITY BIT LOW | PA | MASTER | SLAVE | SAME AS DATA | PA PB 0  0 NO ERROR 0  1 PARITY ERROR 1  0 (RESERVED) 1  1 (RESERVED) | 1 | |
| PARITY BIT HIGH | PB | MASTER | SLAVE | SAME AS DATA | | 1 | |
| PRIORITY TRANSFER SIGNALS (FOR TRANSFER OF BUS CONTROL TO A PRIORITY – SELECTED MASTER) | | | | | | | |
| NON-PROCESSOR REQUEST | NPR | ANY | PROCESSOR | ASYNCHRONOUS | HIGHEST PRIORITY BUS REQUEST | 1 | |
| BUS REQUEST | BR | ANY | PROCESSOR | ASYNCHRONOUS | REQUESTS BUS MASTERSHIP | 4 | |
| NON-PROCESSOR | NPG | PROCESSOR | NEXT MASTER | ASYNCHRONOUS | TRANSFERS BUS CONTROL | 1 | UNIDIRECTIONAL |
| BUS GRANT | BG | PROCESSOR | NEXT MASTER | AFTER INSTRUCTION | TRANSFERS BUS CONTROL | 4 | UNIDIRECTIONAL |
| SELECTION ACKNOWLEDGE | SACK | NEXT MASTER | PROCESSOR | RESPONSE TO NPG OR BG | ACKNOWLEDGES GRANT & INHIBITS FURTHER GRANTS | 1 | |
| BUS BUSY | BBSY | MASTER | ALL | ASSERTED BY BUS MASTER | ASSERTS BUS MASTERSHIP | 1 | |
| INTERRUPT | INTR | MASTER | PROCESSOR | AFTER ASSERTING BBSY (NOT AFTER NPR), DEVICE MAY PERFORM SEVERAL TRANSFERS BEFORE ASSERTING INTR | TRANSFERS BUS CONTROL TO HANDLING ROUTINE IN PROCESSOR | 1 | |
| MISCELLANEOUS SIGNALS | | | | | | | |
| INITIALIZE | INIT | PROCESSOR | ALL | ASYNCHRONOUS | CLEAR AND RESET SIGNAL | 1 | |
| AC LOW | AC LO | POWER | ALL | ASYNCHRONOUS | INDICATES IMPENDING POWER FAILURE | 1 | |
| DC LOW | DC LO | POWER | ALL | ASYNCHRONOUS | INDICATES DC VOLTAGES OUT OF TOLERANCE, AND SYSTEM OPERATION MUST BE SUSPENDED | 1 | |

bus use the same form of communication. Further, devices, device registers, and so forth appear to the bus as memory address space, thus simplifying interfacing.

Bus arbitration is handled via priority techniques. Devices on the bus may be masters (allowed to control the bus) or slaves (a device which is receiving information). Some devices (say, a processor) may operate as either a master or a slave. Every device capable of being a master has a priority. When the current master passes control to a new master, the highest-priority device requesting to become master gains control of the bus. In the case of priority ties, the device closest electrically to the current master receives control. Communication on the bus is via an asynchronous request/acknowledge interface.

The lines summarized in table 7–3 may be grouped into three major categories—data-transfer lines, priority-transfer lines, and miscellaneous signals for bus initialization and voltage tolerances. Since the data-transfer and priority control lines are distinct, bus assignment can proceed in parallel with data transfer on the bus. Further, all lines, except the five lines BG and NPG, are bidirectional. Thus, the same interface registers may be used for both input and output to the bus. Since device registers are addressed as memory, all instructions which address memory become, in effect, I/O instructions. The ability to effect data transfers between devices, for example, between a disk and memory, without processor supervision is a consequence of the multiple-master capability. Device interrupt capability is also provided by the bus.

Details of bus operation, timing, and interfacing may be found in reference 13.

## Standards of the Institute of Electrical and Electronics Engineers

Clearly, there are many possibilities for bus communication. To give some structure to this area, various standards have been proposed. In particular, the Institute of Electrical and Electronics Engineers (IEEE) standard digital interface for programmable instrumentation [14] deals with systems incorporating byte-serial bit-parallel techniques for digital data transfer. Its objective is to define a general-purpose, easy-to-use system that ensures that messages are accurately communicated between two or more devices in the system. The document that delineates this standard encompasses all aspects, from functional specifications through electrical and mechanical specifications. This section focuses only on the functional aspects of this standard. The terminology of the following discussion is that of the standard itself [14].

The objective of an interface system is to provide a communication network over which messages can effectively be carried among a group of interconnected devices.

Messages basically belong in one of two broad categories: (1) those that manage the interface system itself (interface messages) and (2) those messages carried by the interface but used by the interconnected devices (device-dependent messages).

For a communication network to effectively organize and manage information, it should contain three elements: (1) a device acting as a listener, (2) a device acting as a talker, and (3) a device acting as a controller. Figures 7-25 and 7-26 illustrate listener, talker, and controller capabilities in devices interconnected by the interface system.

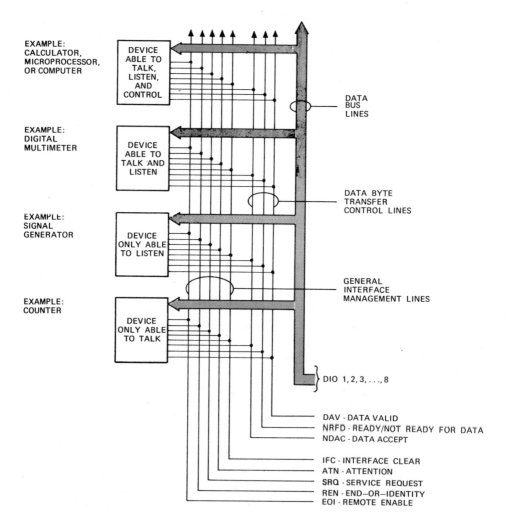

**Figure 7-25.** Communication Network Devices.

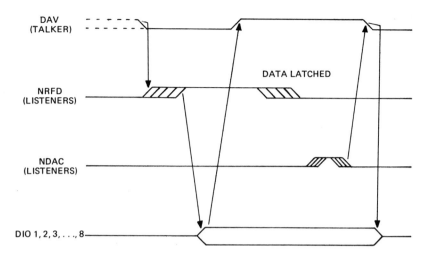

**Figure 7-26.** IEEE Standard Interface Timing Diagram.

The interface contains sixteen lines to carry all communication. Messages are coded on one line or a set of lines, depending on the message.

The bus is divided into three sets of lines: data bus (eight lines), data byte transfer control bus (three lines), and general interface management bus (five lines).

The data bus carries all interface messages and device-dependent messages. Messages are carried on the data input/output (DIO) lines in a bit-parallel byte-serial manner: asynchronously and bidirectionally.

The data byte transfer control bus is used to carry out transfer of data from an addressed talker to all addressed listeners. The three lines DAV (data valid), NRFD (not ready for data), and NDAC (not data accepted) work in a handshake manner to transfer data on the data bus through the interface.

The five general interface management lines—ATN (attention), IFC (interface clear), SRQ (service request), REN (remote enable), and EOI (end or identity)—are used to maintain an orderly flow of data through the interface.

A device is a physical object designed to perform a specific application. Conceptually, it may be divided into three major functional areas: device functions (application-dependent), interface functions (application-independent), and message coding logic. Figure 7-27 illustrates the functional partitioning of a device.

Device functions pertain to the application at hand and thus are not considered within this section. A designer usually has complete freedom to define device capability.

The interface function is the element through which a device receives, processes, and sends messages. Table 7-4 lists the available interface functions.

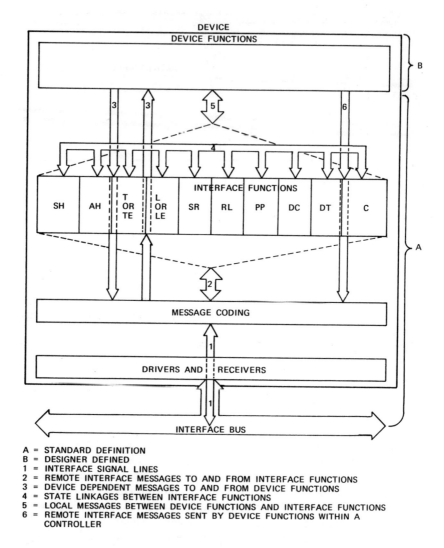

A = STANDARD DEFINITION
B = DESIGNER DEFINED
1 = INTERFACE SIGNAL LINES
2 = REMOTE INTERFACE MESSAGES TO AND FROM INTERFACE FUNCTIONS
3 = DEVICE DEPENDENT MESSAGES TO AND FROM DEVICE FUNCTIONS
4 = STATE LINKAGES BETWEEN INTERFACE FUNCTIONS
5 = LOCAL MESSAGES BETWEEN DEVICE FUNCTIONS AND INTERFACE FUNCTIONS
6 = REMOTE INTERFACE MESSAGES SENT BY DEVICE FUNCTIONS WITHIN A
     CONTROLLER

**Figure 7-27.** Functional Partitioning of a Device.

A designer is given the choice of selecting a particular set of interface functions for the device application.

Each function is defined in terms of a group of interconnected, mutually exclusive states. Only one state can be active at any given time. For each state, an interface function is defined by the following: (1) messages that can or cannot be sent while the state is active and (2) conditions under which the function must leave the current state and enter another.

**Table 7–4**
**Available Interface Functions**

| INTERFACE FUNCTION | MNEMONIC SYMBOL | RELEVANT MESSAGE PATHS |
|---|---|---|
| SOURCE HANDSHAKE | SH | 1, 2, 4, 5 |
| ACCEPTOR HANDSHAKE | AH | 1, 2, 4, 5 |
| TALKER OR EXTENDED TALKER | T OR TE | 1, 2, 3, 4, 5 |
| LISTENER OR EXTENDED LISTENER | L OR LE | 1, 2, 3, 4, 5 |
| SERVICE REQUEST | SR | 1, 2, 4, 5 |
| REMOTE LOCAL | RL | 1, 2, 4, 5 |
| PARALLEL POLL | PP | 1, 2, 4, 5 |
| DEVICE CLEAR | DC | 1, 2, 4, 5 |
| DEVICE TRIGGER | DT | 1, 2, 4, 5 |
| CONTROLLER | C | 1, 2, 4, 5, 6 |

Every message is a quantity of information which is received either true or false. All communication between an interface and its devices is through messages.

Messages sent between device and interface functions are called local messages. In figure 7–27, local messages flow through message route 5.

Messages sent between interface functions of different devices are called *remote messages*. Remote messages are either device-dependent or interface messages. Device-dependent messages are passed between the device functions and message coding logic by way of specified functions (figure 7–27, message route 3). An interface message is sent to cause a state transition within an interface function (figure 7–27, message route 2).

Message coding involves the translation of remote messages to or from interface signal line values. The following is a description of the repertoire of available interface functions.

The source handshake (SH) interface function provides a device with the capability to transfer multiline messages. Along with the acceptor handshake (AH) function, a handshake sequence provides for asynchronous multiline message transfers. The SH function controls initiation and termination of the handshake sequence. It makes use of the DAV, RFD, and DAC messages to transfer each message byte.

The acceptor handshake interface function provides a device with the capability to accept multiline messages. As discussed earlier, it executes in conjunction with the SH function. It may delay initiation or termination of a multiline message until it is ready to continue. The AH function also makes use of the DAV, RFD, and DAC messages.

The talker (T) interface function provides a device with the capability to transmit device-dependent data through the interface to other devices. There are two alternate versions. The normal uses one-byte addressing, and the extended version uses two-byte addressing.

The listener (L) interface function provides a device with the capability to receive device-dependent data through the interface from other devices. As with the T function, the L function has either normal or extended addressing capability.

The service request (SR) interface function provides a device with the capability to asynchronously request service from the interface controller.

The remote local (RL) interface function provides a device with the capability to select between a choice of two sources or input information. It simply indicates to the device whether console input information (local) or interface input information (remote) is to be used.

The parallel poll (PP) interface function provides a device with the capability to provide to the controller one bit of status without being previously addressed. Lines DIO1 to DIO8 are used for this purpose, with a setup of either one device per line or a sharing of lines to accommodate any number of devices. The PP function requires the controller to conduct periodic parallel polls.

The device clear (DC) interface function provides a device with the capability to be cleared (initialized).

The device trigger (DT) interface function provides a device with the capability to have its basic operation initiated.

The controller (C) interface function provides a device with the capability to send device addresses and commands to other devices through the interface and to conduct parallel polls. It can operate only when it is transmitting the ATN message over the interface. If more than one devcie has the C function, then all but one must be in a "controller idle" state at any given time. The one active controller is called the *controller in charge*. The standard provides a protocol to rotate controllers in charge.

Basically, then, these functions along with the message coding and routing comprise the functional aspects of the IEEE standard for digital interfacing. Within the interface functions, a number of options have been left to try to keep as much flexibility as possible.

Practically speaking, the standard stipulates fundamental functions that all interfaces usually contain while also introducing a communications hierarchy. It is the communications network which really defines the standard, and rightly so. Most problems of interfacing arise in device efficiency being constructed by poorly designed interfaces which impedes efficient thoroughput between noncompatible devices. These functions and communications comprise a fully capable, flexible system which can be adopted for interfacing almost any device and may eventually bring some sort of standardization to this field.

### Permutation Networks of 2 X 2 Cells

In the following, a special case of the $v$ $(m,n_1,r_1,n_2,r_2)$ network is considered; where the network consists of interconnected 2 X 2 cells, the assignment of interest is $C(2,2)$. Such networks are attributed to Waksman [15] and Opferman and Tsao-Wu [16]. Such a network is designed in detail here for the case where there are eight input terminals and eight output terminals, that is, where $n_1 r_1 = n_2 r_2 = 8$. As will be seen, such networks result from the repeated application of Hall's theorem [17].

Now, suppose there are eight input terminals and eight output terminals, and it is desired to construct a minimal rearrangeable interconnection network for which any of the 8! permutations from the inputs onto the outputs can be realized. This is schematically shown in figure 7-28. Then consider figure 7-29. Effectively, in figure 7-29, two subproblems have been formed, each one-half the size of the original. But the question which must be answered here is, Why can this be done? The answer is because of a fundamental property of all 8! permutation relative to figure 7-29 which is made apparent by Hall's theorem. For any of the 8! assignments, if any $k$ of the output cells are considered, then the input terminals are to be connected to the $2k$ output terminals, or these $k$ output cells come from at least $k$ input cells. It was previously seen by Hall's theorem that since the two output terminals of each output cell must be assigned to two input terminals, each of the output cells can be connected to one of these input terminals in the assignment through the upper permutation network of figure 7-29. Likewise, each output cell can also be corrected to the other of these input terminals through the bottom permutation network. In

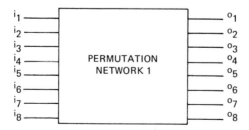

**Figure 7-28.** Permutation Network.

INPUT CELLS                                          OUTPUT CELLS

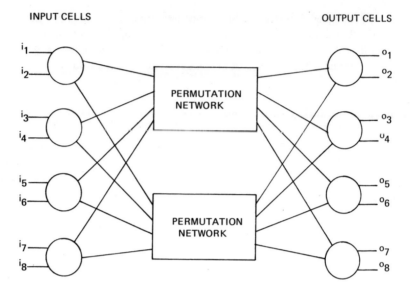

**Figure 7–29.** Partitioned Permutation Network.

other words, a subassignment consisting of one-half the total assignment can be satisfied by the upper permutation network, and the subassignment consisting of the other half of the total assignment can be satisfied by the lower permutation network.

As an example of this, consider the permutation of figure 7–30 which has been realized in the above sense. But note that the states of all the input and output cells could also be reversed, and the permutation would still be satisfied in the above sense. It should be clear that either an input cell or an output cell can be eliminated from the network at the expense of giving up this flexibility. For the permutation being considered, this is illustrated in figure 7–31. The elimination of this cell is obviously equivalent to freezing the corresponding cell of figure 7–30 in the parallel or noncrossing position.

The decomposition leading to the desired permutation network consisting only of 2 × 2 cells should now be evident. This decomposition is accomplished by repeating the above procedure again on the upper and lower permutation networks of figure 7–31. Doing so yields the network of figure 7–32 where the particular assignment being considered is shown still only partially realized. Finally, the final network with the assignment fully realized is shown in figure 7–33.

If such a procedure were performed in general for a network design where the number of input terminals and the number of output terminals were each equal to a power of 2, say, $2^r$, then by the above it should be clear that the

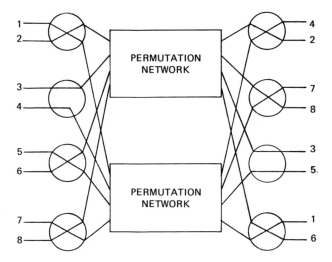

**Figure 7-30.** Example Realization.

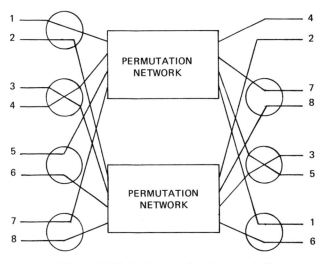

**Figure 7-31.** Deletion of an Output Cell.

number of cells in the outermost level of the network would be $2^r - 1$. The next level would consist of $(2)(2^{r-1} - 1)$ cells, and the level after that would consist of $(2^2)(2^{r-2} - 1)$ cells. If this were continued, it would be seen that the innermost level would require $(2^{r-1})(2 - 1)$ cells. This is graphically illustrated in

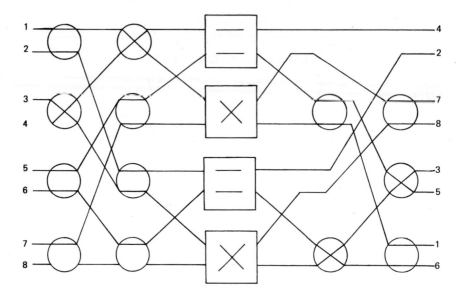

**Figure 7–32.** Second Partitioning of the Permutation Network.

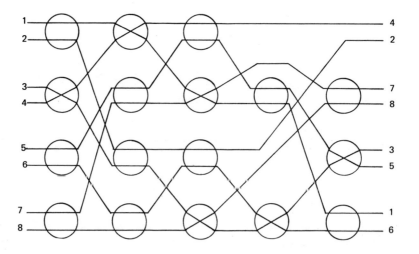

**Figure 7–33.** Third Partitioning of the Permutation Network.

figure 7-34. Summing the number of cells needed in general, then, it is seen that the total can be expressed as $r2^r - 2^r + 1$, or $N \log_2 N - N + 1$. In other words, since each cell contains four crosspoints, this procedure based on successive application of Hall's theorem has resulted in a network containing a number of crosspoints which agree asymptotically with the information-theoretic minimal.

At what cost has this number of crosspoints been obtained? Recalling that this is a rearrangeable network, it should be suspected that the cost is in the implementation of permutations through the network and the degree to which the existing state of the network would have to be rearranged to satisfy a new request for a correction. Indeed, that is precisely the cost, and the reader should consider some incremental realization of some eight input terminal to eight output terminal permutations to sense this difficulty.

## Summary

This chapter has attempted to illustrate a number of important design examples of standards and systems from the viewpoint of their communication architectures. No attempt has been made to develop a complete survey of such systems. Rather, representative systems were considered.

A further subject that could have possibly been covered in this chapter is I/O techniques. However, these techniques are beyond the scope of this book. The interested reader should see Ref. 18 for a summary of such techniques. Additionally, details of the Bell System's advanced communication system (ACS) are just beginning to emerge and may be of interest to the reader, particularly in comparison to IBM's SNA concept [19].

## Exercises

1. Categorize the PDP-11 UNIBUS in terms of the bus parameters given in chapter 5.

2. Categorize the IBM SNA in terms of the network protocol hierarchy given in chapter 3.

3. Categorize the MU5 crossbar exchange network in terms of all applicable parameters (system, bus, or circuit switch) given in this book.

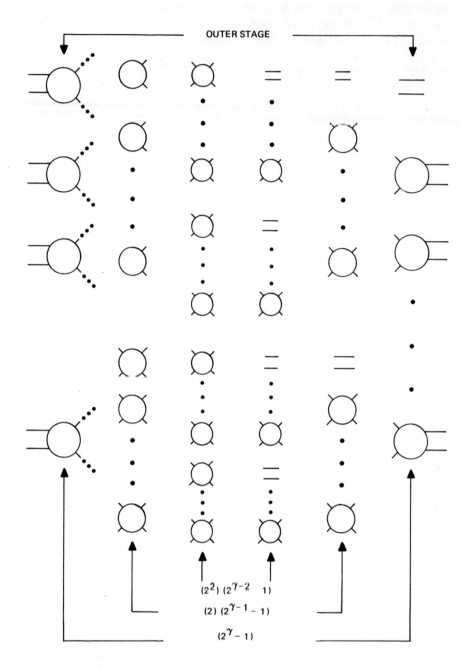

**Figure 7-34.** Generalized Partitioning of a Permutation Network.

## References

[ 1] IBM, *Systems Network Architecture General Information*, GA27-3102-0.

[ 2] IBM, *Advanced Function for Communication Systems Summary*, GA27-3099.

[ 3] IBM, *Systems Network Architecture Introduction*, GA27-3116-0.

[ 4] IBM, *IBM Synchronous Data Link Control General Information*, GA27-3093.

[ 5] IBM, *Introduction to Data Communications Systems*, SR20-4461.

[ 6] IBM, *Data Communications Primer*, GC20-1668.

[ 7] S.H. Lavington, et al., "MU5 Multicomputer Communication System," *IEEE Transactions on Computers*, January 1977.

[ 8] J.H. Brady, D.F. Witte, and J.W. Anderson, *Analytic Study of Decentralized Hardware Modules for Tracking and Display*, Honeywell Inc., Marine Systems Division, CEL-01, April 15, 1973 for NELC contract no. N00953-73-M-2750.

[ 9] L.G. Newcome and D.F. Witte, *Feasibility Demonstration of Distributed Processing for Small Ship Command and Control Systems*, Honeywell Inc., Marines Systems Division, CEL-01, February 4, 1974 for NELC contract no. N00123-74-C-0891.

[10] E.D. Jensen, "The Honeywell Experimental Distributed Processor — An Overview of Its Objectives, Philosophy, and Architectural Facilities," *Computer*, January 1978.

[11] R.S. Lim, "A Barrel Switch Design," *Computer Design*, August 1972.

[12] R.L. Sharma et al., "C-System: Multiprocessor Network Architecture," *Proceedings of the IFIP*, 1974.

[13] DEC, *PDP-11 Peripherals Handbook*, Maynard Mass.: Digital Press, 1973.

[14] Institute of Electrical and Electronics Engineers (IEEE) Bus Standard 488-1975; Daryl E. Knoblock, Donald C. Loughry, and Chris A. Vissers, "Insight into Interfacing," *IEEE Spectrum*, May 1975.

[15] A. Waksman, "A Permutation Network," *JACM* 9 (January 1968): 159-163.

[16] D.C. Opferman and N.T. Tsao-Wu, "On a Class of Rearrangeable Switching Networks, Part I: Control algorithms"; Part II: Enumeration Studies and Fault Diagnosis," *Bell System Technical Journal*, 1971, pp. 1579-1618.

[17] P. Hall, "On Representations of Subsets," *Journal of the London Mathematics Society*, 10 (1935): 26-30.

[18] J.F. Wakerly, "Microprocessor Input/Output Architecture," *Computer*, February 1977.

[19] *Data Management*, "ACS: Data Comm Service," January 1979; pp. 16-20.

# 8 Conclusion

## Summary of Architecture Issues

Attention on new architecture concepts has tended to focus on distributed systems and on networks [1]. The concept of distributed systems is not particularly new; however, the cost tradeoffs of projected processor devices are driving computer architects to conceive of systems with many more than four processors [1 to 7]. This represents a large departure from previous concepts which tended to involve less than four processors. Networks are a new system concept which evolved from trying to develop effective computer-to-computer communication techniques [3, 5, 8]. Further, some researchers have suggested that the same types of operating systems can be used on networks and general-purpose distributed systems [9].

Three researchers, Siewiorek [10], Chen [11], and Anderson [4], have developed computer architecture classification taxonomies. The taxonomies classify architectures based on a variety of parameters. Notably, these classification taxonomies tend to emphasize the system architecture as seen via the types of communication allowed between processors rather than the processor architectures. It appears that the trend in new system architectures will be to develop systems based on their communication requirements rather than their detailed processor requirements.

A number of technologies are currently important in the development of distributed and network-oriented system [12]. From a study of these technologies it appears that the design of a distributed system can be approached as either a computer architecture or a data communication problem or both [13]. The key technologies are:

1. Processor Interconnection
   Bus structures
   I/O techniques
   Circuit switching
   Message and packet switching
2. Process Communication
   Software protocols
   Standard operating systems for both tight and loosely coupled systems
3. Process Partitioning
   Application mapping
   Application reconfiguration

The problems of processor interconnection were extensively studied before the advent of distributed processing. Key technologies involve bus structure design; I/O techniques; transmission techniques including circuit, message, and packet switching; and nontraditional computer interconnection techniques such as satellite and radio communications techniques [14]. These technologies involve many design disciplines. For example, in the design of a system bus structure, the designer must be aware of communication considerations (for example, topology, deadlock possibilitics, probabilities of usage for each device, queuing at the sender and/or receiver, transmission frequency, and so on) and architecture considerations (topology, deadlock possibilities, data-transmission rate, and so forth). The topology of the system could be a function of tradeoffs of both the system architecture and the desired communications facilities. Fault-tolerant architecture issues may also impact the desired topology by requiring that alternative system topologies be available. This would only increase the number of tradeoffs that must be made between providing a good communications topology and a fault-tolerant system architecture. It is virtually impossible to design an efficient computer system with multiple processors without extensive use of communications theory and the attendant analysis (modeling and simulation) capabilities [15, 16]. Further, classification studies of computer architecture will serve only to clarify the relationship between architecture and communication because as architectures become better understood, they tend to be modeled via their communications facilities.

Process communication in some contexts is well understood. In the context of interprocess synchronization, significant work has been done [17]. Network designers and operating-system designers have done much work on large systems with protocols [5]. Currently, a number of researchers are trying to design operating systems which can run (without significant changes) on both loosely coupled and on tightly coupled distributed systems [9, 18]. Communication networks and distributed architectures both need operating-system software. Such software typically is layered and must have protocols, protection mechanisms, scheduling mechanisms, and so on. Some researchers have indicated that there are not necessarily any intrinsic differences between the types of operating systems which should be used on these various systems. It appears possible, through the use of layered highly structured operating systems, to construct an operating system that is useful for both network (loosely coupled) systems and multiprocessor (tightly coupled) systems. The differences would primarily be in the performance levels achieved with such a common operating system. If, however, the primary reason for use of a network or multiprocessor is availability, redundancy, and/or other fault-tolerant considerations (in contrast to a strictly high-performance goal), then such an operating system seems reasonable and able to be developed. There may, however, be some questions of economy that must be addressed, particularly in the communications area.

The issue of process partitioning has been studied to a limited extent for multiprocessing systems. Techniques to decompose at the instruction, process, task, and job levels have been considered. Jensen, to date, has performed the most extensive study in this area [12]. However, because of the difficulties involved in process partitioning, little hope can be expected for automatic process partitioning techniques useful for distributed processing in the near future. The analysis necessary to structure the system architecture must involve the definition of modules of software. Using Jensen's scheme, significant analysis of the information transfer between modules must occur. Further, if, as Jensen suggests, the best means of assignment is dynamic via the operating system, then the designer may end up setting up the framework to be used via the operating system for module assignment. In this case there will be a tendency for the architects to specify only communication protocols and a system strcuture for the distributed processor.

## Research Trends in Distributed-Processor Interconnection Systems

Distributed processing entails a processing load partitioned across multiple processors which intercommunicate. A number of motivations exist for distributed processing, including modularity, fault detection and recovery, improved throughput and response time, load leveling, and resource sharing. The development of distributed processing has been retarded by the high cost of processors. Multiple-processor configurations have been largely confined to those few applications which could afford the potential advantages. The resource-sharing network is an exception, since it is relatively insensitive to processor costs. Rapid advances in semiconductor technology are reducing the portion of system cost represented by processors. This provides impetus to distributed processing and elevates the interconnection mechanism to a critical status. Research and development in processor interconnection have proceeded in several many contexts, for example, logic design, computer architecture, and digital data communications. Approaches and results which have evolved in one context may be beneficial in others, but often they are either couched in special terminology or inextricably woven into the particular application. A more coherent perspective is needed to facilitate the migration of ideas among these various contexts.

Here we have viewed the interconnection mechanism as a host device-independent communicating structure. Important research trends on the interconnection problem are discussed.

### Interconnection Structure

The topology of interconnection mechanisms has been driven by two main forces—computer architecture and digital data communications. The computer architecture perspective may be characterized as constructing a large machine from smaller ones, while that of data communications is the interconnection of separate machines. Typically, computer architects of distributed systems have used mainly bus and circuit-switching techniques. Designers of networks have typically utilized circuit, message, and packet-switching technologies [5, 14].

The first significant contribution toward characterizing the topological structure of distributed computer system architectures was by Chen [11]. While primarily concerned with the design of computer system internal data paths, Chen also considered configurations of these paths. The nodes were assumed to be any PMS-level elements. The logical and physical switch structure diagrams of figure 13 of Bell's book [19] are a comprehensive catalog of PMS configurations. A specific interest in distributed processing was evident in the Siewiorek [6] taxonomy. The emphasis was on geographically local structures of processors, memories, processing elements, paths, and switches. The dimensions went beyond the PMS level and included switching discipline and deadlock handling.

The most explicit *attempt* thus far in the direction of a systematic approach to the analysis of distributed-processor interconnection structure is Anderson and Jensen's model [4]. The model is concerned with the topology of interconnected processors. Aspirall [20] has slightly altered the model to correct "deficiencies" he noted.

For digital data communication systems and computer networks, the topological issues and alternatives are slightly different from those for computer architecture. Geographical distances raise the cost of the communication paths and usually limit the paths to point-to-point concepts. The nodes in computer networks could be terminals, multiplexers, concentrators, host computers, and gateways. From the standpoint of distributed processing, multihost computer networks are the most interesting. The issues which relate network topology to the particular constraints of networks are illuminated in Frank and Chou [21].

*Paths and Buses*

Paths and buses have evolved in three different contexts—logic design, computer architecture, and data communications. Consider logic design. Typically small quanta of data are transferred at a high-duty cycle over very short distances using very simple protocols. The paths are usually bit-parallel and may be either dedicated or shared. The nodes are functional elements, such as registers and arithmetic units. The second context is computer system architecture. Here are longer distances (on the order of 1 to 10 meters) and somewhat more complex protocols. Last is the digital data communications context, in which fewer and longer messages are transmitted, at lower speeds, over distances ranging upward from 1,000 meters, on dedicated bit-serial paths having elaborate protocols.

Path sharing and communication are straightforward in digital engineering and logic design. The growing level of LSI integration and the consequent trend toward functional decentralization are increasing the intersection of logic design and computer system architecture. The first publication which considered path sharing in the computer system architecture context was by Thurber et al. [22]. That paper discussed six arbitration schemes. The only other document which deals methodically with PMS-level bus arbitration is by Chen [11]. Chen picks and categorizes four common arbitration algorithms (which are referred to as fixed priority, snapshot, round robin, and first-come-first-served).

The same two papers responsible for bringing order to bus arbitration are also the major contributors to organization of path communication in the computer system architecture context. Thurber et al. [22] discuss the more common communication methods and provide a simple classification scheme. An extensive taxonomy in path communication is the major contribution of Chen [11]. Neither synchronous techniques nor broadcast (that is, one-to-many) communications are included, but he includes a detailed examination of deadlock prevention, avoidance, and detection and recovery algorithms from the standpoint of interconnection mechanisms.

In data communications, paths are usually point-to-point links characteristic of common carrier systems. Sharing these paths (line sharing) involves the use of multiplexers and concentrators for connection of nodes to the path. The shared paths in logic design and computer system architecture often use "implicit" multiplexing. Doll [23] provides an explanation of network multiplexers and concentrators. Methodology for analysis and synthesis of asynchronous time-division multiplexers is rapidly developing.

The advent of communication satellites has opened Pandora's box to radio links and buses [24]. The random-access arbitration algorithm concept used for the Aloha [25] radio bus is now being used on wire buses [8].

## Circuit Switches

Common examples of circuit switches are crossbar arrays [26], rearrangeable arrays of crossbar switches [27], sorting networks [28], permutation networks [29], and time-division multiplexed circuit switches.

Circuit-switch characteristics include relative sizes of the input- and output-line sets, portal-to-portal time delay, switch setup time, rearrangeability of the switch, blocking or nonblocking characteristics, extra functionality (such as data masking), number of crosspoints, basic crosspoint module design, construction of the switch from the basic modules, and algorithm (that is, control unit) complexity.

Research and development in circuit switches have primarily been in three different contexts. The first and foremost is telephone networks [27]. The emphasis here has been on derivation of the minimum number of crosspoint multistage rearrangeable networks. The reason for the use of crosspoint networks is ease of implementation and representation. Multistage networks evolved as a technique for building larger networks (in terms of connection lines) from smaller crosspoint building-block modules or time-division multiplexed building blocks. Multistage networks introduce the issue of blocking and nonblocking network configurations. Typical research on rearrangeable networks has concentrated on determining how to construct the network, calculating the control algorithms, and bounding the number of required crosspoints and circuit modules.

The second context has been the interconnection of PMS-level devices in computer systems architecture [28]. While crossbars were the primary mechanism initially, other switch forms have been receiving more attention recently. Motivations for these switches have included slower growth rates in the number of crosspoints as the number of input and output lines increases, more complex or dynamic connectivity, inclusion of functions other than routing, integration of the switch into the computer or memory system architecture [30], performance of processing during routing, construction of highly modular switches that can be recursively constructed from basic building blocks, and requirements for very simple switches such as perfect shuffle networks.

Finally, in the context of semiconductor large-scale integration (LSI), researchers have pursued the design of highly regular nonblocking switches with varying topologies [29]. These networks typically were constructed from two input–two output elements capable of permuting or passing the input leads onto the output leads. The studies were motivated by a desire to construct basic LSI modular building blocks, to minimize the LSI circuitry on each building block, to investigate the modularity of the building blocks, and to detail the control of each switch topology.

Design strategies exist for each of the various different switch types, but no tools exist to systematically relate their design tradeoffs to their characteristics. The most relevant survey [31] of circuit switches includes some parametric comparisons. Kautz [29] provides a graph-theoretic development of some of the most important switch characteristics. Masson and Marcus also provide an up-to-date overview of this area; however, they concentrate mainly on rearrangeable networks [32, 33]. A special issue [34] of the *IEEE Proceedings* covers the area of circuit switches. Some modifications of the basic rearrangeable concept [35] such as iteratively time-sharing a single stage to effect the connection have been investigated, as well as designs of time-slot interchangers [36]. A number of techniques that show how a network may be constructed with different cost measures have been documented [37, 38].

*Message and Packet Switches*

The environment of a computer network is ideal for the use of message and packet switches. In the literature, these switches have been variously referred to as message switches, packet switches, or front-end processors. Whereas in other distributed processing environments, the switching and communication functions are handled by separately identifiable and independent units, the computer network message switch typically handles the entire spectrum of switching and communication responsibilities — path arbitration, message routing, and low-level communication problems across physical circuits.

The only current systematic classification solely of the area of message-switch design is a survey [39]. Newport and Ryzlak take an architectural approach in which the entire set of message management operations is divided into a series of well-defined, disjoint functions (for example, input queue handler). The classification of front-end processors (FEP) is then based on the division of responsibility for these functions between the host and the FEP. This partitioning leads to the development of five distinct classes: (1) the FEP as an emulator of hard-wired controllers, (2) the FEP as programmable network controller, (3) the FEP in a shared mass memory configuration, (4) FEP-managed message functions, and (5) the FEP in a shared-memory configuration.

Jensen, Thurber, and Schneider [14] relate buses, message, packet, and circuit switches. The basic paradigm of the programmable network controller (message switch) was first described in references 40 and 41, papers reporting on the initial design of a generalized message switch for the ARPA network. The message-switch design that emerged from this work is called an interface message processor (IMP). An overview of the specific communication responsibilities of the FEP and the tradeoffs inherent in their design can be found in Refs. 5 and 39.

The message-switch software which has the responsibility for implementing the attendant problems of communications is termed the *communication protocols*. The first attempt to systematically define the responsibilities of communication protocols was by Heart et al. [41]. For reasons very similar to those raised within the context of structured programming, Heart et al. viewed these protocols as multilayered with each lower-level layer being entirely transparent to all higher-level layers.

The lowest-level protocols are related to supporting direct switch-to-switch communication along a physical circuit and are termed data-link controls (DLC). They can be considered somewhat analogous to the path communication function described earlier for other contexts. While there have been numerous attempts to standardize data-link control methods, there is currently no single industrywide standard. Currently popular data-link controls include IBM's BISYNC and SDLC, the American National Standards Institute DLC, and Digital Equipment's DDCMP. Overviews of the subject can be found in Gray [42] and Stutzman [43]. Both papers discuss the relationship between network transmission requirements (delay, overhead) and the resulting DLC structure.

The level 1 protocols are concerned primarily with establishing a logical (that is, virtual) channel between the source and destination packet switch that corresponds roughly to the switching functions described earlier for other contexts. This generally involves such problems as routing, message assembly and disassembly, and flow control. A thorough examination of these level 1 problems is presented in Gray [42] where they are discussed under the generic term *source/destination functions*.

There are commonly considered to be two higher levels — the interprocess communication and user-oriented protocols. However, in most networks, these functions are performed by the individual hosts and are more properly considered within the context of the operating system.

A general overview of the entire subject of message and packet switches and their incorporation into the design of resource-sharing computer networks can be found in Refs. 44 and 45.

### Open Problems

To date, the entire field of distributed processing is just beginning to achieve a level of maturity in which researchers can describe competitive systems. Yet there is no common basis for making comparisons of such concepts. Further, there is no real cost-effectiveness proof of the concept of distributed processing itself. That is, is a distributed processor really more cost-effective than a centralized computer system? Our recommendations as to the main open problems are:

1. Development of accurate life-cycle cost comparison to demonstrate or disprove the cost-effectiveness of distributed processors versus large-scale centralized machines such as CRAY-1.
2. Development of categorization and comparison techniques to allow for design and comparison of distributed system concepts, bus structure, circuit switches, and packet switches.
3. Resolution of detailed design tradeoffs in any given design protocol level; for example, (1) development of a "standard" vocabulary and nomenclature for distributed systems, (2) development of detailed models and comparative tradeoffs for circuit, message, and packet-switched systems and competitive cost-effectiveness data for each major protocol level, (3) whether certain circuit-switch concepts are special cases of other circuit concepts, (4) techniques to compare fault-tolerant buses, (5) determination of the relative placement of "distributed" architectures in an overall architecture taxonomy [18, 49], (6) development of interface standards.
4. Development of enough distributed systems concepts with built-in performance monitoring so that performance measurements can be taken to prove or disprove system effectiveness. Much of this type of work has been done for networks, but little has been done of a substantive nature for very large multiprocessors.

## Exercise

1. For each of the generic architectures STAR, irregular network, and central main-memory multiprocessor, develop a complete system interconnection structure design including line protocols, bus arbitration, message-switch parameters, and so on, where applicable.

## References

[ 1] E.D. Jensen, "The Influence of Microprocessors on Computer Architecture: Distributed Processing." *ACM*, 1975.

[ 2] B.C. Searle and D.E. Freberg, "Tutorial: Microprocessor Applications in Multiple Processor Systems," *Computer*, October 1975.

[ 3] F.E. Heart et al., "A New Minicomputer/Multiprocessor for the ARPA Network," *NCC*, 1973.

[ 4] G.A. Anderson and E.D. Jensen, "Computer Interconnection: Taxonomy; Characteristics, and Examples," *ACM Computer Surveys*, December 1975.

[ 5] S.R. Kimbleton and G.M. Schneider, "Computer Communications Networks: Approaches, Objectives, and Performance Considerations," *ACM Computing Surveys*, September 1975.

[ 6] D.P. Siewiorek and M.R. Barbacci, "Modularity and Multiprocessor Structures," *Infotech State-of-the-Art Report on Distributed Processing*, 1976.

[ 7] R.J. Swan, S.H. Fuller, and D.P. Siewiorek, "Cm* − A Modular, Multi-Microprocessor," *NCC*, 1977.

[ 8] R.M. Metcalfe and D.R. Boggs, "Ethernet: Distributed Packet Switching for Local Computer Networks," *CACM*, July 1976.

[ 9] R.H. Eckhouse and D.L. Nelson, "Distributed Computing − Networking or Multiprocessing," *Distributed Computer Workshop*, (Providence, R.I.: Brown University, 1976).

[10] D.P. Siewiorek, "Modularity and Multi-Microprocessor Structures," *Seventh Annual Workshop on Microprogramming*, October 1974.

[11] R.C. Chen, "Bus Communication Systems," (Dissertation, Carnegie-Mellon, 1974).

[12] E.D. Jensen and W.E. Bobert, "Partitioning and Assignment of Distributed Processing Software," *COMPCON East*, 1976.

[13] K.J. Thurber and G.M. Masson, "Recent Advances in Microprocessor Technology and Their Impact on Interconnection Design in Computer Systems," *ICC*, 1977.

[14] E.D. Jensen, J.J. Thurber, and G.M. Schneider, "A Review of Systematic Methods in Distributed Processor Interconnection," *ICC*, 1976.

[15] L. Kleinrock, *Queueing Systems,* vol. 1: *Theory* (New York: John Wiley & Sons, Inc., 1975).

[16] L. Kleinrock, *Queueing Systems*; vol. 2: *Computer Applications* (New York: John Wiley & Sons, Inc., 1975).

[17] E.W. Dijsktra, "The Structure of 'The' Multiprogramming System," *CACM*, May 1968.

[18] P.J. Fortune, W.P. Lidinsky, and B.R. Zelle, "Design and Implementation of a Local Computer Network," *ICC*, 1977.

[19] C.G. Bell and A. Newell, *Computer Structures – Readings and Examples* (New York: McGraw-Hill, 1971).

[20] D. Aspinall, "Multi-Micro Systems," *Infotech State-of-the-Art Report: Future Systems*, 1977.

[21] H. Frank and W. Chou, "Routing in Computer Networks," *Networks*, 1972.

[22] Kenneth J. Thurber et al., "A Systematic Approach to the Design of Digital Bussing Structures," *Proceedings of the 1972 Fall Joint Computer Conference* (Montvale, N.J.: AFIPS Press, 1972).

[23] D.R. Doll, "Multiplexing and Concentration," *Proceedings of the IEEE*, November 1972.

[24] J.W. Schwartz and M. Muntner, "Multiple-Access Communications for Computer Nets," *Computer Communication Networks* (Englewood Cliffs, N.J.: Prentice-Hall, 1973).

[25] N. Abramson, "The Aloha System," *Computer Communication Networks* (Englewood Cliffs, N.J.: Prentice-Hall, 1973).

[26] C. Clos, "A Study of Non-Blocking Switching Networks," *Bell System Technical Journal*, March 1953, pp. 406–424.

[27] V.E. Benes, *Mathmatical Theory of Connecting Networks and Telephone Traffic* (New York: Academic Press, 1965).

[28] K.E. Batcher, "Sorting Networks and Their Applications," *Proceedings of the SJCC*, 1968, pp. 307–314.

[29] W.H. Kautz, "The Design of Optimum Interconnection Networks for Multiprocessors," *Structure et Conception des Ordinateurs (Architecture and Design of Digital Computers)* ed. Guy Boulaye, École d'été de 1 O.T.A.N.A N.A.T.O. (Advanced Summer Institute 1969) (Paris: Dunob, 1971).

[30] L.R. Goke and G.J. Lipovski, "Banyan Networks for Partitioning Multiprocessor Systems," *First Annual Computer Architecture Conference*, Gainsville, Florida, December 1973, pp. 21–28.

[31] K.J. Thurber, "Circuit Switching Technology: A State-of-the-Art Survey," *COMPCON*, Fall 1978.

[32] G.M. Masson, "On Rearrangeable and Non-Blocking Switching Networks," *ICC*, 1975.

[33] M.J. Marcus, "The Theory of Connecting Networks and Their Complexity," *Proceedings of the Institute of Electrical and Electronics Engineers*, September 1977.

[34]  *IEEE Proceedings*, Special issue on circuit switching, September 1977.

[35]  M.J. Marcus, "Space-Time Equivalents in Connecting Networks," *ICC*, 1970.

[36]  M.J. Marcus, "Designs for Time Slot Interchangers," *Proc. 1970 NEC*, pp. 812-817.

[37]  G. Masson, "Generalized Multistage Switching Networks," *Networks*, December 1972.

[38]  N. Pippenger, "The Complexity Theory of Switching Networks," M.I.T. Technical Report no. 487, December 1973.

[39]  C.B. Newport and J. Ryzlak, "Communication Processors," *Proceedings of the IEEE*, November 1972.

[40]  L. Roberts and B. Wessler, "Computer Network Development to Achieve Resource Sharing," *Proceedings of the SJCC*, 1970.

[41]  F.E. Heart et al. "The Interface Message Processor for the ARPA Computer Network," *Proceedings of the SJCC*, 1970.

[42]  J.P. Gray, "Line Control Procedures," *Proceedings of the IEEE*, November 1972.

[43]  B.W. Stutzman, "Data Communication Control Procedures," *ACM Computing Surveys*, December 1972.

[44]  D.W. Davies and D.L.A. Barber, *Communication Networks for Computers* (New York: John Wiley & Sons, Inc., 1975).

[45]  N. Abramson and F. Kuo, eds., *Computer Communication Networks* (Englewood Cliffs, N.J.: Prentice-Hall, 1973).

[46]  H.J. Siegel and S.D. Smith, "Study of Multistage SIMD Interconnection Networks," *5th Annual Computer Architecture Symposium*, IEEE Computer Society.

[47]  *Computer*, Special issue on circuit switching, June 1979.

[48]  D.D. Clark, K.T. Pogran, and D.P. Reed, "An Introduction to Local Area Networks," *Proceedings of the IEEE*, November 1978.

[49]  K.J. Thurber and H.A. Freeman, "Local Computer Network Architectures," *COMPCON*, Spring 1979.

# Index

# About the Authors

**Kenneth J. Thurber** is a senior staff scientist in the advanced hardware development department of Sperry Univac's Defense Systems Division, St. Paul, Minnesota. He currently acts as a consultant to the signal processing group on advanced computer architectures. His current interests include high-performance systems and distributed-processor architectures.

**Gerald M. Masson** is an associate professor in the department of electrical engineering at The Johns Hopkins University. He received his Ph.D. in electrical engineering from Northwestern University in 1971 and was an assistant professor of electrical engineering at the University of Pittsburgh from 1971 to 1975. His research and teaching interests center on digital systems theory, fault-tolerant computing, and computer communication and interconnection. He has served as a consultant to both government and industry in these areas and has published and presented research papers in journals and conferences dealing with associated issues.